# A Generation Speaks

## Voices of the Great Depression

# A Generation Speaks

## Voices of the Great Depression

### The Writers' Discussion Group

### Chapel Hill Senior Center

Lucy Rodgers Watkins, Chief Editor

The Chapel Hill Press, Inc. • Chapel Hill, NC 27514

Published by The Chapel Hill Press, Inc.
600 Franklin Square
1829 East Franklin Street
Chapel Hill, NC 27514
Phone: 919–942–8389

ISBN 1–880849–21–6

Library of Congress Card Number: 00–102014

Printed and bound in the United States of America

# Dedication

This book is dedicated
to the people who experienced
the Great Depression

# Table of Contents

# Acknowledgments

The members of the Writers' Discussion Group wish to express special thanks to The Orange County Department on Aging and The Chapel Hill Senior Center staff for all their support and for making meeting space available to the group, and to The Friends of the Chapel Hill Senior Center. In particular, we thank Libby Lefkowitz and Marie Spinner for their fundraising.

Cover designed by Heather Hille

Interior design, layout, and typesetting by
The Chapel Hill Press, Inc.

The writers also wish to thank the following individuals and businesses for their support:

Bank of America, NA
Baum Diamonds
Roger and Farley Bernholz
Branch Banking and Trust Company
Catharine Carter Photography
Central Carolina Bank and Trust Company
Centura Bank
Chapel Hill Press, Inc.
Coffee Mill Roastery
Coldwell Banker
Crown Honda–Volvo
First Citizens Bank
First Union National Bank
Glaxo Wellcome, Inc.
Josh and Robin Gurlitz
(continued)

Shelton and Mary Edna Henderson
Hewlett-Packard Company
Julian's Home
McFarling's Exxon
Office Supply and More
Prudential Carolina Realty
Mary and James Semans
Viking Travel
Wachovia Bank, NA
Weaver Street Market
Wellspring Grocery
Whims Cards and Gifts

# Songs of the Great Depression

Winds will break trees, unless the body bends,
And the tree sighs and turns and springs
Back on itself, almost a dancing endurance.
Such are we common people,
Leveled by storms of a time that blew
Us all alike, and we bent back to ourselves—

And did simple things:
Bent to a crackling old Philco
In a circle of awed and silent children,
Played kick–the–can, and risked
Hundreds of Monopoly dollars,
The only precious money we had,
For a little green house on Broadway;

Gave handouts to hoboes, soup to the cold,
Shared shelter with homeless cousins,
And early corn with neighbors;
Dug ditches and planted trees,
Filled highway holes and painted
Huge, hopeful murals, forever coloring
Post offices in our senses.

To bend and turn back to ourselves,
To endure, is a courage of the ordinary,
The common people,
Who emerged, perhaps gnarled or torn,
To tell their ordinary stories.

Lucy Rodgers Watkins

**Lucy Rodgers Watkins**, of Chapel Hill, has worked for thirty–two years in non–profit education and community and human development programs. Her poems have appeared in *South Today, Echoes*, and the *UNC–Greensboro Alumni Magazine.*

# Background

## Willie Mae Jones

On Black Thursday, October 24, 1929, the stock market took a five–day plunge that resulted in the loss of over \$32 billion worth of equities. From the Wall Street crash to the outbreak of World War II was a period marked by the Great Depression at home and dark war clouds abroad. This was the era of soup kitchens, breadlines, and bank failures, of bonus marchers and dust bowl storms, of painful labor gains and rampant lawless gangs.

The Thirties had other tragic headlines. In 1932 the Charles Lindbergh baby was kidnapped and murdered. In 1937 the zeppelin Hindenberg, the world's largest dirigible, crashed on landing with the loss of 22 lives. In 1936 a gossip–hungry public was intrigued with the decision of Britain's King Edward VIII to abdicate the throne to marry American divorcee Wallis Warfield Simpson. Prohibition was repealed. Franklin D. Roosevelt was in the White House energizing a dispirited nation with his New Deal programs (National Reconstruction Act, Civilian Conservation Corps, Public Works Administration, Works Progress Administration) and his broadcast fireside chats. Radio became the major provider of entertainment in the Thirties. The coverage was broad enough to include news events, comedy programs (Jack Benny, Amos and Andy, Little Orphan Annie and her dog Sandy had their own radio serial).

In 1938 Orson Wells scared listeners with his dramatization of H. G. Wells' *The War of the Worlds*, and there were musical variety shows. Among those who popularized songs over the air were Bing Crosby (singing

3

his theme, "Where the blue of the night meets the gold of the day"), Rudy Valley ("Nevertheless"), and Russ Columbo, ("Love Letters in the Sand").

The Broadway theater was blessed by contributions by Jerome Kern, Richard Rogers, Irving Berlin, George Gershwin, and Cole Porter. *Porgy and Bess*, the folk opera, gave us the lullaby, "Summertime." Woody Guthrie wrote over 1,000 songs, most of them about working men. Among his most famous songs are "So Long, It's Been Good To Know You" and "This Land Is Your Land." Margaret Mitchell wrote the novel *Gone with the Wind* in 1937. John Steinbeck wrote the classic of the Great Depression, *The Grapes of Wrath*. He received the Nobel Prize in Literature. Carl Sandburg and W. H. Auden set the pace for poetry throughout the 1930's. In his collection (1936), Sandburg celebrated America by affirming his faith in democracy and in the human ability to endure. His bold conversational style captured the pulse of American life.

Hollywood dominated arts and entertainment with both fantasy and morality plays. *The Wizard of Oz* symbolized Hollywood's impact during these years. Beaten down by the joblessness and breadlines, people needed relief. Young Shirley Temple reigned as top box office star from 1935 to 1938. Disney produced the first full–length animated film, *Snow White and the Seven Dwarfs*. Jimmy Stewart attacked corrupt politicians in *Mr. Smith Goes to Washington*. Orson Wells directed and starred in *Citizen Kane*. It is a masterpiece of light and shadow. Hollywood did produce a number of war films. Some were realistic, like *Bataan*, but most were sentimental stories meant to stir patriotic feelings. The Federal Theatre Project, established under the New Deal's WPA, employed about 10,000 and brought the stage to over 30 million people in twenty–nine states. One successful production was *The Swing Mikado*, a black jazz version of Gilbert and Sullivan's operetta.

In the 1930's American art went through a major transformation. One reason for the change was that the federal government, through the Federal Art Project of the WPA, began to fund art. The project made art part of America and developed the talent of many artists like Jackson Pollock. By 1939 project artists had completed 1,300 murals, 48,100 paintings, 3,562 sculptures, and many more works. These were placed in many public buildings being constructed by the Works Progress Administration.

The dominant style in architecture was "streamlined modern," which stressed simplicity, lots of glass windows, smooth surfaces, and little decoration. Classical and Gothic reflected a new emphasis on simplicity and less detail—as in the Jefferson Memorial in Washington, D. C. In 1937 architect Frank Lloyd Wright produced one of his most famous home designs. His belief was that buildings can link people with each other and with the natural environment.

In sports, Joe DiMaggio thrilled baseball fans and became a hero to all Americans. Other baseball stars included Lou Gehrig and Bob Feller. Boxing was dominated by the "Brown Bomber," Joe Louis. Americans thrilled to the Olympic Gold Medal performance of Sonja Henie in ice skating, and both Babe Dedrikson and Jesse Owen in track and field.

Magazines helped people escape from their cares with illustrated glimpses into the lives of well–known entertainers, sports personalities, and wealthy society "stars." Many millions of people explored the worlds of science and technology exhibited at two World Fairs, one in Chicago and one in New York City.

The Great Depression forced most Americans to devise inexpensive forms of entertainment. Parlor games, jigsaw puzzles, card games, and Bingo became leisure time activities. With improvement in the highway system, Americans were increasingly lured by the romance of the open road and their country's scenic wonders. After investing in a trailer and hitching it to their car, the family could enjoy a rather inexpensive camping vacation.

Many people believed that the crash of the stock market did not cause the Great Depression. That slow, severe economic collapse started in mid–1929 when purchasing declined and construction dropped. Many industries, such as coal, railroads, and textiles, had slow growth and weak profits. Farmers were already in an economic depression. Their decline in purchasing power was felt throughout the country. The unequal distribution of income added to the problem. The supply of goods exceeded demand. Poverty became a way of life for forty million people. On the individual level, wages fell sixty percent. Between 1930 and 1937, 86,000 businesses failed, and by 1938, 11,000 banks had failed.

When America entered World War II on December 8, 1941, the entire country—its people and industries—had to be organized into a single war effort. Once Congress declared war, the U.S. government moved swiftly to transform the economy. The heroines of the home front were the proud, patriotic women who went to work in arms plants while their husbands or boyfriends fought in the war. By 1944, three and one half million women were working in the defense industry along with six million men.

President Roosevelt believed that children's emotional lives would be affected by the deprivation of the Depression. He maintained that it was the duty of government to secure the rights of children as well as to help the parents secure jobs and maintain stable families.

Studs Terkel in his book, *Hard Times, An Oral History of the Great Depression, A Personal Memoir*, wrote: "The suddenly–idle hands blamed themselves rather than society. True, there were hunger marchers and protestations to City Hall and Washington, but the millions experienced a private kind of shame when the pink slip came. No matter that others suffered the same fate, the inner voice whispered, "I'm a failure."[1]

True, there was a sharing among many of the disposed, but, at close quarters, frustration became, at times, violence, and violence turned inward. Thus, sons and fathers fell away, one from another. And the mother, seeking work, said nothing. Outside forces, except to the more articulate and political rebels, were in some vague way responsible, but not really. It was a personal feeling of guilt.

The Depression affected people in two different ways. The great majority reacted by thinking money is the most important thing in the world. Get yours. And get it for your children.

And there were a small number of people who felt the whole system was lousy. You have to change it. The young

1    Studs Terkel *Hard Times* (New York, Random House, 1970), p. 462.

people came along and wanted to change it, too. Whatever
changes are needed should be responsive to people's needs.
And it has to be done using our democratic process, they
thought.

•••••

**Willie Mae Jones**, a native of Louisiana, was a teacher
and an administrator for forty years in the Louisiana
education system. She retired to Durham, North Carolina,
in 1992, and has studied writing at the Duke Institute for
Learning. She has published in *Dreaming*, *Metaphor*,
and *Echoes*.

# Values in the Depression Years

## Annie Morrall Kinghorn

I was born in 1919. It was four months before my eleventh birthday when the stock market crashed in 1929. So I lived all my teenage years during the Great Depression.

My family lived in Beaufort, South Carolina, a pleasant little coastal town that had many longtime residents. The United States Marine Corps training base of Parris Island was nearby, and it brought newcomers and also provided employment for many of the local citizens.

I do not have many bad memories of the Depression. One reason for this, I believe, was the personality of my father. He was always in a good humor and would not let anyone disrupt his good humor. He loved to joke, have fun, and keep everyone laughing. If something unpleasant was going on, or if an argument was about to develop over anything at all, he would reach for his hat and immediately walk out of the door. This meant someone else (usually my mother) had to work through all the household situations that did not qualify as "fun" or "happy!" In a family with five children there were plenty of concerns, but my father held the position of the lighthearted parent, and so for me as a child he was a source of play and not of "depression."

My father was inventive in a way that children appreciate. One day during the Depression there was a day so cold and rainy that water was thickly frozen on the streets. My father brought home a sturdy wooden packing crate from his furniture store. He nailed some runners on it and towed it on a rope behind his car. He took each child, one at a time, for a ride down the street. None of us had experienced an icy sled ride before and we thought it was wonderful fun! I realize from my vantage point of today that it sounds dangerous, but in those days there were few automobiles to compete for space on our small town's streets in bad weather.

My father once devised for all of his children another ride of exceptional high excitement. At that time we lived in a small house in an area called "The Bluff," high ground with a grand view of the Beaufort River. From a height of about thirty feet there was a steep slope down to the water. Our father secured one tall post at the top of the bluff and another at the water's edge. He hung a heavy wire between them, arranged a pulley on it and attached a horizontal rod for a handle. We children had great times riding this contraption to the bottom of the bluff. There was a string attached in a way that would permit the pulley to be yanked back to the top of the bluff for the next passenger. It took our mother to see the dangers inherent in this enterprise: a heavy pole requiring careful timing at the bottom of the ride, and a dangling string to become tangled around a child's neck on the way down! As a young woman, our mother had the benefit of a good education which had included nurse's training. I think it made her more cautious. Anyway, all of the children survived our father's inexpensive "inventions."

Other favorite pastimes that kept us from feeling deprived during the Depression were related to pleasurable activities on the river. We all loved to swim and to row a flat–bottomed wooden boat, referred to locally as a "bateau" (pronounced "batt–oh"). I particularly loved to go crabbing. I made my own crab lines of about eight feet of heavy string weighted with a sinker on one end. Any old thing would do for a sinker: a piece of broken brick, an old bolt, or a jagged stone. A wooden stick was needed on the other end of the string. It served as a place to wrap the string as the crab line was being pulled in with a crab, or when the line was to be stored. And it kept the line afloat until it could be retrieved if it dropped overboard.

The crab bait was tied near the sinker. The best bait was an old chicken neck, the smellier the better! Care had to be taken in holding the baited crab line. Usually there was no way to see the crab coming. We had to wait quietly until we felt the crab seize the bait. Then we slowly pulled the line toward us and upward until we could place the net under the crab.

The crab net was designed on a long wooden pole with the net portion hung from a metal hoop on one end. With a quick swish the crab was captured in the net and dropped into the waiting wash tub. In those days before commercial fishermen were catching so many of the crabs, we could fill half of the tub with large adult crabs in an hour. They are not so plentiful today.

After a successful crabbing expedition, we would take our catch back to the house. Our mother would boil crabs for twenty minutes, pick them, and make the best deviled crabs I have ever eaten anywhere. There was much sport associated with crabbing. It also put good food on the table.

My father was a great fisherman. He kept his fishing rod in the trunk of his car and knew all the best places to fish. If the tides were good and the weather seemed right, he was ready. He would come home with a string of six to eight fish, each about ten inches long, any time he surmised the time was right to fish. This was more good food for us. If there was a surplus, he would share with the neighbors.

My most vivid memory of sensing the trouble and worry of the Depression came from one short sentence from my mother. She was a faithful church member and believed in making her donation to the church every Sunday. The church provided a box of small envelopes for each family's offering, one for each Sunday of the year. My mother always placed her weekly offering in an envelope early in the week in anticipation of the following Sunday. She kept the enveloped on the fireplace mantel in her bedroom. One weekday I overheard her say to herself, "Money could not be any more scarce." And she took her money out of the little church envelope and went to buy groceries. The following week the local bank failed, and with it went our savings.

My older sister Julie reminded me of this story that we heard in Beaufort during the Depression. The telegraph office employed a delivery boy who worked hard and had tried to save some money. He was given a telegram to take to the bank. He knew that it read: "Close the bank!" He walked into the bank and asked to withdraw all of his money. After he was given his money, he delivered the telegram.

My younger sister Mae told another Depression story about our father. Although savings were gone and times were hard, he kept his furniture store open. No one was buying new furniture, but those who had bought furniture on credit before the Depression wanted to pay what they owed, but most found it impossible.

The only real income for our family during the Depression came from the funeral business my father operated. Families of people who had bought insurance policies to pay for their funerals before the Depression had the resources to pay for funerals when the time came, while in the furniture business there was only the hope of collecting some small amount of money owed for previously bought furniture. Our father would call on customers to collect payments.

Once when Mae was a little girl, he took her with him when he went to the home of an old woman in a poor neighborhood. The woman was lying sick in the same bed she had been paying for with credit. She owed a payment of fifty cents. "Mr. Willie," she said, "You will just have to take this bed I'm lying in because I can't make the payment."

Our father was quiet for a minute and looked around the room. He saw a little stack of official looking papers beside the bed. He asked, "What's this?"

The woman answered that those were prescriptions from the doctor who had been making house calls and that they were of no use to her because there was no money to pay for medicine. Our father picked up the prescriptions, went directly to the pharmacy, paid for the medicines, and took them back to his customer. And, I suppose that is another reason money was scarce at our home during the Depression.

•••••

**Annie Morrell Kinghorn** graduated from Columbia College in South Carolina. She lives in Beaufort, South Carolina. She still enjoys crabbing and keeps her friends supplied with crabmeat.

# Family Sharing in the Bronx

## A Chapel Hill Resident

In 1929, when Wall Street crashed, I had just finished elementary school in the Bronx. From 1924 to 1930, I attended school in PS6 on Madison Avenue in Manhattan. These were hard times for people, but we children never felt deprived because our parents shielded us, and, too, everyone else was in the same predicament.

Our part of the business area of the Bronx was occupied by the clothing industry. In 1929 our mother had to go to work as an operator in the clothing factory. Our father kept his small clothing factory going on a shoestring.

Mother's sister had two children. Our uncle was a bookbinder who lost his job. So all eight of us lived in our four–room apartment.

Sleeping arrangements included Mother and Father on a day bed, an aunt and uncle on a single bed, my cousin and I on the other single bed, and two boys (my brother and a cousin) on the floor. Cooking and cleaning were done by my aunt.

The older boy suffered the most because of lack of money. He was the brightest, and so he tried to go to City College at night, but was not financially able to finish.

At Christmas time we had saved our pennies, and eight of us had a total of eight dollars. But out of that money, we all had presents. And they were wrapped. My uncle eventually got a job and had money for moving to Brooklyn.

I had been working every summer as a waitress in a children's camp. This job got me out of the city. One summer I came home with $17 in tips. When I gave it to my mother, she cried because she had no money for food. The next summer I worked as a camp bookkeeper. On weekends we went as a family to Coney Island and to Central Park.

An interesting result of the Great Depression for us is that my Cousin Ruth and I are frugal. But the two boys are spendthrifts and never learned to save.

# Doubling Up with Relatives

## Katherine M. Kaman

From the time I was born until the stock market crash in 1929, life was pretty normal. My parents bought a home on Southern Avenue at Rozelle in Memphis. I entered first grade at Rozelle School which was about two and one–half blocks from home. I could walk to and from my school. My favorite person was Mr. Burke who was a uniformed crossing guard at my school. My first grade teacher was Ms. Armistead (I'm sure she was a spinster). I hated school, but I had no brothers and sisters, and school meant friends and the company of my peers.

My dad ran into bad health and a series of surgeries. Before he could recover, the stock market crashed, and we lost our home. The next four or five years of my life were pretty desperate, Depression years—the abomination of desolation and utter hopelessness.

## The Depression

I first noticed that things were not the same when we moved from our lovely brick home on Southern to a clap–board cottage on McLemore. Sensing that my mother was upset, I tried to console her that I liked our new home better. There were no social programs, no unemployment compensation, no aid to dependent children. Everyone was on his or her own "root hog or die." The armies of the unemployed marched on Washington, D. C., but it did no good—they were ignored. Men and women tried to sell apples and pencils on street corners. My dad, being a railroad man, had no work; the railroads were barely operating. No one else would hire railroad men, as they knew when the economy improved and the railroad resumed full scale operations that the men would go back to the railroad.

We lived for a short time in Amory, Mississippi, my mother's home town. At this time, things were not too bad; I was in the third grade, and we were happy in Amory. By the time I was in the fourth grade, we came back to Memphis. Mother took in a boarder to help with the expenses and occasionally got a day's work in a grocery store demonstrating Humko products. For this, she made $2.00 a day, quite a handsome sum at that time.

Things got worse, and Daddy went to Mississippi to look for work. Mother and I moved in with Aunt Genevieve and her family. We lived on a screened–in porch (it was winter). Genevieve's husband hung tarpaulins over the screen wire to keep out the cold. We had a little space heater to keep warm, and Mother took in sewing to have money to provide for necessities. During this time, my mother took some of her sewing money and bought fabric to make me a dress to be entered in a department store sewing contest in the hope of winning a cash prize. (If she didn't win, all was not lost as I needed a dress anyway). The dress was cotton, green and orange, very fine plaid, made in princess lines with a choir boy style white collar with scalloped edge and a split into which she inserted handsome fagoting with white thread. It was a pretty dress, but before it was over, I really grew tired of it. It was a great disappointment when she did not win. She got Honorable Mention (a ribbon but no cash). I wore this dress to school every day. Mother laundered it at night so it was always clean.

One day, Aunt Genevieve was gone for the day, and there was no food in the house; we had no money to buy food. I came home to lunch every day so I could eat whatever was available. That day Mother found an onion, the heel ends of a loaf of bread, and some rancid butter. She diced the onion, sautéed it in the butter, toasted the bread ends, and served the onions over the bread. I believe we had iced tea to drink. When I came in, we sat down to eat. We said grace and ate the meager meal. When it was over, I told my mother I enjoyed my lunch! Unknown to me, my mother cried all afternoon.

I tell you these things as they are symbolic of the times in which I grew up. We were not alone. Other people were suffering as well.

During this period, Mother walked seven miles to town to deliver some sewing she'd finished and anticipated collecting her modest $2.00 fee. The lady did not pay her, so she had to walk back home, since she didn't have the five–cent fare to ride the street car home.

When school was out, we went to Tupelo to live with my daddy's mother. She had a small home, and five people already lived there. We fared better there, as Mommie had a garden, some chickens, and a small cow. The women cooked on a wood stove. We had no electricity, no running water, no plumbing. We pumped water from a well and had a "two seater" outdoor privy. Entertainment was to sit on the porch in the evening and have the adults tell ghost stories. We never got tired of it, the same stories over and over, and we'd get so scared we'd want to sleep with Mommie in her feather bed. You'd burrow down in the softness, cuddle up against Mommie, and be safe from the world and all the demons!

The highlight of the day was to walk (barefooted) the half mile up the road to the highway where the "mail rider" delivered the mail to rural mail boxes. I don't know what we thought we were going to receive. I was always expecting a summons from Hollywood asking me to be a movie star (it never arrived), but I was pretty sure it was just a matter of time. Don't ask me why I believed this. One day Jack and I were the first ones to the mail boxes, and we found a sample of "Feen–a–Mint" in our box. We thought it was chewing gum! We entered into a conspiracy to raid the mail boxes, take all the gum, and chew it (we did not consider this to be stealing, since it was free, and no one knew it was there). This turned out to be a classic story of "Crime and Punishment." It's a wonder we didn't die, but we did sit out on the two–seater all afternoon looking at Sears, Roebuck Catalogs and being punished for our sins. We knew better than to tell the adults what we'd done.

That summer, the couple next door took me to a movie to see *Alibi Ike* with Joe E. Brown. I'll never forget it! They also bought me a double dip ice cream cone. What a treat!

Hoover was president. When he gave a speech, it was always the same, "Prosperity is just around the corner. There will be a chicken in every pot in every home." Some people up the road had electricity and a radio; I guess they were rich. When the President spoke, they'd invite the neighbors to their house. It was standing room only in their yard; they'd open the windows and play the radio real loud so everyone could hear. Everyone was anxious for good news that never came.

I think all the above is why I don't like Tupelo, Mississippi. I just associate it with hopelessness. This was the summer that Mr. Shands fell on hard times and burned his house down. He was a close by neighbor—we woke up during the night; his house was blazing. We feared our house would catch fire too, but fortunately we were spared.

# The Metamorphosis

It was 1932, the year I would be nine years old. The Democratic Party nominated a "dark horse" candidate to run for president of the United States, Franklin Delano Roosevelt. Once again, there was hope.

As soon as he took office, Roosevelt declared a bank holiday and closed every bank in America to prevent runs on banks. He introduced the New Deal and unemployment compensation. He began to rebuild the confidence of America. He founded the HOLC, Home Owners Loan Corporation to reinsure homes and stop foreclosures. The railroads began to move again with bargain fares called "Excursion Rates." We moved back to Memphis, a humble beginning, but we had a rented home, and our little family was together again.

Daddy had a "run" (trip) per week, but it meant he was back to work on the railroad again, and things were getting back to normal. We rented a small three room "shot gun" house (one room straight behind the other) on Philadelphia, near the Fairgrounds. The house was in poor condition, so the owner gave Daddy some free rent in exchange for his labor painting the house inside and out. I began school at Peabody School in the fifth grade. We didn't have much money, but these were happy days. We had a radio, and my favorite shows were *Gail & Dan*, who had a monkey named "Snodgrass," and *The Little Theater Off Times Square*. Don Ameche was the host, and the programs featured a three–act play once a week. While we were living here, I had an emergency appendicitis attack and had to have what was then major surgery. I was out of the school for about six weeks, but with the help of a kind teacher, Mrs. Douglas, I was able to make up my work and pass to the sixth grade. I finished grammar school at Peabody School and began the seventh grade at Fairview Junior High, a brand new school at the corner of Parkway and Central.

We moved over onto the next street, which was called New York, and began to buy another home, a five–room clapboard house with a nice porch. I completed the seventh grade at Fairview and started the eighth grade. At this time, I had a darling dog, a screw tail Boston Bull named "Miss Fannie Brown." I loved Fannie, and she was a great companion. My Daddy's brother, Scott, lived with us from time to time; he was a "rounder" and not too reliable, but he was a wonderful cook and occasionally cooked "chili mac" (a chili and macaroni dish that was really quite good).

In the spring of 1936, a very serious tornado struck Tupelo, Mississippi. My grandmother passed away in October before the tornado struck in April. My grandmother's home and its contents were destroyed. My Aunt May and Aunt Lottie were killed. My cousins, Jack and Billy, were left orphans, and they began to take turns living with us from time to time. In the fall of my eighth grade year, we moved to Nashville, as it looked like Daddy would be there permanently. However, after only a few months, his work took us to Amory, Mississippi. I loved Amory as much as I despised Tupelo. It was a pretty little town with a parking lot in the center of town, and the trains coming and going were the town's excitement.

We attended the Methodist Church, where we had an active youth group and had many good times. By this time, both Jack and I were thirteen years old, and I for one thought I was grown. By this time, we had a car, a Chevrolet, and Mother learned to drive. This was an especially happy time. Life in a small town is just about

Utopia for a teenager. My best friend was Carolyn, a willowy blonde, who grew up to marry a Baptist minister and become a very proper lady.

While we were living there, Amory celebrated her Sesquicentennial. It was quite a celebration. My Mother's half–brothers came with their families to help celebrate. Uncle John was a good cook, and he made a large pot of the most delicious chicken Brunswick Stew I ever tasted. I wish I had his recipe; it was delicious! I got to take part in the official celebration as a dancer in a little group of teenage girls who dressed in gauzy Roman style togas. My uncle, who owned some motion picture theaters, brought his motion picture camera and recorded the celebration. I just knew this would be my big break into the movies, but, of course, it wasn't.

## High School Daze

From the mid–to–late thirties on until Pearl Harbor, December 7, 1941, life moved at a serene and leisurely pace. My folks were able to buy a new home in 1938—1800 Mignon, near Overton Park, the zoo, and Southwestern College. This was a brand new home in a new subdivision, two bedrooms, one bath, living room, dining room, eat–in kitchen, and a porch. Total purchase price $4,200 financed for thirty years at four percent interest! New cars cost $500 to $600. Most people didn't have one. A car was a luxury used for pleasure and Sunday driving. People used public transportation, street cars and buses, to go to and from work, downtown shopping, etc. The fare was seven cents, and the service was excellent. In a way, this was an era of excellence, as the economy emerged from the Depression, people were grateful, valued their jobs, and worked hard. It was a safe time; the crime rate was low, and the races seemed to live in harmony and supported one another. You could buy your groceries by telephone, and a delivery boy delivered them. You could even call the drug store, and they'd deliver a Coca–Cola and a box of aspirin. If you were sick, doctors made house calls; if you needed to go to the hospital, the doctor would take you in his car. A doctor was a trusted, honored, and respected family friend. Our doctor was Dr. Jimmy Owens, a wonderful man. He was short, slightly chubby, had balding white hair, a round, well–scrubbed face, a pleasant smile, and a flower in his lapel. When he showed up, you knew everything was going to be okay!

The only place in the entire world that was air conditioned was the movie theater. They had hanging banners outside that looked frosty and that read "Cool Inside." People sat through bad movies just to be cool.

There was an outdoor theater in Overton Park called "The Shell." Seating was under the stars. During the summer, a local theatrical group produced musical comedies and light operettas at The Shell. The chorus, dancers, etc., were local volunteer amateurs. Big name stars came to Memphis and played the lead roles. Productions included *The Merry Widow*, *The Chocolate Soldier*, *Show Boat*, and many, many more. It was pleasant and cool outdoors under the stars. I'll always remember Dorothy Kirsten of the Metropolitan Opera singing "I'll See You Again." What beautiful memories!

•••••

**Katherine N. Kaman** died in 1998. This is a section of her biography, which was submitted by her son Chris Kaman.

# About Hoboes

## Cherry Parker

Hoboes did not suddenly appear when the Great Depression (October, 1929–December, 1941) hit America. With the growth of the railroads from 53,000 miles by 1870 to 230,000 miles in 1930, transient Civil War veterans were the first to hit the rails to find temporary employment in the West. When the numbers of unemployed increased during the economic panics of 1873 and 1893, more hungry men hopped freight cars. Then, later, during the Great Depression when countless able–bodied workers were jobless, many banks had closed, and hometown soup lines were cut back, it has been estimated that more than one million men as well as thousands of young boys, girls, and women joined the hobo ranks. Before this, the hobo culture had consisted mostly of unmarried men who often were the prelude to today's migratory workers. This group did not want to be called "tramps" or "bums" because they often worked for a meal and a place to sleep rather than begging for a handout. According to Charles Elmer Fox in his *Tales of an American Hobo*, "Who else but a hobo would travel a thousand miles to make a dollar a day harvesting wheat?" Other hoboes picked fruit, felled timber, raised railroad beds, or did farm work during their travels; and some with an artistic bent carved and made intricate boxes, picture frames, and small furniture, often using cigar boxes. Today, these sought–for collectibles are called "tramp art."

"Bums," according to Fox, "were usually found on street corners, mooching...from passersby". He wrote, "Hoboes will work. Tramps won't and bums can't."

Fox and other hobo writers told of the perils and discomforts of boxcar travel: the dust and grime, the sliding cargo which hit the riders, the fumes as the trains passed through tunnels, the dangers of swinging aboard a rolling train without slipping under its wheels to get maimed or killed. At the peak of the Depression, 6,500 illegal railroad riders met this fate in a single year.

Another threat was the fear of railroad yard cops, some with clubs, who tried to keep hoboes off the trains, or to herd them into jail.

Cold and hunger added to the miseries. Fox described the hobo bed, made from a roll of newspapers: some to lie on, some to cover with, all tucked under, especially under the head so the wind would not blow the paper away. He also described the hobo "jungle" where men lived in groups in makeshift shelters, cooking over an open fire.

A few of the Depression hoboes became well known. Writers Jack London, Carl Sandburg, Louis L'Amour all rode the rails, as did folk artist Woody Guthrie, and TV host Art Linkletter. Eric Sevareid also made a hobo trek, as did Supreme Court Justice William O. Douglas.

World War II drastically changed things for hoboes. When the railroads changed from steam to diesel in the 1950's, with fewer trains on longer runs and fewer stops where a hobo could swing on board, the hobo lifestyle slackened. Some of the Depression survivors had settled in towns they had liked as they passed through, but others stayed on the road to become old, even to die there.

More recently, Ted Conover, who left college to ride the rails for four months, describes some veteran hoboes that he came to know in his book, *Rolling Nowhere*.

Conover writes, "To understand (hoboes)...you have to understand that people cannot always do what they are told. Maybe you are told to get a job, but there aren't any; maybe you return from a crazy war and are told to carry on as though nothing ever happened. Maybe you live in a small room on a smaller pension, spending each day doing nothing....Many tramps' careers on the road began when the tramp told society, 'You can't fire me—I quit.' "

Conover ends his book about hoboes by telling us what he learned on the road. He says, "The hobo is not 'one of them.' He is one of us."

●●●●●

A native Kentuckian, **Cherry Parker** is a widow with two children and three grandchildren. An R.N., she has a degree in Public Health Nursing. She has been published in many professional journals and lay magazines. For a number of years she wrote a weekly newspaper column called *With Cherry*. She is co-author of *The Hand-Me-Down Cookbook*.

# Personal Encounters with Two Hoboes

## Cherry Parker

Down in the Village in New York the summer of 1960, I bought a paper called the *Hobo Express News*. Ben (Hobo) Benson, its editor, publisher, and news–vendor, was hawking it on the square. "Read all about it," Ben was crying, "Find out why hoboes don't marry."

I talked with Benson briefly, then bought a paper. Besides burning to know why hoboes don't marry, I've always had a personal interest in hoboes.

My cousin Douglas was one. I remember first meeting Douglas when I was a kid living at my grandpa's in Elkton, Kentucky. Grandpa was a retired Methodist preacher, and when Douglas was visiting, he was fed and bedded but regarded with some distrust. Grandpa tried his best to keep us children away from Douglas. But he couldn't. Douglas was too fetching. He was in his middle or late twenties at the time and very handsome in spite of the fact that he possessed what we have always described as "the Cherry nose." I recall that he wore turtle–necked sweaters and brindle–colored corduroy trousers, and he told us about how he cooked stew over an open fire in a hobo jungle, using a rusty coffee can, as well as how he rode boxcars from Louisville to Los Angeles and then back again. He also wrote lovely, complicated poetry which he read to us, gesturing dramatically. He liked for us to applaud loudly, and we did. And we all laughed a lot, but I always felt sad when the laughing was over.

After Douglas took back to the road, every hobo who meandered by along the Hopkinsville Pike came to our house asking for a handout. Grandpa accused Douglas of leaving some kind of mark near the vicinity of the mailbox to let them all know that Grandma had food available.

But, getting back to Benson's hobo paper——

On its title page, the *Hobo Express News* proclaimed, "All the Hobo News Fit to Print."[1] It went on, "The left ear gives a hobo weather forecast: June—Bridal Weather, July—Hellish Weather, August—Hobo Weather". On the front page also was a large picture of Ben (Hobo) Benson himself. He closely resembled the late Jimmy Durante. A smaller photo described two hobo Queens (women) from Iowa who hitchhiked to California but paused long enough in their tracks to write a book about it.

On the editorial page, along with other things, an article called "Social Security, Relief, and Jobs Have Ruined Hobo Profession" was featured, while a letter dated January 18, 1960, from Mrs. Roosevelt read as follows:

"Dear Mr. Benson, May I thank you very much for your letter and the copies of the Hobo periodicals. It is most kind of you to send them to me and I was interested to hear about your many activities. With kindest regards and best wishes, Eleanor Roosevelt."

This page also contained art show dates, the Skidrow–Bowery news, and a letter to Mayor Wagner from a "Sober Bowerite" who felt that the most crying need in New York was for a Bowery curb market.

1    On page 2, the *Hobo Express News* it says "No copyright, poems, or jokes. In Public Domain."

Much of the other copy, including verse, was written by editor Benson. A signed ditty by Henry Herbert Knibbs has a stanza:

> *"But there was the road windin' mile after mile...*
> *And nothing...to do...but go.*
> *So beat it, Bo, while your feet are mates;*
> *Take a d— good look at the United States."*

Another called "The Dying Hobo" by Overland Red started off:

> *"Beside a western water tank, one cold December*
> *day,*
> *Inside an empty box–car, a dying hobo lay;..."*

Pictures and this announcement covered the last page, "For Vice–President Vote for Famous Ex–Hobo King Benson. Ex–Official King of the Hoboes. Former Editor–the Hobo News. Vote for Leisure and Prosperity." It proclaimed the stated platform includes: four work hours a day, four work days a week, three–month vacation with pay, and so on.

The key article, "Why Hoboes Don't Marry," was also by Benson. I read it twice but did not find out anything too sensational. I did discover that Benson wanted "the free life—no hits, no runs, no errors." And that Benson, at 75, was "still a single man and proud of it."

The story of my cousin Douglas turned out a little different. Douglas never did marry either. But he reformed, and so Grandpa's prayers were answered. I think Douglas even went back to college. When World War II came along, he joined the army, and we heard that he got some ribbons. But we never saw Douglas in his army khaki, or in his brindle–colored corduroy pants again. Never heard his lovely, complicated poetry which made us laugh while we felt like crying.

Douglas was killed in action somewhere in Germany.

And it seems rather ironical that, after all, the last ride he ever took was in a boxcar.

•••••

A native Kentuckian, **Cherry Parker** is a widow with two children and three grandchildren. An R.N., she has a degree in Public Health Nursing. She has been published in many professional journals and lay magazines. For a number of years she wrote a weekly newspaper column called *With Cherry*. She is co-author of *The Hand-Me-Down Cookbook*.

# Who Is Poor?

## 1928 Until 1934

## Lucy Rodgers Watkins

Who is poor? *Until she was three, she had never heard the word except in the abstract: "Blessed are the poor in spirit, for theirs is the kingdom of heaven".*

• • • •

They had lived in the Little Red Brick House in Greensboro from as early as she could remember, with a sandbox beside it to play in; and she had her own kiddy car to ride on the sidewalk. Mama let them play boat or car in the two valises her Daddy used to take on trips. They had a cabinet radio then, so that she could sit on a stool before it, open the doors, and pretend to play a piano on the ledge as the music came from inside. Once she looked behind the radio to see if she could see whether there were people inside it playing the music and talking.

Her father and mother liked the Little Red Brick House and worked to make it nice. Her mother bought them a little wooden table with three chairs, just the right size for them to eat at. Her father planted two trees in the front yard and kept it clean and raked. Once when he was in the side yard burning branches, she called to him through the closed window, but he couldn't hear her. So she sang to herself,

Nobody loves me, everybody hates me,
I'm going in the garden and eat worms;

Long, slick, slimy ones, big, fat, juicy ones,
Golly, how they tickle when they squirm.

When she had double pneumonia—*it was sometime in late 1928 or early 1929*—they put wrap–around mustard plasters on her and gave her caster oil in orange juice. When her Daddy came in one night with her caster oil and orange juice, she told him, "I'll take it like a man." *But it tasted so bad that she was almost grown before she could stand to drink orange juice again.* She was very sick, but she passed what they called "the crisis;" and it was a long time before she could even sit up. She lay looking at her wooden bunny pulling a cart that her mother had put on the windowsill, and she felt her tiny doll's rubber water bottle under her pillow. *Oranges cost ninety cents a dozen that year, and a week's supply for her illness must have taken a fourth of her father's salary every week.* Shortly after that, her father was offered a job on a newspaper in Chicago.

•   •   •   •

They rode the train to Washington, and she felt very small standing under the enormous high ceilings of the Washington Union Train Station. Then they rode all night on the train to Chicago, and she slept in a curtained berth with her sister, Mildred. Her mother tucked them in and closed the curtain. It was cozy and comfortable. Her sister, Winnie, slept with Mama.

They lived in a second floor apartment in Rogers Park, a block from Lake Michigan, which was across Lake Shore Drive, the biggest street she'd ever seen. They were not supposed to let anybody in the front door, which had a little peek hole for grown–ups to see who was knocking. Since they didn't have a car, her father went to work on a train called the El, up above the street, which roared over the underpass half a block away. Sometimes her mother let the three of them run down the street to stand under it and "let the train run over us," or meet their father coming home from work.

*Were they going alone on this adventure? Or was her mother watching them from behind? She felt she was going alone.* One day their parents took them to ride on the El, and they squatted down on the floor beside the El windows to try to see the tops of the skyscrapers down town.

On summer days near dusk, their mother took the three of them, in their matching pink summer pajamas that she had made, down to Lake Michigan, where they set small wax paper boats, each with a lit birthday candle, on the water's surface and watched them sail out onto the vast lake.

Some summer days when they were going to the beach, as an adventure her mother let her older sister go alone down the back steps from the apartment to the alley (while the rest of the family went down the front steps), then down the alley to the right and out into the side street where she met the others. One day, she persuaded her mother to let her go on the adventure instead of her sister. She went very proudly, her first time alone. It seemed farther than she had thought it would; and when she stuck her head out around the corner of the building at the end of the alley, her mother and sisters weren't there. It was all strange looking, and she felt not so much afraid as very alone and small. *She had turned the wrong way at the bottom of the steps.* A big policeman saw her and took her back down the alley again to find her frantic mother and sisters at the other end. *Chicago could be alien.* But the alley was a friendly and bustling place, full of activity. The vegetable man, the fish man, the banana man all came along it, shouting what they had to sell. The organ grinder man came through the alley too, and his little monkey danced to the music and held a cup for pennies, which the three of them tossed down from the dining room window. But after the day she had made the wrong turn down there, she didn't go down alone again, only stood on the back porch and listened and looked.

In the winter the snow banked up to the second story of the apartment house, and they opened the window and tasted the snow or gathered a bowl for their mother to make snow cream. Lake Michigan, which was a lake but looked like an ocean because she couldn't see anything on the other side, was frozen in waves, as if it were the ocean held still in a picture. On the beach the firemen sprayed water on the tennis courts to freeze so children could skate. It was very cold. They were blown down coming from the grocery store one windy day: *Chicago could be cruel.*

At Christmas time they went to visit people who had a son just a little older than they were. She saw the large living room from under the grand piano, where she sat on the floor watching the boy's new electric train come around a gold–backed chair on tracks laid all over the side of the room and winding around her private seat under the piano.

From that day on, she wanted an electric train every Christmas.

That year she saw the poor. A family friend was taking them across the city in his car one cold day in downtown Chicago, and she saw men lined up for over a block to get something to eat at a soup kitchen. They had no overcoats on, and their collars were turned up around their hunched shoulders and necks. Across the street under an overpass, men lay on the sidewalk on newspapers with newspapers covering them. *Later in her life, she learned that Chicago's notorious gangster, Al Capone, had opened soup kitchens all over the city to feed the poor.*

* * * *

*At the end of the year in Chicago, her parents decided to go back South, where her father was promised a managing editor position at a newspaper to be started in Richmond.* They rode the night train again, and she got to sleep in a berth again and see the statues around the ceiling in the Washington Union Train Station, *the first copies of classical art that she was to know.* In Virginia they went to her mother's family farm until her father could find a place for them to live in Richmond. They lived for the next six months on the farm with her boy cousins, Bobby and Johnny, and her aunt, uncles, and grandmother. It was wonderful, her favorite place, *and she always felt safe and secure there.*

They ate quail, turkeys, squirrels, and rabbits her uncles had brought in from hunting. When it was sheep shearing and killing time, they had mutton from the sheep in the pasture. They ate fried and roasted chickens that she

helped feed, and their eggs that she helped gather. She also helped pick up apples from the orchard, and Aunt Nancy and her mother picked and canned vegetables from the garden. Potatoes came from the cold storage room in the basement. Her aunt made tea cakes and pound cakes; and for breakfast they always had streak–of–lean, streak–of–fat bacon that was kept from one meal to the next in the corner cupboard in the dining room. Hams for dinner came from the smokehouse with its smoky smell and hard–packed red clay floor. She watched her uncles milk the cows, and drank the milk either warm just after milking, or cold as it came from the underground icehouse with blocks of ice covered by straw, or was pulled up in the bucket from the dark old open well on the back porch where they kept it chilled. She and her sisters and boy cousins took turns churning the milk 400 turns of the handle, slowing down gradually toward the end so the butter would gather as her aunt added cold water.

She helped bring in wood for the wood stove in the kitchen, and sat behind it on the wood box and ate apples on cold or rainy days. Old Alice, who was black and lived down the road with her sister, Mary, the cook, washed their clothes in a black iron pot over a fire by the backyard woodpile. Mary always gave them cookies, but Alice talked under her breath and would grumble at anyone of the children who sneaked up on her from behind the woodpile to hear, and send them running in fear. *It was an almost real fear.*

Kerosene lamps lit their evenings, and the regular Bible reading and prayers before bedtime. At night she lay snuggled down in a featherbed, and in the morning, she heard Uncle Henry chopping wood that he brought in to make a fire in the bedroom fireplace while she snuggled down farther until it was warm enough to dress. In the spring and summer, her mattress was made of corn shucks instead of feathers. Corn shucks were hard to sleep on and rustled when she turned over. Winter or summer, everybody washed his hands in the back porch entry, where she had to avoid the wasps and dirt daubers that built their nests in the corner of the ceiling. The towel hanging from a nail seemed always to be wet. She helped Bobby and Johnny pump water from the well outside to bring in and set on the shelf beside the basin. Everybody drank the nice, cold water from the dipper in the bucket. Winter or summer, they went to the toilet in the Johnny house, down the path between the milkweed plants to the end of the yard. It had three holes, large, medium, and small; and usually the old Sears, Roebuck catalogue served instead of toilet paper. Her mother and aunt used feed sacks to make towels and aprons. Feed sacks often came with nice flower patterns printed on them.

They played in an old car up on blocks in an open shed, making car noises and imagining they were driving all over the country. On Sundays they went to Sunday School and church in the buggy, four miles over the red clay roads to Meherrin.

When her mother got sick, the doctor had to be sent for and came eighteen miles to see her. *She didn't know that it was pneumonia.*

*She didn't know that the job her father was promised didn't come through, because the man lost his money and couldn't start a new newspaper in the middle of the Depression. She didn't know that the only money her father had—$100—was used by the whole family that half-year for coffee, sugar, shoes, and other absolute necessities. She didn't know that her father's trips all up and down in three states were for looking for work or doing temporary, short-term jobs.*

• • • •

And then, one day, they moved to Greensboro, where her father went to work for the *Greensboro Record* . They lived in a nice house on North Eugene Street, just across the street from the elementary school where she would be going the next year.

There was a furnace in the kitchen to heat the whole house, and a heater for hot water that Mama lit with a match when anyone needed to take a bath. When painters came to paint the house, she went around the corner alone to watch. The man standing at the top of a ladder suddenly turned around and shifted his top false teeth out of his mouth and back in again, making a hideous face. She ran as fast as she could back inside the house. But other times she played outside with Mildred and Winnie, *feeling very safe.* She climbed trees and up the garage doors to the roof to sit astride the roofline. Once when she was coming down a tree in the front yard, she slipped down, but her heel caught between a branch and the trunk. Her mother came running out of the house and climbed the tree to get her loose.

When they played hide–and–seek, sometimes her mother would unfold the sofa and close her up inside so that nobody could find her, or hide her under the clothes in a dresser drawer. They made trains with the dining room chairs and occasionally used the extra table leaves to make airplane wings to turn their trains into planes. Mama put blankets over card tables to make houses, and cardboard boxes became cars and boats.

Lela Ramsey and Brother Ramsey lived next door, on the side where the painter had scared her. Mrs. Ramsey sat on the front porch in a swing a lot and fanned herself and watched the cars go by. The three sisters didn't exactly play with Lela and Brother: Lela was a little older than they were, but that wasn't the reason. Brother was a mean little boy, but that wasn't the reason. Although she didn't know why and never thought much about it, she seemed to feel that they weren't exactly the kind of children she was supposed to play with. *Later in her life, she would have heard her father refer to people like them as "common."*

One hot summer day Brother Ramsey hid their newborn kittens under a washtub in the back yard. When she and Mildred and Winnie finally found the kittens, they were dead from the heat. *She learned that people could be cruel*. But her father used to bring home stray kittens whenever he found them, once in the rain one night with its little black head sticking out between the buttons of his coat. "Oh, no, not another one," her mother said. "I'm sure that must be the neighbor's kitten." But sometimes they couldn't find the owner, and once her mother let her keep a butter–colored one. When it was only a little bigger, one day it ran in the street and was hit by a car and killed. She cried and couldn't go to sleep that night. Her father brought her crackers and a glass of water and sat beside her while she ate them. Then she slept.

Sometimes a washer woman would come and scrub clothes on the scrub board in the washtub in the kitchen, but once a week her mother gathered all the sheets and towels into a big pile in the hall where she and her sisters would jump into them until the pile was complete, and then her mother tied them up for the laundry man to pick them up. On washday, if the weather was bad, the washer woman had to hang the clothes inside, and sometimes her pajamas weren't dry by bedtime. So her mother would put them in the oven to dry, standing there to make sure they didn't burn. She had two pairs of socks, so having dry socks wasn't a problem. She had a Sunday dress and, when school time came, she had several school dresses. But she liked her sweater best, one with colored stripes, which she named her "Joseph coat of many colors." She had one pair of shoes, which she polished on Saturday night along with her father's shoes. He gave her a nickel to polish his. If she had a hole worn in the sole of her shoes, her mother cut cardboard in the shape of the shoe and put it inside until they could go to the shoe repair man to fix it. In the summertime, she went barefooted except for wearing sandals to Sunday School and church. Every spring, she loved the first day she could take off her shoes and socks and walk in the cool, green grass. As spring went on, she toughened her feet by walking, then running, across dirt, then plowed ground, then rocks, until nothing would hurt them, unless she stepped on someone's carelessly thrown cigarette butt or a yellow jacket in the grass.

Several times every year, various aunts would send their children's outgrown clothes, and she and Mildred and Winnie would have a great time sorting out who got what. She always got her cousin Nancy's shorts, because they fitted her best. That was wonderful for summer and Saturdays.

They got ice for the icebox by putting a sign in the window for the iceman to see. It was a diamond–shaped sign that could hang by any corner, so that the number on top—15, 25, 40, or 50—told the iceman how many pounds her mother wanted. The iceman came in a wagon drawn by a horse. When he went inside to take the huge block of ice with his tongs to put in the icebox, she and her sisters sneaked around front and got chips of ice out of the wagon to eat. They didn't know whether he would be angry at them taking it, but they were afraid he would be. She wasn't sure, but maybe it was stealing. She did it anyway, but ran before he came back out.

That summer she saw her first total eclipse of the sun, looking at it through old negatives. It was a very important occasion. That summer also, men often came and knocked on the back door and asked for something to eat. Her mother always managed to find them a plateful of food, and they sat on the back porch and ate.

Once her father made something liquid in the bathtub—all very mysterious to her—but it was a drink called gin. She seemed to feel her mother didn't like his doing it.

She grew old enough to sing in the children's choir at church that year, and at Christmas time to go caroling. She walked across the street and started school and learned to read. She learned to skin the cat and do chin–ups on the acting bar on the playground. She learned to dance the minuet for a play about George and Martha Washington, but was sick and had to give her part as Martha to a schoolmate. She and her sisters had measles and mumps, and she was very sick. No one could come to see them, because there was a sign on the door with "Quarantine" written on it. Her mother was glad their sign didn't also say "scarlet fever." That year everybody had vaccinations for the first time, for diphtheria and smallpox, a very grown up step to be taking, she felt. That year, she and her sisters also went to the dentist for the first time, and he wrote each of their names with his drill on glasses for them. That was also the year she and Winnie had their first operations: the doctor put them to sleep in his office and took out their tonsils. She had a bad dream from the ether and was sick when she woke up, but the nurse gave them balloons and ice cream.

That spring, in 1933, one warm day her father was home from work and had the Philco radio turned on, with the window open. She sat on the moss under the tree outside and listened to President Roosevelt give his inaugural address. *She didn't remember what he said.* She knew he was the new President, and that it was an important occasion.

Big news came in editions of the newspaper that newsboys came around at night to sell, shouting, "Extra!" Her father bought one which had big headlines about the

Yangtze River flooding and drowning thousands of people. There was another Extra when a school exploded in Texas and killed a lot of children. *Years later, in another town, a magazine salesman with only one arm came to their door to sell magazines. He told them he had been in that explosion.*

They went to Banner Elk that summer, the nicest vacation they'd ever had, and the first one that was somewhere else than Bobby and Johnny's farm. They saw Blowing Rock, Looking Glass Falls, drove along the gravel one–lane Yonalossee Trail with hairpin curves where the car had to back up to get around the curve, and to the top of Roan Mountain, and ate buckwheat cakes for breakfast in the dining

room. *She didn't know that her father was being paid in "pink slips" instead of money, that the trip was paid for by advertising in the newspaper, and that her father was writing a big article for the paper as part of his pay. She didn't know that her mother had to use the pink slips at stores that advertised in the paper, and that any change she got back if the bill wasn't exact was almost like gold. Her mother talked later in life about having ten cents a week to buy small necessities, a cooking spoon or fork, and save for larger necessities from stores that didn't take pink slips. She didn't know* that during the Depression years, her parents lost her mother's share of the family farm and two houses they were trying to buy.

That fall, one night she woke up and found her little white iron bed pushed back out of the children's room and standing at an angle in the back bedroom. She called her mother, and her father came and picked her up and carried her into their front bedroom. There on the bed her mother lay with a tiny baby girl beside her. She didn't say a word. Her father put her back to bed. The next morning, she told everybody that she had been the first one to see her new baby sister, Suzanne.

• • • •

Halfway through the next year, when she was in the second grade, they moved to Salisbury, to another nice house. *She didn't know that her father could no longer manage to pay for everything with pink slips, and that, although he wanted to remain a newspaperman, he had to leave the newspaper and take a government job.* Moving was exciting. When all the furniture was gone, they could run around the house and shout and hear echoes like the ones they'd heard when they shouted in the mountains.

In the new house, there was an extra room that could be their playroom. There were children across the street, and they started going to a new school, where she led a children's rhythm orchestra and learned about birds in the Audubon Club. They all had whooping cough that spring and stayed home from school for a month, with another quarantine sign on the front door. The doctor came to see them at home and even had to pierce Suzanne's ear drums on the living room sofa because she was so sick. Once, her mother was so tired, she went to take a nap and said, "Don't wake me up even if the King of England comes." So when the doctor came, they told him what she said, and he examined them all and left without waking her up.

The only thing she ever got tired of was soup for lunch every day for a week or two. *She didn't know that the government hadn't paid back her father's business travel money, and that food money was scarce.*

● ● ● ●

*Who is poor?*

She only knew the men lined up at the soup kitchen and sleeping on the street under newspapers and the men who came to the back door asking for something to eat were poor.

*But she didn't know the real meaning of the word; she only had the sight of them etched in her memory.*

●●●●●

**Lucy Rodgers Watkins**, a native North Carolinian, has published poetry and worked for over 32 years in non–profit education and community development programs, at the U.S. Department of Labor, with the Ford Foundation, and as an education lobbyist in Washington.

# The Twenties, the Crash, and Hope

## Marian Walsh

Growing up in the midst of the depression that began in the fall of 1929—I was ten years old at the time—I have vivid memories of many happenings both before that date and on through my college years, when World War II finally brought prosperity (and a vastly changed society). During those pre–college years I lived in a farming community, population less than three hundred: Genoa, New York, near Cayuga Lake and Cornell University.

Until I was five years old, I had lived on a farm owned by my paternal grandfather, near Albion, New York and Lake Ontario. My Black Day came when I was told that we would no longer live on the farm. My grandfather had died and the marketing of Eastern apples was being usurped by the dark, red beauties coming from the state of Washington.

In Genoa, my maternal grandfather was a VIP, owner of a successful agricultural supply business and president of the Bank of Genoa. My Aunt Marian, whose husband had received a large family inheritance, lived across the street from us in a beautiful brick and stucco house that they had built—the townspeople called it "the mansion." Her husband had been diagnosed with a severe mental illness soon after their marriage in 1916—a blight on my grandfather and all their lives. And my father, who had aspired to college teaching, began to sell insurance. This business, The Genoa General Insurance Agency, is still in operation. My grandfather's business was dissolved in the mid–seventies.

In 1920, over half the United states population lived in cities or small towns.

Farming was dwindling rapidly. Business was dominant; the business man was lauded. Industrial production had grown sixty percent since the closing years of the nineteenth century. Advertising, beginning at the turn of the twentieth century, grew in importance as a means of luring people to buy industrial products. At the same time, growth of the automobile industry, motion pictures, and radio set standards for manufactured products and cultural activities, as did magazines, newspapers, books, drama, and music.

Women, who were liberated from the household by kitchen appliances and processed foods, worked outside the family; the divorce rate rose; they changed their dress, drank, and smoked; they competed with men. The Prohibition enactment of 1919 led to crime and lawlessness. The Scopes Trial in Dayton, Tennessee, July 10–21, 1925, upheld the belief in the Divine Creation of man against the Darwinian evolution theory. Works of literature and painting were recording views of the rapidly changing world.

For a time in the 1920's there seemed to be a golden age of progress. I remember the comfortable, unchanging ambience of my community, set in the midst of a beautiful countryside where there was a good school, a well–stocked store, a hotel, and even a small hospital. The Catholic and Presbyterian churches faced each other across the street. Next door to one church was a building which was used as a theatre on the second floor. The ground floor had accommodated horses and carriages. The hotel, beside the theatre, did not feature, during those years, the tavern offerings of its old past. My only inkling then of any clandestine activity was a view I had through the rear window of our car during a trip to the farm. I saw a suspicious–looking roadster speeding along behind us. I guess it reminded me of pictures I had seen of pirate ships. Besides our Essex, a little black box on wheels, it was the only other car on the road. I mentioned it to my parents.

"Probably bootleggers coming down from Canada," they said.

Of course, I gathered from their voices that this was a threat to what is right and that it was fascinating. Since I had, in my family, no experience with the evils of alcohol, I only vaguely connected bootlegging with their lofty attitude toward people who "drank."

My aunt bobbed her hair and wore kneelength dresses with a dropped waistline around her hips. She had a shiny navy blue satin dress made for me in that style with a bright red corsage of imitation berries at the shoulder. Why she did this I don't know. There must have been a special occasion. I hated the dress. I saw myself in the huge full length mirror in her front hall with my sober brown hair cut in bands and my black patent leather Mary Janes, and I longed to be sitting high up in an apple tree wearing my khaki shorts.

My grandparents had a Victrola, which I liked to wind and hear recordings of classical music. My parents took me to the Bailey Hall Series every year at Cornell. I heard Yehudi Menuhin, a chubby eleven year old with long golden curls. Wearing a black velvet suit with white lace ruffles at the neck and wrists, he played a full length concert. My experience with other kinds of music was limited to hymns and the songs in the book, "I Hear America Singing," that our music teacher put us through twice a week, singing solfeggio before we were allowed to use words. My introduction to jazz was unpleasant. The young man next door, who kept leaving his young family, sat on his front porch one day playing a saxophone. I found the slippery sound of the instrument and the music disturbing to my pre-teen senses.

There was very little drama for me to see during those years. A minstrel show was done at the Gem Theatre. My father played the part of Uncle Sam. I remember my mother sewing red striped on his white trousers. He sang to a high-stepping march beat and tipped his tall star-spangled hat. Of course, I thought that was wonderful.

Another memory remaining vivid for me is a production of *Hamlet*, done by a traveling company, the Ben Grete Players, in Auburn. I can still hear the boom of the cannon and the pacing of the heavy boots on the dim stage as the curtain opened. And I can seeing an actor unearthing skulls and saying, "Alas, poor Yorick... ." And I heard the music of Shakespeare's language.

There was no movie theatre nearby. In Moravia I did see a silent movie of the life of Christ. And my grandfather, along with the proprietor of the store, had a radio. I can hear the squeaking door, the menacing voice saying: "Who knows what evil lurks in the hearts of men? The shadow knows... ." Then there was old Ma Perkins selling Oxydol. People came to the store around dinner time to hear Amos and Andy and the Kingfish (pronounced. *Keeng*).

A Fuller Brush salesman visited my grandmother. She said he could sell to a hitching post. He would open his carrying case and spread his wares on the living room carpet. My grandmother always bought something. He talked about his son of whom he was proud. Several years later his son was killed in World War II. The man lost his buoyant spirit. He never came anymore.

In April 1929, the United States was so prosperous that President Hoover was quoted: "Mankind may triumph over poverty."

But advertising and installment buying techniques which had been stimulating mass consumption could not ultimately balance mass production. The economy was unsound and business men were becoming pessimistic. Tariff policies had hindered the growth of foreign trade. Nothing had been done to limit speculation in securities. Nothing had been done to increase farmers' purchasing power.

On September 9, 1929, the panic began. My aunt and uncle, arriving from Florida in the Piece Arrow, pulled up under their *porte cochere,* and my aunt stepped out of the driver's seat announcing the approaching crisis. On October 24, Black Thursday, 13,000,000 shares of stock were sold and prices dropped fast. During the next two years, two–thirds of foreign trade fell. Factories closed. Mortgages were foreclosed. There were runs on banks and many banks, including my grandfather's, failed. Dividends were unpaid. Buying power became paralyzed. Deflation in Europe further cut foreign trade.

From May, 1931, to July, 1932, the depression became worse. In January, 1932, Congress approved a federal loan agency, Reconstruction Finance Corporation, which later served as the principal lending agency during the New Deal, World War II, and the period of post–war reconversion. Hoover kept saying that prosperity was just around the corner, but the number of unemployed was as high as 13,000,000. One–quarter of the farmers had lost their farms. There were long breadlines in the cities. More than $1,500,000,000. had been drawn from banks that were still open throughout the United States.

The urgency of economic issues made Prohibition a minor matter. In February, 1933, Congress proposed that the 18th Amendment be repealed. On December 5, 1933, Utah became the 36th state to ratify the 21st Amendment, repealing the 18th, which had been unenforceable from the outset.

In his inaugural address on March 4, 1933, Franklin Delano Roosevelt tried to reassure the nation, saying: "...let me assert my firm belief that the only thing we have to fear is fear itself:" (I put that colon there to indicate a split–second pause). I heard him say those words over a neighbor's radio as I walked back to school after lunch and instantly felt a surge of energy. I will always remember the sound of his voice. He was a superb speaker.

Roosevelt immediately initiated legislation, all passed by Congress in ninety–nine days. Measures included unemployment relief, federal supervision of investment securities, creation of Tennessee Valley Authority, prevention of mortgage foreclosure on homes, railroad recovery, and an industrial recovery program. Ultimately, it was a three–year drought, rather than the Agricultural Adjustment Administration (AAA) that aided the farmers, causing increases in commodity prices. (My grandfather, a permanent Republican, said that Roosevelt was trying to do God's work for Him.)

State relief agencies received grants for which Congress appropriated $500,000,000. In administering these grants, the states had to meet federal standards. The Civilian Conservation Corps (CCC), popular throughout the 1930's, employed young men in reforestation and similar projects. I recently heard an elderly farmer, now the patriarch of a large family, praising the CCC program in which the took part in Washington State.

(The CCC cut down all the apple trees on my one grandfather's farm and the surrounding region. Perhaps for some good reason I never understood.)

In spite of the New Deal efforts, the Depression continued. In 1935 Roosevelt began to introduce reform measures. Replacing direct relief with work relief, Congress appropriated $1,400,000,000. to establish the Works Progress Administration (WPA). Between 1935 and 1941 an average of 2,100,000 were carried on the WPA rolls, engaged in projects varying from digging ditches to writing travel guides.

The Social Security Act, passed in 1935, was the beginning of a permanent, expanding national program. When I began to teach after graduating from Syracuse

University in 1940, I was paid twenty–five dollars a week. I had a Social Security number, for which I now give thanks.

Once when FDR was campaigning in Syracuse, I saw him up close, riding in his open roadster, smiling and waving, talking to the person sitting beside him. He radiated warmth and I felt his greatness. Having been insulated from national concerns in a community where no one was rich—not even my aunt and uncle after 1929—and having graduated from the Genoa Union Free School with the twelve students, class of 1936, I found college a great adventure. My family had fretted exceedingly about Roosevelt's policies, but I had been absorbed in the bewildering state of being a teenager. New York State Regents courses had prepared me well for college. A wealth of information and ideas was available to me there, after my previously circumscribed experience.

During my junior and senior years at Syracuse, the imminence of war was growing. One night in the summer of 1939, when I was a counselor at a Girl Scout Camp, the staff took cots out beside the lake. As we gazed up at the sky, crammed full of stars, we heard Hitler's insane screaming coming from our little battery radio. We shivered. Soon the whole world was at war, which ended the Great Depression, but at what a price.

●●●●●

**Marian Walsh** is a native New Yorker who grew up in the farming community of Genoa, which had a population of less than three hundred people.

# Fear

## Martha Drake

My memory of the Depression was of fear—fear of not having enough money for food. We had been well–educated as a family and prominent as having the best house in the area. Our grandparents were affluent and important people in Michigan. Rather unexpectedly, there was no income for our family. We lived in a college town where all of the professors had their salaries reduced to $100 a month. But they had the $100, and we had almost nothing. My father had a big Cadillac dealership, but no one could buy cars. He could not pay his taxes and lost his dealership and the building he owned where it was housed. And he became sick. I heard my mother call her brother for fifty dollars for food.

Mother made over old coats and dresses for us. I remember one dress that had a removable flounce so that it could be either a long dress for evenings or short for afternoon parties. My aunt gave me one of her old coats and bought a new hat and gloves to go with it. We lived in a college town so that I could go to college and live at home and work on the campus for my tuition of thirty dollars a term. I had pledged a sorority but had to drop it because I couldn't have the college job and belong to a sorority.

My husband–to–be had just one sports coat which had the elbows repaired and rewoven several times. It was so bad that my mother and sisters went together and bought him a new jacket to graduate in. We had no cars. We hitchhiked. We were often real tired and hungry. There was no safety net—no social program. I think of the Depression as being a frightening time.

**Martha Drake** and her husband retired to Chapel Hill from Michigan. Martha graduated from Northwestern University with a degree in business and worked as an accountant. She has been an avid activist for various groups all her life.

# Learning Thrift

## Elizabeth Bolton

When I graduated from high school in 1929—in Hendersonville, North Carolina—it was a wonderful time to be alive. I had made good grades, had a leading role in the senior class play and George S.—the boy all the girls seemed to like—was dating me. All that summer, I was preparing to enter Agnes Scott College in Decatur, Georgia, near Madison where I had lived many years. Mamma was making several dresses for me—even a wool suit.

In September, Mamma and Daddy drove me to Decatur and helped me to get settled in my room. Soon, I heard—everyone was talking about it—a crash on Wall Street. At first I did not realize what was meant, but gradually the results of the crash became evident. Fathers of families were committing suicide because their lives seemed to be ruined.

My brother who had jerked sodas at Jackson's Drug Store for several years to make money for college had put his savings in First Bank of Hendersonville. When it closed, he lost all his savings.

My father, a minister, had a good position as field secretary for the Louisville Baptist Seminary. His work carried him around the country collecting money for the institution. Soon, there was no money to collect because supporters lost their money. Then my father lost his position.

At the end of my sophomore year, I transferred to the University of North Carolina at Chapel Hill because expenses were less than at Agnes Scott. Papa didn't want this. I didn't want it either. But I didn't want to borrow a lot of money for my education and have a big debt to pay off when I graduated.

I lost credits in the transfer to UNC, and my friends at Agnes Scott. But I tried to make the best of everything.

There was no money now to buy new dresses. Mamma was making over some of the old ones I had worn in high school. My father now had a new position as pastor of a church in Colerain, North Carolina, but his salary was less and we had to "scrimp" in many ways.

I borrowed some money to finish college and graduated from Carolina in 1933. At one point, I remember University President Graham speaking to us students, "You don't have money to pay your expenses, but if you leave college now and go home, you won't get your education. Try to work at odd jobs; do anything you can to stay here and get your degree."

I got my degree on time and got a position as teacher of English and French in Welcome High School in Welcome, near Lexington, North Carolina. My salary was seventy dollars a month—the state salary. I was glad to have a job. I paid twenty a month for room and board and managed to survive on fifty that was left.

I could buy a postage stamp for three cents. An ice cream cone cost a nickel. So prices were relative. I never once thought of trying to buy an automobile.

The Depression really did not end until the arrival of World War II in 1940. Since then, everything has been different. We are much more affluent now. I am constantly amazed at the way the new generations spend money. You would think "money grows on trees," as the saying goes.

However, I find that I cannot change my attitude toward money. It is ingrained. I always consider the cost of everything I buy because I am a child of the Depression and always will be.

•••••

**Elizabeth Bolton** is a native Tar Heel, born in Charlotte in 1912. She obtained degrees in English, French, and Library Science. She taught in several military dependents schools in Europe and was later a librarian at UNC. She has published one book of poems, one book of short stories, and a memoir, *Papa Was a Georgia Preacher*.

# Everyday Friends in Hard Times

## Aurelia Brown

Growing up in Ridge Spring, a small town located in the Ridge Section of South Carolina where there was a real spring behind the Baptist Church, seemed very ordinary to me, but I don't believe any children today will have similar memories. The Ridge Section marked the division where an ancient ocean shore gave way to the red clay of the Piedmont. Between the two was dark, rich farm land, and farming was the main occupation of the residents—all Democrats, except for one man who was the Postmaster.

Other residents included Mr. Long, the barber—hair cuts, twenty–five cents. Girls and boys sat on a board across the arms of the chair and left with a dash of "smellum–sweet" on their hair. Then there was Mr. Milford who could pull a quarter, which he never gave me, from behind my ear. Mr. Durham had a hardware store. Out front was a peanut parching machine. How good they smelled! I've heard that he once had a monkey, but I never saw it. It was whispered that Jim Fallaw's father had a liquor still. Jim always seemed to have dimes which made him different from the rest of us. There was Lybrand's gas station where A.G. pumped gas for us and then put it on our "charge."

I was the second girl in the family with two younger brothers. Elizabeth, my older sister, born when my father was thirty–one, was a special favorite. I heard many stories of how I, a colicky baby, cried the first year of my life. Elizabeth and I had been so happy to have a baby brother that when Joe was born we called him "Boy" until my grandmother came for a visit and reminded us that he had a name. My earliest memory is of the day Joe learned to walk, which meant that I was about three. Michael (Mickey) was youngest, and his sensitive nature made him join in when any of us cried.

Our house was set off the highway at the edge of town by a horse–shoe curve of pecan trees. My Father's sister, Sallie Lou, who lived across the road had designed the plan for herself, but gave it to her brother when her husband wasn't interested in building it. To me, it is still the prettiest house in the world, red brick with a large porch with white columns across the front and a covered drive way and a glassed porch to the left and right of the main building. Upon opening the front door, downstairs you saw a large central hall from which a wide curving stair ascended to the second floor. The hall was bordered on the right by a family sitting room (the nursery) and a bed room (Mama's room) and a bath, and on the left was our formal sitting room and the dining room. The kitchen, the butler's pantry, and a back porch with an adjoining well completed the first floor. Upstairs another hall was bordered by four bedrooms, two baths, and a sleeping porch where the four of us were put to bed early enough to see pictures in leaves at the large oak tree outside before quieting down and going to sleep.

A stair led up to an attic which extended across the length of the house. The attic plays a mixed role in my memories. As a child, I was afraid of the monsters who lived there and threatened to come and get me during the night. Later, on rainy days, it was a great place for skating and hunting through all the things stored there. As we grew older, each of the four of us had a corner for storing mementos and unused wedding presents.

The house was surrounded by a grape arbor and garden at the side and back. Also, nearby was our large log cabin play house. This was completed one Christmas Eve, and Santa left one of his sleigh bells for a dinner bell. Beyond were the smoke house, the chicken house, the asparagus packing house, the cotton house, the blacksmith shop, weighing scales, barns for mules, pigs, and cows, and a gear house.

Beyond these buildings and of much interest were two houses where black families lived. The adults worked on the farm as "hands" and the children were often our playmates. Living in one of these houses was Fanny, a "wash woman". I often talked to her while she washed clothes in a large tub with a rub board, hung them on a line, and then ironed them. It was amazing to see her work with two flat irons, one heating in the fireplace while she used the other. She would carefully wipe the ashes off the hot one and beautifully iron a starched white shirt. She wasn't our wash woman, however. On Monday Mama would gather all the dirty clothes and linen into a split bottom basket and send them to "Aunt Laura," an aged black woman who told me that she was the first to have ever "helt" my newborn father in her arms.

Christmas was an exciting time. Benny, the overseer, would take the four of us on a wagon through the woods to find just the right tree which he would nail on a base and bring inside to the nursery. Earlier, we had used lighted candles for decoration, but after several trees ignited and one of my first grade friend's gown had caught fire, they were judged too dangerous.

There was no central heat in the house, and usually we had a fire in the nursery and only one of the bedrooms, Mama's, downstairs. On Christmas Eve we dressed for bed there, said our prayers at Mama's knees, and after Father read *The Night Before Christmas*, we rushed upstairs to bed.

We were allowed to come down on Christmas morning as soon as we woke up. The first one awake would call to the others. We had decorated the tree earlier, but we were anxious to see if Santa had come. First a look to see if Santa had eaten the candy we had left for him ("Thank you, it was fine"), a glimpse at the white hearth to see the black foot prints as he turned to go back to his sleigh, and then to see if he had answered the letters sent earlier to him by a draft up the same chimney. Mama soon appeared, still in her gown with her long hair plaited down her back. Father didn't appear until later. He was home for his bi–yearly visit. After we grew up, we learned that on Christmas Mama and Father, after getting our gifts ready for the morning, would open their presents to each other an then carefully rewrap them, ready to exclaim over them as we watched the next morning.

Our stockings were filled with once–a–year treats: a tangerine, an orange, raisin clusters, and Brazil nuts. Mama had been busy making divinity fudge, salted nuts, stuffed dates (Father's favorite), and orange peel candy (everyone's favorite). Later in the morning the "hands" would come to the side door, call "Christmas Gift," and receive our gifts of warm gloves, food, and sweets.

We took turns with dinner at my Aunt's and Grandmother's: Christmas with them one year and Thanksgiving dinner the next. I always hated to leave my new gifts when it was our turn to be away at Christmas. Christmas at Mama's was fun, though. In addition to my grandmother, I would see my aunt Chloe (Tots) and her children, Paul and "Little Elizabeth," my favorite cousin. We also had a wonderful dinner: turkey, dressing, country ham, macaroni and cheese, green peas, biscuits, celery and olives, ambrosia, pound cake, fruit cake. Virginia, the cook, made the world's best biscuits. Once, one of the grandchildren dropped his biscuit in the gravy, and then we were each allowed to drop one in.

The school house, which was next door to Mama's, had toilets with no running water, and so I always came home with Little Elizabeth at recess to use the bathroom and have a lettuce sandwich. My aunt Tots made her own mayonnaise, and it was even better than Hellman's. A lettuce sandwich is still one of my favorites.

Ridge Spring School was a very good one for a small town. The teachers were outstanding. Mrs. Bonnett was especially good, and so each of us had excellent training in English. Miss Bessie Jones had taught so long that she had taught Father. Miss Bessie and I became good friends. When I graduated from high school, she gave me two sterling silver tea spoons in Marlborough pattern. I liked it so much that I chose it for "my" silver and still enjoy it today. Mrs. Asbill, third grade teacher, had eyes in the back of her head and so was a strict disciplinarian. Plays were given by the Junior and Senior classes. With small classes, we could all take a part. Once the Junior–Senior end–of–the year party was held at our house; another year we had it in a new peach packing house which we christened the "Fuzz Box".

Father had worked as a young man as a banker and then as a farmer. When prices for cotton and peaches, the crops which brought in money, plummeted, it was necessary to obtain work which would bring in cash in order to pay the workers on our farm and for fertilizer, spray, and taxes. Mama began teaching in the seventh grade and Father got a job with one of the New Deal agencies. He was very soon transferred to Kentucky. He and Mama wrote often, but he was only able to come home twice a year. Every Sunday, during the seven years he was away, he gathered funny papers from papers in his hotel lobby, rolled them up and sent them to us.

When Father needed surgery for cancer on his face, it was impossible for Mama to leave us, the school, and the farm or to afford the trip to be with him. A kind nurse held his hand as he went under anesthesia. She said that he kept calling her "Aurelia," my mother's name.

Wallace Steadman was a young Wofford graduate when he came to Ridge Spring as superintendent of the school. He hired Aurelia Cunningham, a Winthrop graduate as one of the teachers. Later he married Frances Anderson. Miss Cunningham married J. Cal Watson, and they became our mother and father. The Steadmans and the Watsons each had four children, two boys and two girls, who were fast friends. We had picnics and parties and fish fries together at the Old Shoals.

When Father was away, the Steadmans were especially caring. I remember one expression of true devotion when Mr. Steadman came to our house to work on a broken toilet "because he enjoyed that kind of work."

One day out in the yard, I found a check made out to Father for $5.76. I don't know how this could have been lost as Father was very careful of money. It was immediately decided that the money was mine, and I could spend it as I wished "some day." How many hours I spent leafing through the Sears Roebuck Catalog looking at the many things my money could buy! I'm sure that my math improved as I added up the many ways to get to a total of $5.76. As a young women, I asked about my money and was told that it had been spent of necessity long ago—no matter, I had had full value.

My mother was tall, and so she had a problem finding clothes with skirts long enough—and the right price. She had a navy suit which she wore to teach during the week, and then on Saturday she would sponge and press it and wear it to church the next day. When she stood in front teaching a Sunday School Class, I would dream how "when I grew up" I would buy her a fine outfit. However, Mama taught Elizabeth and me not to depend on clothes as much as a clean face and a sweet smile; these were more important. Our shopping consisted of what we could afford rather than the prettiest, but I always felt all right.

Mama gave the four of us lots of books and often read aloud to us. I remember being afraid and going out of the room to skip Mama's reading when the funny papers told of Chester Gump's being captured by cannibals. A special time was when we gathered on the front porch to hear Mama read from the *Saturday Evening Post* serialized Mary Roberts Rhinehart mysteries. Our cousin George would come across the street to hear.

There were several men in town who had large orchards of peaches. When peaches were ripe, "Peach Season," all high school age young people, white and black, worked in the packing sheds. It was hot, sticky work with long hours, as peaches had to be de–fuzzed and packed and shipped immediately in large refrigerated trucks. I remember how when we had to work into the night, the blacks would sing Negro spirituals.

Peach season was eagerly anticipated. For the young people, it meant being together with friends and money for new clothes or a permanent. For the farmers, it meant a chance to be repaid for money spent through the year on cultivation, fertilizer, labor for thinning, picking and packing, and the cost of sending the crates to market. Some years were great. In others, cold snaps killed most of the tiny peaches. When all peach growing states had bumper crops, the market was flooded, and the price at times didn't pay for transportation to market.

Mama couldn't have managed the peaches and other parts of the farm without Bennie, our overseer. He was a large black man we all loved. I remember leaving a baked potato in the gear room as a surprise for him. He only went as far as the eighth grade in school, but he had lots of true wisdom, common sense, and a way with people. When the "hands" were thinning peaches and were afraid of snakes which might be in the grass, Bennie assured them that the train which passed about a mile away twice a day shook the ground so much that snakes couldn't stay around. He kept records of the hours workers put in and suggested to Mama what each should be paid. There was great respect between him and my parents. Though Father would have been surprised to say it, Bennie was Father's best friend. He came to work for us the year I started to school and was still there to help Frank and me move to Atlanta for our first home.

We had very little cash. We all picked up pecans after school, and Mama sold them for Christmas money. I remember that my grandmother felt Mama was too open in telling us children of our poor condition, but Mama felt that it was impossible to disguise. Once when a traveling circus came to town, she made a chocolate cake so we wouldn't ask to go.

We always had plenty to eat: vegetables from the garden, pork from the hogs raised and butchered, and eggs and milk from our chickens and cows. We seemed to eat a lot of cabbage and green beans. Neighbors shared special treats. I can remember very few times when we ate at a restaurant.

Our family had many good times. I remember our church had a "white elephant party." Each person was to bring something he or she had but couldn't use. Young people had fun playing Rook, Parcheesi, Pick–up–Sticks, Gossip and Spin–the–Bottle. On many Fridays nights, a group of high schoolers would meet at someone's home and play "dates." The girls had cards and would spend ten minutes or so with a boy who asked her. Later, we danced to records and enjoyed punch and cookies. This was a time of many great popular songs, and we learned the words of them all. Movies were twenty–five cents and wonderful—a very special treat. Once I was taken to see the movie *Hurricane* by my aunt in the afternoon. When a boy asked me to go to the same movie that night, it didn't occur to me to refuse—two hurricanes in one day! We never spoke of young people as "kids," as kids were young goats.

Vacations were always visits to family. Only once did we go to a beach, and that was a day trip with friends. Earlier, we had wonderful trips to the mountains, but that was before Father went to Kentucky.

I believe that Mama's monthly pay as a teacher was $85.00, but soon teachers were paid in certificates instead of cash. It was hard to find someone who would redeem them for full value. Once when Mama's Study Club was having a very special meeting in our house, Mama borrowed $5.00 from her brother–in–law to have the piano tuned.

We had a friend in Batesburg whose discouraged father killed himself. Mama once shared with me that she didn't want Father to hear what a hard time we were having, as he might do the same. Another friend, one of a family of eleven children, lost property twice; once, their home in town and, later, the farm which was so important in growing food. The whole family finally went to live with grandparents.

Hard times lasted a long time for me. After I was married and Frank was in graduate school, our weekly food budget was $12.50. The depression did make a lasting impression on my life. I'm still very frugal, remembering when we couldn't afford a measuring cup at twenty–nine cents.

There are many ways that my generation had a really hard time; however, there were good times also. We had the all–time great movies and classic actors and beautiful actresses who wore wonderful clothes. We could go to see movies with a date without being embarrassed by off–color material, and follow a wonderful romance. The songs we liked so much, people still sing. I remember the night when we all drew close to our small radio to hear the blow–by–blow description of the Joe Louis–Max Schmeling fight. How proud we were to have the winner an American who was fighting a man encouraged by Hitler. We were proud of our country, and later everyone supported the men serving it.

I always felt that we had companionship during the hard times. We weren't in this alone. In Ridge Spring and later in graduate school, others had the same challenge. I am glad, though, that in later years, that is behind us. I would hate to go through the Depression again at this stage of life.

**Aurelia (Pat) Brown** was born in Ridge Spring, South Carolina. She graduated from Columbia College, Columbia, South Carolina, and taught school until she married. She resides with her husband Frank in Bethesda, Maryland.

# A Banker's Family

## Franklin Brown

I'm not sure exactly when I first became aware of the Depression and the enormity of what was going on. I knew my father was worried about something, but for me, in the late 1920's, things seemed to be going pretty smoothly. I was going to school (in the 5th grade), playing ball with guys after school, eating a lot, and fully enjoying it.

For my father, however, things were not going well. As a banker in North Carolina, my father was very attuned to the ups and downs of the economy. His father—my paternal grandfather, Joseph G.—was owner and CEO of the major bank in Raleigh at the time, and there was every expectation that my father—at that time cashier—would ultimately inherit the job in the bank. So to me, at the tender age of ten, our family future looked pretty secure.

That was 1929.

I don't remember any of the economic events that occurred in October of that year, so I didn't really understand why my father was so concerned. The Bank Holiday was the first clue I had, and at first it seemed to me that that wasn't all bad. A holiday was always a pretty good idea. But afterward, when many Raleigh businesses began getting into trouble, other aspects of the Depression began to hit. There were stories in the paper about New York executives jumping out of windows, companies going bankrupt, farmers having trouble selling their produce, people starving. But for me, all that seemed very far away, at first. And I wondered why all the excitement.

I went to school every day—usually walked the three miles each way or rode my bike. We went to Church every Sunday, and I remember my grandfather was Superintendent of the Sunday School, leading all of the combined Sunday School classes in a joint session before they broke up into separate classes.

We had just had a new house built, in the mid–1920's, next door to my Mother's parents, who lived just across Hillsboro Street from the college. That put us about four doors closer to Hillsboro Street than our first house, both on Maiden Lane. Things were pretty peaceful there like a small college town today. Hillsboro Street (US Route 1) was unpaved, lightly traveled, nothing like the "Old Bloody" reputation it acquired later.

My grandfather died soon after the Depression hit, and I wondered years later if the bank's problems had somehow precipitated his death. His bank was having some Depression–related problems, as were all banks, but there was no thought in the minds of the family that anything really serious could happen to "our" bank. He was leading the Sunday School classes one Sunday morning when he had a stroke and died suddenly. It was the first death I knew anything about, and it really shook me up.

The bank lasted another two years before the accumulation of other people's bankruptcies forced it to close. The seriousness of the thing had finally hit home about 1931. It was then that our bank went under, and my father was given the job of handling the receivership. To him, the future, looking beyond the receivership assignment, seemed very bleak. My grandfather had been hit particularly hard. As owner of the bank, he was subject to "double liability" if the bank got into trouble. So he not only lost his bank, but his family savings.

The strain on our own family finances kicked in then. I remember it made my father physically ill. I often woke up in the morning to the sound of my father being sick in the bathroom. The bank receivership was a temporary blessing, but beyond that, there was no visible job security.

The family began to economize, although as a ten- to twelve–year–old, I wasn't very aware of the extent of it. I just remember eating a lot of macaroni and cheese. And a lot of grits and potatoes. I'm sure we ate a lot of other things, but somehow, in retrospect, the plethora of macaroni, peanut butter, and cheese has become a sort of metaphor for hard times.

The magic trip that my father had promised, and that we children had all looked forward to, was to drive to Atlanta. That never happened. We *did* make several one–day trips to Wrightsville Beach though, and, really, I liked that better than I would have liked Atlanta, I'm sure.

My grandfather on my Mother's side was Professor R.E.L Yates. He was head of the mathematics department at North Carolina State University. He had tenure at the College, so the Depression didn't pose a risk of his losing his job, but of course it *did* affect his salary—everybody's salary was being cut as the economy worsened. Fortunately, though, he also owned a large farm and a dairy outside of Raleigh. This turned out to be a very fortuitous combination as the Depression began to bite. Frequently, we had dinner with them, and I remember my grandfather Yates bragging that everything on the table—ham, turkey, beans, sweet potatoes, ice cream—all came from his farm.

There was a lake which was part of the Yates farm, which had an operating mill that ground corn meal. But the best part of the lake from the kid's viewpoint was the opportunity to paddle a boat around and across the lake. We also swam in it, despite the squishy-feeling mud on the bottom.

We kids didn't feel at all underprivileged during this time. My father took us out to the lake frequently. He also took other children with us, including both my friends, my sister's friends, and a bunch of kids from the local orphanage where he was on the Board. These kids from the orphanage weren't having much other recreational fun at that time, so they always enjoyed the outing.

We expanded the scope of the rowing adventures to include frog-gigging, which not only gave us kids some excitement in our lives, but also provided some variety from macaroni in our diets. The most exciting time we had frog-gigging was when my father invited the superintendent of the girl's division at the orphanage, an eighty-year-old woman, to go out on the lake with us. She had the seat of honor in the prow of the boat, and everything went well until one of the frogs on shore became frightened and jumped. It turned out that he jumped directly into her lap. The frog seemed to realize that no one would gig him as long as he sat there. We kids fully enjoyed the spectacle, but I don't think she ever went again.

I joined the Boy Scouts when I was twelve. This was 1931. The Depression was well underway, but I never associated scouting with the Depression, and I never felt deprived. Scouting was always upbeat; we spent our time working on merit badges and going on camping trips and cookouts. Camping always seemed to focus on Yates Pond, but it never occurred to me that this happened because going to Yates Pond was cheaper than going away to a regular camp. It was also more fun. We built a log cabin on the side of the lake with the help of a mule from the Yates farm. And as far as I know, the cabin outlived the lake, which was destroyed when hurricane Hugo washed out the dam in the late eighties.

The lake and the mill have been set aside for historic preservation and are now being repaired.

My main buddy during these years was Billy Bridgeforth, who also lived on Maiden Lane. Our recreation was to walk the three miles into downtown Raleigh on Saturdays and go to see the cowboy movie for ten cents. The show also had a continued serial feature which went on for months, and "added short–subjects," all of which kept Billy and me busy for the whole of a Saturday afternoon. I remember when the streetcars were first put in on Hillsboro Street, running directly into town. It cost a nickel, but Billy and I didn't want to take so much money out of our movie budget.

School was about two miles away from our house. Of course, there were no such things as a school bus or school cafeterias. Mother fixed a sandwich—probably macaroni—and I walked two miles to school, cutting through fields, along rutted paths, and through a woods. Today that would be viewed as dangerous, I suppose, but I don't remember there being any concern about crime. In fact, we never locked our front door.

It was in 1933 that the receivership project at our bank was finished. My father had gotten to know the regional bank examiner during the period, and through him had landed a job in the regional office in Columbia, South Carolina. For me, the principle trauma involved in the move was changing schools and meeting a whole new set of friends. I entered Columbia High School in my sophomore year and was lucky enough to be assigned to a geometry teacher who was terrific. I think it was Mr. Greene who set the whole focus of my career development into math and science, and later into physics and operations research.

The Depression was still having its effects. My father had a job—a pretty reliable one—as regional bank examiner. He did a lot of work–related traveling all over South Carolina and would be gone for days at a time. We broadened beyond macaroni in our menus, but we were still living in debt left over from the Raleigh bank failure. In order to help finance my college education, I got a job running an elevator in a Columbia office building, on the night shift. I was planning to go to the University of South Carolina in Columbia, where local students got a tuition break, and I could live at home.

The elevator job was okay. The local wisdom was that it was good work, but it had lots of ups and downs. Actually, it proved to be a wiser move than we had anticipated. It not only provided some income, but since I was working on the night shift, things were pretty quiet, and there was a lot of time left over for studying school assignments. There was nothing more exciting to do. This helped me to become class valedictorian at Columbia High School in 1939 and to get into Phi Beta Kappa.

My interest in physics and astronomy (started by Mr. Greene) led to a part–time job, when I entered the University, of opening the University's astronomical observatory to the public. This was a magnificent experience, one for which I would have paid *them* if I had been able. We had a sixteen inch telescope, and I was totally responsible for it. My interest in physics and astronomy blossomed even further.

Looking back on it, I realize there *was* one major up–side to the Depression, as it affected me personally. Without the Depression I would never have left Raleigh, or moved to Columbia, or gone to the University of South Carolina. And if that had not happened, I would never have met Pat. We both attended the Wesley College Fellowship at Washington Street Church, I from the University, she from Columbia College, a woman's school. I started attending when I was a senior—Pat was a freshman. This was 1938, the Depression was ending, but World War II was on the horizon.

Pat and I were married in 1943, just a few months before I left for Europe as part of the war effort.

•••••

**Franklin Brown** graduated from UNC with a Ph.D. in physics. He founded a research operations company in Bethesda, Maryland, and recently retired.

# Finding Jobs

## Dorothy Salemson

Having been born in 1912, I was a teenager when the Depression struck and the banks failed in 1929. We had always lived a very comfortable life. My father had been a very successful business man. We lived in our own home in a pleasant upper–middle–class residential area in Louisville, Kentucky. My mother had full–time help, and the four children wanted for nothing. So it was with surprise and resentment that our perfect world fell apart.

There was no money for college. A two–year normal school course with free tuition seemed the logical course to pursue, although teaching was the last thing I wanted to do. Having graduated from high school at age sixteen, I was ready to teach by the time I was eighteen. But a job was not available in 1930. Teaching was a preferred profession, and there was an overabundance of previous graduates who were not about to relinquish their jobs.

At home things had taken a turn for the worse. My father lost his business. Payments on our home could not be met, and the house was taken over by the bank that held the mortgage. We had never been wealthy. Now we were downright poor.

My mother was the real strength in the family. Her cool head prevailed, and she set about trying to solve the many problems that seemed insoluble. She investigated businesses that she could run, since my father had gone on the road trying to buy and sell silver and gold. She settled on a delicatessen that was for sale. My mother was an excellent cook and felt she could put her culinary art to good use. We all worked long, hard hours. I had left the "nest" to go to work in a local department store, working six days a week for $9 per week. Most of the employees were paid $7 weekly, but the owner was a friend of my parents and made an exception in my case.

It wasn't until 1933 that I finally received a call from the Board of Education that there was an opening for a fifth grade teacher in a local elementary school. The salary was $900 a year; but due to the Depression, there was a ten percent cut in the salary, resulting in my receiving $810 annually. However, since I still lived at home, the money was a windfall.

My first summer vacation arrived, and a friend asked me to accompany her on a trip to California. The trip by tourist Pullman would cost $100 round trip, traveling through Chicago, north through North Dakota, into Canada, west through the Canadian Rockies, to Vancouver, by boat to Seattle, then again by train to San Francisco and Los Angeles. The meals cost $1 a day!

The trip was even more memorable since it was in Hollywood, in 1936, that I met a delightful young man who was to become my husband.

You might wonder how was it possible to survive on so little. My adult life was really just beginning. Everything was an adventure, and I certainly did not feel deprived.

(Note: I didn't marry the young man until 1942. I returned to Kentucky to teach. He remained in Hollywood. World War II brought us together for what were to be forty–six years of a wonderful life.)

**Dorothy Salemson** taught in elementary school from 1931 until 1942. She married a writer while he was in the army. After the war she lived on Long Island and raised two children. From 1961 until 1989 she worked for the Association for the Help of Retarded Children, after which she retired and moved to Chapel Hill as a widow.

# The Gold Coins

## Samuel R. Marks

As we were newly arrived immigrants, the Great Depression did not change our lives for the worse; they were already bad enough. My father had a poorly–paid job which provided only the bare necessities for our family of eight. Some months, when the rent was due, he had to scrounge around among his "landsleit" to borrow the $25 to pay it. My mother did her share by shopping around for the cheapest cuts of meat, the lowly–esteemed carp, and the day–old bread for our daily meals. She was an excellent cook and was able to make some of the best tasting soups from the low–priced vegetables and scraps of meat. Coal for heating was used sparingly, and the use of electricity, especially when one forgot to turn off the lights on leaving a room, brought loud condemnation from my embittered father. This was not the Golden Land he had been induced to immigrate to.

Every penny counted, and I must shamefully confess that when I surreptitiously took fifteen cents from my mother's change purse to go to the movies, she was immediately aware that someone had been in her purse. My morals, at the age of ten, had been overpowered by desire to see what had happened to my favorite cowboy, William Duncan, who had been left hanging off a cliff in the previous episode. Unfortunately, my concern was not relieved, as the next chapter had him in the hands of the black–hatted villains.

We, of course, had to walk to school, rain or shine, carrying our lunches, which usually consisted of jelly or tomato sandwiches, with two cents in our pockets for candy.

I soon learned that by buying the candy store's "Grab Bags" I would get more for my money, though the candy would be crumbled or sun–spoilt.

One of my most painful memories is tied up with our neighbor's offer of two $2 ½ gold pieces in exchange for five dollars in bills. He was a manager of an A & P store, and his company had paid all its help in gold pieces, urging them to circulate them around among their neighbors so that the powers that be would appreciate the company's importance to the city. I had never seen a gold coin, and the sight and touch of these coins awakened in me the memory of my early impression that the streets of America were paved with gold, a belief that even some grown–ups had.

I handled the coins gingerly, and ran over to our apartment to show them to my mother and the other children. We stared at the coins, amazed that such small coins would be worth so much money. Even my practical mother was carried away by their beauty. She went to her purse, but in our straitened circumstances she could not find the five dollars needed. Between her and the two older children they came up with only $2.50, enough for only one of the coins.

We kept that coin for a whole week, admiring it every day, but soon had to part with it to the neighborhood grocer for our food bills. We were all sorry to see it go, feeling as if a little magic had gone out of our lives with it.

When I recently sold my coin collection, an old five–dollar gold piece brought $250. It was no longer a symbol of the Golden Land for me. It brought to mind only the sad thought that the $250 would have been enough to pay the rent of that shabby first apartment for ten months!

Today teen–agers will find it impossible to believe that we could have been happy to go to school with only two cents in our pockets for candy, or that an entire family could not come up with five dollars in exchange for two much–desired gold coins, then a symbol of our new, if not Golden Land.

It was only after the Great Depression that the Golden, image returned to our new land.

•••••

**Sam Marks** was born in Russia and emigrated to Cleveland, Ohio, with his family in 1923. After retiring in 1981, he moved with his wife Ann to Chapel Hill. His memoirs of life between two world wars numbers over one hundred stories, one of which has been published in his army division's book of war stories.

# College

## Samuel Kaplan

The only time my parents ever fought was during the Depression.

They were childhood sweethearts growing up in Russia. My father arrived in the United States in 1913, and proceeded to Detroit to the boarding house run by my mother's sister who had come a few years earlier. He obtained a horse and wagon and sold fish, riding down back alleys where the housewives could come out of their kitchens and choose what they wanted from the wagon. Within a year, he had saved enough to send my mother the money for steamship passage. They were married in her sister's parlor.

It was a loving marriage to the day he died. By 1929, they had five children. My father had his own fish stand in a corner he rented in someone's grocery store. He was secretary of the Jewish Fish Handler's Union (being the only member who had taught himself to read and write English), and they had bought a house, (the dream of every immigrant), with an upstairs flat to rent out. I was thirteen and had never heard a harsh word pass between them.

Then came the stock market crash and the Depression. Sales at the fish stand dropped lower and lower to the disappearing point. And it was the fish my father didn't sell that became our diet day after day. At the beginning of each week, it would be fresh. The same could not be said by the end of the week. Our clothes became shabbier and shabbier. My mother spent more and more of her week mending and sewing. My father took to selling vegetables and fruit on weekends at a local farmers' market. He would get up at 4:00 a.m. on Saturday and Sunday and go down to the produce outlet downtown to pick up what he needed. It didn't seem to add much to our income. Then he became a school bus driver. We three eldest children attended a Hebrew school weekdays after public school. It was run by the Jewish community of Detroit. I think we went free, the powers–that–be feeling than more important than money was the need to preserve Jewishness in the younger generation. My father went to the director of the school and attained the job of driving the bus. It was, of course, a part–time job. He would close his fish stand early, and I think the bus job paid him about ten dollars a week. I remember feeling proud, when I boarded the bus, that the driver was my father.

We were, of course, losing the house. There was no way of making the mortgage payments. I heard my father talking to our upstairs tenant, who was in the same boat as we were. He told him to forget the rent, that the bank was in the process of foreclosing, which might take about a year.

Then the fighting started. My older brother and I had sold newspapers since I was eight. At first, we had sold on street corners but had eventually graduated to having our own news route. Every Saturday we would make the rounds of our customers to collect for the week, deduct what we needed to pay for the papers, and dutifully give the rest to our mother. And every week she religiously deposited the money in a special savings account so that we could go to *college*. My father wanted to tap that account. (It was only much later that I realized how desperate he must have been.) My mother said *no*. My father became more pressing. My mother was adamant that money was for *college*. I was kept awake nights listening to them arguing bitterly in the kitchen. One morning I found her crying, and she told me she might take the children and leave him. (I have no idea where she thought she might go.)

Our survival was guaranteed from (to me) an unexpected source. And with it, the bitter quarrels disappeared. The company supplying my father with fish agreed that no matter how little he sold, he would be allowed, as a loan, to take twenty–five dollars home every week. (By 1935, when his fortunes changed again, he had run up a very large bill.)

The *college* account wasn't large. But the tuition and books at the city university were about eighty–five dollars a semester (we, of course, brought our lunch from home), and the account paid for four years' expenses for my brother and two years for me.

It was after my second year in college that a new market opened up in a new area of Detroit. My father obtained a fish stand there, which was immediately successful. The first night at the kitchen table, they sat counting the money they had taken in that day with a sense of wonder. We all watched them count. I said "Pa, I want to go to the University of Michigan in the fall." "Don't bother me," he said and kept counting.

But the Depression was over for them. I received my Ph.D. in mathematics from the University of Michigan in 1942, just before being drafted into the U.S. Army.

**Samuel Kaplan** was born in Detroit, Michigan. He spent all of his working life as a professor of mathematics. Since his retirement, he can be found at coffee shops on Franklin Street, still pursuing mathematics.

# Those Were the Days and Years

## Vignettes of the Great Depression

### Carl Armin Viehe

I walked up Main Street and stopped at the bank. It was called the People's Bank. The shade was drawn at the front door. In the window the sign read: "Closed by order of the United States Government." This was the Bank Holiday ordered by President Franklin Delano Roosevelt shortly after he took the oath of office as president of the United States on March 4, 1933. We were in the depths of the Great Depression.

I was a teen–ager, growing up in Hamburg, New York, a semi–rural village some fourteen miles from Buffalo. Those Depression years bring back vivid memories.

In downtown Buffalo I saw World War I veterans, their American Legion caps firmly pulled down on their heads, selling apples for five cents each.

Veterans from across the country marched to Washington in the Bonus March. President Herbert Hoover ordered troops to disperse them from their tents in Lafayette Park. This act was one more reason people were to vote for Roosevelt in the 1932 election, despite a prediction by periodicals, such as the *Literary Digest*, that the Republicans were sure to win. After the Democratic landslide, that popular magazine went out of business.

The Depression was a time of low prices and much do–it–yourself. When the soles of our shoes wore out, as they did frequently in those days, I would be sent to the five–and–ten cents store for a shoe mending kit—a rubber half–sole along with a small tube of glue. Men who smoked bought loose tobacco with cigarette papers and "rolled their own."

When I consider today's prices, I am amazed at what things cost in those days. We could go to the Palace Theater and see a movie for twenty–five cents. When I was sent to the grocery store I would give the clerk eleven cents for a quart of milk and nine cents for a loaf of bread. We could buy a lovely necktie for a dollar and a pair of shoes for two dollars and a half. But if we wanted expensive footwear we had to lay out five dollars. At that time, a workman's average wage was one dollar an hour.

I vividly remember being sent to Walters' Meat Market (Mr. Walters also handled a few grocery items) to buy a quart of milk for lunch. Mr Walters had a large hand–lettered sign in bright red in his store window which read "Porterhouse steak, 18 cents a pound." But even at that price my family could not afford porterhouse steak.

In the 1930's "going to the store" meant being personally waited on by the clerk. As we told the grocer what we wanted, he would pull the items from the shelf. Going to Altes' Meats meant watching the butcher cut your order. And, oh, how I loved George Altes' home–made sauerkraut, which my family with a German background often bought along with a roast for Sunday dinner!

Church giving was also quite low. Many church–going parishioners would put ten cents in the collection plate on Sunday. But I remember seeing one so–called wealthy woman put in twenty–five cents as the plate passed her. It was not unusual for my father, the minister, to be given a two and one–half dollar gold piece for performing a wedding or a baptism. My wife, Mary Louise, now wears one of those gold heirlooms on a chain as a necklace.

In the 1930's, airplanes were becoming more common. I was first aware of an airplane high above our house on Hosea Avenue in Cincinnati in 1919 when I was two years old. Later, I learned that two pioneer airmen, Sir John William Alcock and Sir Arthur Whitten–Brown, had made the first non–stop flight across the Atlantic in 1919 in a twin–engine Vickers Vimy. They flew from St. Johns, Newfoundland, to Cliften, Ireland.

But my memory of planes and airmen really began in May, 1927, when one day my father showed me a newspaper with large black headlines. I asked what it meant. He replied that Charles Lindbergh had just made the first solo flight across the Atlantic from New Your to Paris in thirty–three hours. Lindbergh immediately became everybody's hero, and mine, too. Then I began hearing on the radio of other attempts to span the Atlantic, some successful, some not. Two Germans attempted an east–west crossing but crashed in Labrador. Wiley Post made the first solo round–the–world flight. And, of course, there was "wrong way Corrigan," who took off from Long Island, supposedly headed for California, and then landed in Ireland.

In the late 20's and early 30's radio became a part of my life. On Thursday nights at eight o'clock, I would listen to Rudy Vallee and the Fleischmann's Yeast Hour. He began each program with his theme song: "My Time Is Your Time."

One family ritual at our house involved radio listening. Each evening my parents and I would sit down to dinner about 6:30. Promptly at 6:45 would come "S-U-N-O-C-O,

Sunoco brings you Lowell Thomas and the news." This was followed at seven o'clock by Amos and Andy. No one left the table until the last program ended.

The Depression years turned everyone's interest to politics which were closely tied to the economic situation. In late February or the early days of March, the sitting Congress was about to adjourn prior to the inauguration of the new president. As my father and I sat listening to the radio, he turned to me and said, "Now listen. He will adjourn the Congress *sine die*."

Sure enough, Vice President Charles G. Dawes, whom the press called "Injun Charley" because he had Indian ancestry, intoned, "I declare this Congress adjourned *sine die*."

My father explained that the Vice President adjourned Congress without a day set for reconvening. This Congress was finished. After the inauguration a newly–elected Congress would be in session. It was that new Congress that would carry out Franklin Roosevelt's New Deal legislation. To meet the needs of the population in economic depression, there would come into being many new governmental agencies, such as National Recovery Administration (NRA), Civilian Conservation Corps (CCC), Works Progress Administration (WPA), Tennessee Valley Authority (TVA), FCC, FDIC, and many more, some of which are still in existence today.

My parents and I, along with millions of others, would gather around the radio to listen to Roosevelt's Fireside Chats. These gave the nation hope and encouragement. Every Sunday afternoon my father and mother would tune in to Father Coughlin broadcasting very radical ideas from Royal Park, Michigan. He preached a version of social justice, in including such things as inflation and isolationism. My parents disagreed with practically everything the priest said.

Then there was that memorable Saturday afternoon on January 30, 1933. From my high school teacher, Edward Schweichert, I had developed a great interest in current events by the age of fifteen. The political situation in Germany was very unstable, and I followed developments every day in the "Buffalo Evening News." That Saturday, there was a broadcast from Berlin, Germany. President Paul von Hindenburg turned to Adolph Hitler and his National Socialist Party to head the government.

I said to myself, "This is a turning point in history." Little did I realize then the real importance of the event and the tragedy it would bring the world. I remember being excited. I called up my history teacher and told him to turn on the radio.

Another Depression memory concerns prohibition. In 1920 the nation adopted the 18th Amendment to the Constitution, prohibiting the sale and manufacture of alcoholic beverages. As a boy, I was aware of the village drunks and places where they could buy liquor, called "speakeasies."

Breaking the law often became a contest between the rum–runner and the Internal Revenue agents. One day my parents and I drove to Niagara Falls. We went through Buffalo, crossed the Niagara River on the Peace Bridge, and on into Canada, where there were no national laws against liquor. Every night Canadians would try to cross the river by boat with loads of liquor, hoping not to get caught. That day as we drove along the Niagara shore in Fort Erie, Ontario, we saw small boats pulled up on the river bank.

Men were loading the boats with large bags filled with liquor bottles. Each day the newspaper would report the number of people apprehended for trying to smuggle liquor across the border the previous night.

Prohibition ended in December, 1933, with the repeal of the 18th Amendment. It was said that the sale of beer and liquor would boost the economy during the Depression.

In June, 1935, I graduated from Hamburg High School in the middle of the Depression. That summer, I got a job working for the Hamburg Canning Factory for thirty cents an hour. The next summer the rate was reduced to twenty–five cents an hour. In September, I went off to the University of Michigan, where tuition for out–of–state students was fifty–five dollars a semester.

I graduated from the university in 1939. On September 1, 1939, Germany invaded Poland. On September 3, as I waited for a friend outside Hamot Hospital in Erie, Pennsylvania, I heard on the car radio that Britain and France were declaring war on Germany, This marked the end of the Great Depression. From then on things would be different. And they still are.

American would live through World War II, the Korean War, the Vietnam War, enjoy talking pictures, be glued to television sets, see men walk on the moon, and encounter terror of the atom bomb. Yes, we live in a different world from the days of the Great Depression.

●●●●●

Carl Viehe retired from the United Church of Christ ministry in 1991. A former North American alumni secretary for Mansfield College, Oxford University, England, Dr. Viehe's writings include poetry, devotional material, and stories for pre–school children.

# The Class of '33

## Samuel R. Marks

The sad news that the John Adams High School in my home town of Cleveland, Ohio, was being demolished due to old age sent me to my files to hunt up my 1933 classbook, facetiously titled "Senior Owlet—Hoo's Hoo in June '33."

What a mixed group we were! Chudoba, Hamad, Jankovsky, Karlinsky, Levin, Pavelka, Tomasello, Zaremba, *et al*, most of us immigrants from Eastern Europe, just getting started in a new land.

We were in the midst of the "Great Depression," and jobs and money were scarce, as witness the mere eight–page, soft–cover booklet for a class of 375 students, which pictured fewer than two–thirds of the class; most of the others did not have the spare funds to pay for the photos. The same lack kept all of us from appearing in the white flannels and blue coats we had decided on for the graduation exercise. The class faculty advisor nixed this requirement, since many of the students did not have the flannels and could not afford to buy them.

Sixty–six years have gone by, and I can recognize only a small number of the classmates pictured in my book. I left school early in the day for an afternoon job and had little time to get to know most of them. Nor was the time yet ripe for these various nationalities to mix socially.

There on the front page am I, a member of the publication committee, with a head of hair which has long since fled. In the center of the page is Eugene Orban, the class president and fleet halfback for our mediocre football team. The son of a florist, he is to use his fleetness in delivering flowers. Beneath him is the baby–faced Freddie Fennell, our class secretary and musical genius, who played every known percussion instrument from a bell to a xylophone in our prize–winning band and orchestra. He was later to become Dr. Frederick Fennell, nationally famous conductor and composer. Next to him is committee member Ernest Kiss, whose ads in the local papers would soon advertise him as "Kiss the Plumber!"

On the following pages, in alphabetical order, I recognize the Bossin twins, Aaron and Mack, so identical that they substituted for each other in class and in their

jobs as ushers in a movie theater, without anyone ever catching on. They bring to mind their lovely dark–haired sister, my silent love for the two years we were in class together, who shortly after her graduation fell victim to a strange disease and died.

Then there is Ethel Fox, voted the belle of the class, who seldom dated classmates, preferring "older men." Next is Ed Likover, who

# SENIOR OWLET

"HOO'S-HOO»
IN
JUNE '33

John Adams High School
Cleveland, Ohio

103

became an attorney championing liberal causes, only to fall victim to the McCarthy Committee investigation, which made him drop his law practice and become a successful builder. Next to him is Ralph Liss, a big ox of a man, who did not know one end of a football from the other, who was nevertheless cajoled into joining the team and becoming an outstanding guard. And here is the class's other Sam Marks, who received my diploma as I did his, the only difference in the two being my middle initial "R.".

With sorrow, I notice the smiling face of David Miller, the son of close family friends, who eventually took off as a bombardier from an English airport and was never heard from again—it was from his family that I first learned that MIA stood for Missing In Action. Handsome Gerald Rado became an actor and talent scout, and Sam Seifter a highly regarded chemistry professor at an eastern university. Sam never responded to the letters I sent him, because, as he told another friend, he didn't remember me—an absent minded professor indeed! And finally, there is Edith Weisberg, whom I belatedly asked to be my date for the prom, only to be told she was going with the football captain!

Four people who signed my book bring special memories. Masa Kameoka, the beautiful daughter of a Japanese–American couple and darling of the entire class, became an outcast when her father, the leader of the city's small Japanese community, was jailed when bombs fell on Hawaii; and Miss Cora Welday, my favorite English teacher, who wrote on my final report card that I would make my school proud of me when I went to college. Wasn't she aware of my situation? She should have written "if," not "when!" The other two, the only blacks in the class, ended in disparate careers, Donald Shy as a post office clerk and William Mason as a professor of history.

Yes, I finally got to go to the prom, with a blind date selected from the photos in this very same book. Frances Jenkin was a flutist in our orchestra with no date. I was introduced to her at her home in the presence of her mother, whose face lit up with joy at this last minute opportunity for her daughter to be escorted to the prom. Another mother provided the transportation, squeezing three couples into her sedan, from which we all emerged disheveled.

Frances Jenkin went out of my life with the end of the prom. Her tears, shed on seeing her wrinkled gown, have remained to haunt me ever since. Perhaps this is as good a way as any to recall our impoverished but interesting lives in the "Great Depression!"

●●●●●

**Sam Marks** was born in Russia and emigrated to Cleveland, Ohio, with his family in 1923. After retiring in 1981, he moved with his wife Ann to Chapel Hill. His memoirs of life between two world wars numbers over one hundred stories, one of which has been published in his army division's book of war stories.

# The Depression That Wasn't

## Connie Toverud

When you don't know what a Great Depression means, there isn't any. I was a little girl during those years, and although I heard the big people talk about being in the midst of the Depression, I would look around me and couldn't see anything that we were in the middle of except our huge, drafty old house.

True, the old house was cold most of the time because the ceilings were twelve feet high. My father explained to me that heat rises, that we didn't have money to buy enough coal to heat the whole house, and that that was why we had to wear our outdoor clothes inside in the winter. It never occurred to me to ask why we didn't have money. I only wondered why we couldn't fly so we could live up near the warm ceiling.

I remember talk about people who lost all their money. I could understand why someone could lose a nickel on the way to the store to buy an ice cream cone, but I thought a person had to be mighty careless to lose every bit of his or her money. I decided they didn't have parents like mine who made sure I had pockets with no holes so I couldn't lose all my money.

I remember my parents feeling sorry for people who had to "do without." They never specified without what, but I saw it happen to my sister once, so I knew what they meant. My older sister was given an allowance every month so she could learn to manage money and buy only what she needed. There were lectures about frivolous purchases and giving in to fads. Well, one month she gave in, for Dutch wooden shoes were all the rage. She needed a new pair of shoes because her old ones had holes in the bottom, and she decided to buy the wooden ones. My parents told her in no uncertain terms that those shoes would hurt her feet, go out of style as soon as they hurt other people's feet, and she should buy good, sensible shoes. She didn't.

True to their prediction, the shoes caused her agony, and she could wear them only a few days. Back she came to my parents, pleading for an advance on her allowance so she could buy new shoes. "No," they answered. "When you are foolish, you have to 'do without'." So she put cardboard in the soles of her old shoes and wore them until the next allowance came around. My confusion lay in the fact that my parents felt sorry for people they talked about who had to "do without" during the Depression, probably because they bought the wrong shoes, but they never felt a bit sorry for my sister.

Sometimes I wondered why my mother never bought new clothes, but I decided it was a grown–up thing and that only little girls were supposed to have new dresses. Mine were sewn by my mother with huge hems that could be let down as I grew. A new ribbon for a sash made it a new dress.

My mother taught piano lessons in our home, and there was often talk between my parents about "making ends meet." I knew it had something to do with music, so I guessed it meant that when the pupils played duets with my mother, the hope was that they would finish the end of the piece at the same time. I knew one thing, and that was that I never wanted the music to end.

So for me, the Great Depression never happened. I was loved, played with, and prayed with. I had breakfast, lunch, dinner and a cat. I had bedtime stories, a big sister, and hugs. Sure! I heard about a few people who jumped out of buildings because they were so sad, but I knew that if they had my family, they would have been fine.

•••••

**Connie Toverud** is a columnist for the Chapel Hill Herald. She is a former high school guidance counselor and now leads workshops internationally on grief and loss. She also translates books from Norwegian.

# Life in the Dust Bowl

## Wesley H. Wertz

My name is Wesley H. Wertz. I was born March 2, 1922, in Quinter, Kansas. My parents owned and operated a wheat and livestock farm. I received my education in grades one through twelve in the public school of Quinter. My college education was at Kansas State University in Manhattan, Kansas. I graduated with the degree of Doctor of Veterinary Medicine (DVM).

As a pre–teen and teenager, I lived through the Great Depression of the 1930's. In addition to the Depression, our part of the country suffered severe droughts in the early 1930's and was part of the "dust bowl."

Farm crops during those years yielded very low. Some years there was no grain or livestock feed harvested. Many farmers had to sell their cattle and hogs due to lack of feed and money to buy feed. Cattle were selling for ten cents a pound or less; hogs, from three to five cents a pound. My parents were able to keep a few cows to milk and had some hens for egg production.

Milk was separated from the cream so that they had cream and eggs to sell. That money was used to buy staples at the grocery store. We always had a garden. So, with the fresh and canned vegetables, meat that we raised, milk, cream, butter, and eggs we always had plenty of food on our table. However, cash was in very short supply. Mother saved the flour and feed sacks, which she washed and bleached, and used the material to make items of clothing.

Because of the lack of rainfall and the high winds which were prevalent, there was a lot of dust in the air from the

111

cultivated fields. I remember many times there would be clouds of dust in the air from the cultivated fields in the west. When these clouds were especially large and severe, we were barely able to see our hands held at arm's length in front of us. Dirt drifted over fences and farm machinery left outside.

My mother, with very little success, tried her best to keep the dust out of our house. Even taping the windows and weather stripping the doors failed to keep out the dirt.

Financial and weather conditions did improve in the late '30's. By the early 40's living became more normal.

•••••

**Wesley Wertz** retired from the life of a veterinarian. He resides in Missouri.

# A Sense of Neighborhood

## O. J. Gossard

A memory of the Great Depression is a memory of my youth. I was born in Omaha, Nebraska, in 1923, but by the time I entered kindergarten, we lived in suburban Cincinnati, Ohio. My father had lost his job with the M. E. Smith Company, a wholesale dry goods firm, when the Smith company went bankrupt in a pre–Depression business shakedown. He then took his family to St. Joseph, Missouri, and Maywood, Illinois, for short lived jobs before finding a position in Cincinnati. I learned later that he always found the jobs beneath his abilities, but there were few opportunities for better jobs.

I was a happy kid. Life was wonderful for me, growing and playing in a neighborhood of other youngsters my age. But I was always aware of a grim attitude about money. There were parental groans about my growing into new larger sizes of clothing or unexpected rips of my trousers or holes that appeared in the soles of my shoes. My mother spent all her leisure hours darning socks or mending clothing.

But I was a kid and thought that the worry about money was natural, just a natural background to growing up. My father worked the five week days and half a day on Saturday. I remember one summer day during the week when he came home for lunch. He never had lunch with us before, but it was good to have him with us for lunch. My parents seemed subdued that day, and soon after lunch I was sent out to play. Shortly, he left driving his old REO up the street. Years later, I was told that he had lost his job that day and set out to find another one.

Years after, when I was married with two boys, I thought about my father with a family of three children losing his job in a time of economic uncertainty.

Next door to our home lived the Stemlers, two children and a grandfather, who had been the immigrant from Germany. Grandfather Stemler was a short, dour old man with a big mustache. We never noticed him except when he walked up to the streetcar or back in the afternoon. We kids were a little afraid of him, but on New Year's Eve ushering in 1934, we young ones were in a festive mood and swirled up around him to wish him a Happy New Year. He paused, unsmiling as usual, and uttered in gutteral German–English, "1933, no damn good. Too many threes!"

During the great dust storms, I remember looking up at the unusual dark clouds of dust and marveled that I could write my name in the accumulated dust on our front porch. My mother's explanation that the dust was from the top soil of Oklahoma seemed strange. I knew enough about geography to know that Oklahoma was far, far away.

We lived about a quarter of a mile away from the railroad tracks. We were always told to run home if we ever saw any strange men in the woods that lay between our neighborhood and the tracks. But occasionally, a man would knock on the back door seeking something to eat. My mother always fixed a sandwich and a glass of milk. These men were always appreciative and after their lunch, they would saunter back into the woods toward the tracks.

I don't want to leave you with the impression that life in my part of the Depression was always grim. For one thing, there was a great sense of neighborhood. On warm days, after supper, my father would sit in front of our big radio to hear Lowell Thomas and laugh at the antics of Amos and

Andy. He then would go out to the front porch to read the afternoon newspaper. Soon he would be talking with Mr. Keller next door, and then each of them would haul a chair off of his porch and place them near each other on the two concrete driveway paths between the houses. And then another neighbor would join them. And another. Then their wives would have finished cleaning up their kitchen and join their husbands and neighbors in the expanding circle. We kids would play kick–the–can or go–sheepy–go or some other kid game, but eventually we would slip into the circle or lean against the back of a parent's chair. We didn't speak, but in the growing darkness we listened intently to the stories of our parent's youth and other subjects. I think that that was where I first learned to love the sound of the spoken words.

And so my impression of those Depression years was a feeling of neighbors, of time to enjoy life. Yes, it was a time when we had no television, spending money, or credit cards, but those of us who were kids missed the deep stress and worry that our parents experienced. Perhaps it was just that at that early age, I was superficial and failed to appreciate the gravity of our national life.

•••••

**Oliver Gossard (Ollie)** retired from teaching for Elon College, Elon College, North Carolina, and now resides in Seven Lakes, North Carolina.

# People Talking about the Depression

## Lucy Rodgers Watkins

People talking in April, 1999, about their memories of the Great Depression shared common experiences. Most of the African Americans and several whites lived on farms at the time; and being used to growing their own food and hunting and fishing, they didn't suffer from hunger. And their jobs were farming jobs. They didn't seem to feel poor most of the time. A few lived in cities, and their stories are of survival with food package aid, soup kitchens, and the Civilian Conservation Corps and the Works Progress Administration. But there are subtle variations in their memories, and graphic individual experiences.

## Transcripts of Taped Conversations
## April 19, 1999

### Hettie Mae Clark

We were pretty well except...my daddy had his own farm, and plenty of food. We growed cotton instead of tobacco. We didn't have tobacco. We had cotton and corn and wheat and cane—sugar cane—he had his own cane mill, and people would come round there from the country, like if you had cane, you had your pile and that's where they would grind up the cane and make the cane, cook it. It was just as nice, and people would come in there with their wagons, with their cane to be fixed up. I was a little girl then. I was born in '23, so I couldn't have been more than eight or nine. [We grew] all sorts of vegetables, and [we had] pigs and cows and chickens and guineas—they hollered all the time. Would you call that an animal or a fowl? Yes, fowl. Compared to some people, we had it pretty good. [We lived] down in Pittsboro out in the country, right down the Raleigh Road, out in the country. Everybody mostly had their own farm. Some didn't own their home though. They didn't own their farm. Everybody farmed. We didn't have to buy much. Wheat, we had that ground for flour. And milk. Mama sewed [our clothes]. Mama sewed a lot, and after we got up in size, we started buying from the store. We were pretty well equipped. We didn't make sugar, it was molasses. They called it molasses, molasses from the cane. I said about all—pepper, sugar, salt—didn't have to buy very much. We had meat year–round. You'd get some of the best beef then. It was too good to cook. Now I don't know what beef tastes like. Sometimes you think you get a good piece, and sometimes you can't hardly eat it, and sometimes it's good. You know that. [Chicken is not as good as it was.] No, those were good chickens. They don't taste nothing like they used to. I know Mama had chicken cooked... people would come and eat...it was nine of us...but one I never saw. She died before I was born. Now all of them are gone but me. I'm the youngest. The very oldest and number eight died the same day. Number eight died in the morning, and the very first one died about six–thirty. It was a sad day, but now you've got to look at it, nobody killed them. They died. They were all sick. It was really a blow.

[My father and uncle and the boys] they hunted, killed rabbits, squirrels, everything. We raised meat, you know, raised a lot. Went fishing. Oh, they loved to fish, and I was the only one in the family that didn't like fishing, but I went with my Mother all the time, because she liked to fish. But I didn't like to fish; I still don't like to; I like to buy mine in the store.

We had all the equipment to farm with. [got along pretty well.] I thought so. [Everybody raised everything.]

Watermelon, cantaloupes, all that stuff, and all the vegetables, you know, squash, corn, beans, peas, you name it, tomatoes, onions. [Put them up] in the summer. Pickles, jellies, preserves. Old people used to quilt a lot, they'd come to my parents' house, this group of women, they'd quilt all day, then they'd go to somebody else's house. That's the way we got our quilts. That was fun. After you grew up, you looked back at that life. That was the best time. It was, because children now won't work, they be killing their parents before they work sometimes.

I was young, I didn't know who was out of work. I don't know. The WPA. I know something about that. CC Camp. Yeah, I knew some people who were in the CC Camp and that was all, but neither one of my brothers was in the CC Camp. [They worked on the farm too.] And then, they had that sawmill. And then they started scattering around, going different places.

[If needed a doctor], well, we'd get to a doctor. You know you could drive your wagon or buggy up there in Pittsboro. Papa had a wagon, had a buggy. I guess he gave him money, he sure didn't give him no corn or nothing. He paid money. [discussion of barter] Well, we were poor, but thank God, we weren't like that.

Oh, I forgot, we had a big peach farm. Used to sell those peaches, and things, potatoes, sweet potatoes, turnips.

You're talking about CC Camps, a lot of that stuff I don't know much about, swapping food, I don't know nothing about that. Then, when you're in the country, you don't see as many people as you see on the street, so I can't tell you nothing about how people were living in town. They did [have school buses] after awhile. We used to have to walk about four miles—that was high school though. Used to have country schools, and you didn't have to walk that far. But in high school you had to walk, until they got buses coming down. So that was nice.

I've been [lived] different places. Just before the war, I was at my daddy and mama's farm. I hadn't left home, I was in high school.

I guess that's about all. He had his own mules. Never had a tractor. We had that big old mowing machine. And then the children got grown and started leaving, and so he just gave the farm up. [Leave it to anybody?] Ain't nobody out there. I told you everybody was dead. [Land?] Sold it. We were old enough, it was okay.

Photo Credit: North Carolina Collection, University of North Carolina Library at Chapel Hill

Roscoe Gregory

I'm from New York, worked in New York. Born and raised. Moved down here in '87. My son brought me down here. He was living down here. I was in the city fire

120

department, was a captain, seventeen years. Was born November 4, 1919, seventy–nine years old. [I lived through the Depression.] Yeah, I was in the CCC, and the WPA. Went to Elmira, Syracuse, upstate New York. We did forestry work, road work, built roads, beginning of highways, cut down all them trees, [conservation] work. Liked it. I was pretty good at it too. We was poor and I joined up with the CCC. I was in two years, that was about the limit it was. That was 1937. Before that I was in school, was only seventeen. Father worked for the WPA for awhile, but he was a longshoreman down at the docks. He worked down at the docks. He belonged to the longshoreman's union. There were just two of us, me and my sister. He went to the WPA, and had a couple of jobs, and we had it rough some days. We always had food. I used to shine shoes, got a nickel, got tips, pretty good. Helped to support family, especially when my sister took sick with rheumatic fever. Went to King's County Hospital up there. [Pay?] Well, they had some kind of situation in King's County, when you're sick, you go into King's County. When I had pneumonia, I was in King's County, and had my appendix out in King's County. [The medical care] wasn't good, but it was there, and it helped you, you know, the treatment. [Clothes] We got them together somehow. We'd work at it. Mr. Bernstein used to have a tailor shop, making clothes, getting material. We'd pay him about a dollar every two weeks or something like that, and wind up getting the suit out. I was not just shining shoes, you know, working extra work needed to do. I was in my teens, eighteen. The CCC was the first job I had. I come out of school and went in the CCC. [My father in the WPA] He worked at building LaGuardia Airport. He had to take buses, it was two hours of traveling time, but he would do it. [When I got out of the CCC] I went into the WPA. I worked out at the international airport,

Idlewile, helped build it. I worked in the WPA almost two years, then I went in the Army. In the WPA, they paid you according to how you [needed it for] your family. In the CCC we got paid $30 a month. When I made leader, it was $36. Just like a corporal or sergeant or something. Went into the army in 1943; I worked in the WPA until they drafted me.

## Howard Clark

[I'm from] here and about 12 miles from here, down in Chatham County. [I've lived here] in and out, in fact, I was born just down the street here, right up there behind McDonald's. In the Depression in 1929 I was about nine years old. [Remember it?] I sure do. Actually, I didn't live with my mother and father whenever I was round about that age. My Granddaddy took in me when I was about six years old, and I stayed with him until he left and went to High Point. My aunt carried him up there to take care of him, and that was in about '34 or '35. Well, my mother come to Chatham. She was living in High Point, but she come back to Chatham to take care of me herself, so she's been here ever since. We had stopped farming, but it was on the farm where we were living. That didn't leave it up to nobody to farm but me. [Food from farm?] That was a lot of help, because we raised some, we even planted cane, made our own molasses, and so we ate just about what we raised. We raised [chickens], so we'd take some eggs to the store and buy some cheese, take some eggs to the store and buy some coffee, something like that.

## Louise Brunssen

[Lived in Germany during Depression.] I grew up on a farm. I had four sisters. [Lived in] Olgenburg, in the northern part. Near Bremen. I came to the United States in 1953. I was thirty–nine years old. [Depression started much earlier in Germany, just after first World War] I was just four just after the first World War. I was born 1914 [so lived through two world wars] Yes, the first one I was a baby, and that was a very bad time. We lived on a farm, and always had enough to eat after the war, but during the war it was pretty bad. But that's what they say; I was pretty small. My mother got T. B., and she was only forty–six years old when she passed away. I was nine years old. I was the youngest. They had to take care of me. (What made you come to the U.S.?] My husband had two brothers here. They came in 1929. [If you'd come earlier, you would have escaped that second World War. ] Yes, that was awful. We lived just in the north, and all the planes came in to Hamburg, to all the big cities. [They didn't bomb my city] No, then we lived in a small city, and they just wanted to bomb the city where we lived, and then the war was over, and they didn't bomb any more.

[Between the wars, lived on a farm.] Yes, we had cows, and all had to work. We worked in the household. See, sometimes there was not these jobs like there are now. I could find work. It didn't pay very much.

## Esther Evans

In Person County—I was born in Person County—over near Hurley's Mill. In fact, that's where I still belong to the church, Union Grove Baptist Church. And we lived on a farm. My grand dad, my daddy's dad, had a farm, and there were two houses. When my daddy got married, he built him a house up on a hill, and then they had another house that was a sharecropper's house. My daddy rented [land to farm]. He had his own car, so he rented [land to farm], but the man in the other house, whoever lived there, they just worked sharecrop. And we used to walk to school, which was a long ways, about three miles. We walked sometimes; it was cold. My teacher lived up on the hill about a mile from us, and she was a good friend of my dad's, because they all grew up together. So she had asked me when her husband would take her sometimes, especially on rainy and bad days, so they would always pick me up. And I would get to ride.

I can't...to me times never seemed all that bad, because my parents, they raised their garden, and Mother always canned everything, and my...[clothes] oh., yes... no, we didn't have no hand–me–downs, but the only thing that was given to me was what my grandmother would give me, and they was new clothes. They were never hand–me–downs. I was the oldest in the family, and then my brother, I had a brother not quite two years younger than me, and it was just us two for about five or six years, then another, my other brother was born, and we thought he was our little doll. He was our favorite little brother. [Born at home, didn't go to hospital.] My mother had a doctor, Dr. Warren, and my dad had a doctor, Dr. Bain, because my dad would not take pills, and that's what Dr. Warren always gave out, was pills. My mother liked pills, so they had separate doctors. So Dr. Bain, my daddy's doctor, he lived, like, almost joining plantations to my granddaddy's farm. You could walk over, you know, to where his doctor lived. He had had infantile paralysis when he was little, so his daddy sent him to college to be a doctor.

124

He had about seven boys, I believe. Since he had infantile paralysis, he went to college, so he was a doctor, and he built a doctor's office right beside his store. He ran a big country store, so that's where we went. We could walk over there, because it wasn't that far from my granddaddy's house.

And I remember times, then, they got bad. My dad had a car, but—and my grandmother had a car also. My granddaddy finally lost his farm. We moved over in Orange County, right next to my mother's daddy. He had a big farm. He had three or four sharecroppers on his farm. He was one of the well–off black people, you know, so we stayed there for about—we didn't live on his farm, it was joining his farm. And then my granddaddy bought the farm that we lived on. We had moved off farther, Pineknot, right close to the school. And times got tough, so my daddy's car gave out, and he wasn't able to buy another one, so we would use the wagon to go to church, and we went at least a couple of years—I don't know what year it was, back in the thirties, thirty–two or something like that. But to me, I mean, it was okay. My daddy always, you know, he talked about we going on the wagon, and he'd fix it up, you know, straw in it, and to me all that was great. I mean it was like a hay ride or something, and we looked forward to it, you know. We couldn't wait for May to come, to, you know, get out there barefooted. Mama wouldn't ever let us go barefooted 'til the first day of May. Then we could take off our shoes and go barefooted. We always wore shoes to church. My brother—both of us—we always wore shoes to church. It was seven in our family. I was the oldest. And I had two sisters, four brothers. And after we moved over in Orange County, my daddy got sick, of course, and he had to go to the hospital, and they thought he was going to die, but he came out.

At that time, people would help each other, help raise, mind the crops, and neighbors would come in, anybody who needed anything, and when they had gardens, whoever's garden came in first in the neighborhood, they shared it with the neighbors until theirs come in. That's the way they did. So I mean times didn't really seem that bad to me. Like I said, we always had plenty to eat. It wasn't that fancy, but it filled you up, and it was good when you was hungry. Everything was good. We never had a radio. I never had a radio until I married. My husband had one. He had one in his house. But my daddy—we never owned a radio. My daddy didn't ever buy one, but after I got married, all my sisters and brothers, they bought a radio. We'd go out in the yard and play. We had these old tires hanging up in the tree to swing, and rolling tires to play, and hop–scotch and jump rope, and we just had a great time. On Sundays, my parents—they didn't belong to church, but both of their parents belonged to church, same church, so we went to church once a month. We always went on fourth Sunday. They were Primitive Baptists. We looked forward to then. Like I say, when we didn't have a car, we went on the wagon. But as children, we just had, I remember, it was a wonderful time to me.

And after moving over in Orange County, it was not that far from school; in fact, we were close enough if we wanted to, we could walk home at lunchtime, you know, to eat. But we didn't do it often. Most of the time we carried our lunch so we could play during the recess. But we walked to school, you know, all the time. My aunt, my cousin, they lived over on the hill, and my husband's people, who I finally married, they lived not far from us, and so all the neighbors, like I said, they shared; nobody that I know of went hungry out there round in the community where I stayed. It wasn't that tight of a time.

I remember people used to get jobs [WPA]; they'd go work on roads or something or other. [CCC] Not really, I didn't know nobody. I know they had some people, if they wanted, you know, to make money, some people worked on the roads. They didn't go out of the state, It was, you know, around in the community close enough where they could come home. I remember it, something called the CCC, and people would go all around in the state. But none of my family never worked in them. We farmed. My husband's people, they raised a lot of potatoes. They'd always have some of the best sweet potatoes. And I know, when we'd go to school, if we went by there, my husband's mother would,

Photo Credit: The Odum Photo Study, Southern Historical Collection, The Library of the University of North Carolina at Chapel Hill

she'd always cook a big pan of potatoes, and sometimes she'd give us some. We didn't have to go right by there all the time, but sometime we'd go by there. In the afternoons, when we were coming home from school sometimes. My parents raised sweet potatoes too, but they never had a lot of them like my husband's dad did. We always had just plenty of them, you know, to last from spring to when they would come, you know. They used to put the sweet potatoes in the barn, the tobacco barn, and they'd spread them out in there, and they would dry out, and after they'd dried out, they would put them in baskets, like put them upstairs in the attic so they wouldn't freeze. And they would keep most of the time all winter. Now my grand daddy use to—he had all kind of fruit on his farm, every kind of fruit tree, and he had apples, the first earliest apples to come until October—it would be cold—the tree of apples would always get ripe in September. They were the best, and he would put them in, would pull them off, put them in baskets, you know, wrap them in newspaper, and put them in baskets, and they lasted all the winter. At Christmas time, we'd go to visit, and he'd always give all the children a bag of apples. He'd put them all up in the attic, all wrapped in newspaper, and put in these bushel baskets, and they kept up there.

Like I say, I don't remember—you know, to me—it was tough times—but to me it wasn't, I mean, it was a happy time, because we had plenty of food, and we had clothes and we had a way to go, so it was much happier than the people now with everything. Yeah, we enjoyed ourselves, I think


Arthur Dockery

I was born November 9, 1925. I was born in Chatham County. Liable to have been on a farm, cause I was a little young. [My father] worked in Rockingham. I think he worked at some kind of store, something like that. He didn't have no job all the time, because he was up here in the WPA, construction work. I can remember the time when I was in Chatham County, and my mother took me up in Washington, D. C., when we were about—me and my brother, we were round about—he was a little older than I was, I was round about three, and he was round about five years old, and she took us up in Washington, D. C. I was raised up in D. C. That wasn't small. Now I can tell you about the soup line up there. They had a soup line up there. Everybody would go down on Connecticut Avenue and get in the soup line. I remember that now. I didn't stand in line. I can remember that. We got food and stuff, like they'd give you food like ham. Some kind of aid plan. I forget what they called it. I remember being hungry. [Radio?] I don't think we had a radio or TV or nothing. We probably had a radio. [Hear President Roosevelt's fireside chats?] I probably have. I know President Roosevelt. He was in Casablanca. I was over there, I was in Casablanca in the Navy. I went in 1942, and got out January 6, 1947.

I went to school in Washington, D. C. We had some clothes. We wore those bell–bottomed pants, you know, those .... We got our lunch, you know, some of those jars that you carry fruit, you know, that you make fruit in? Well, my mama fixed those jars, and we carried them to school, and for our lunch, we'd go the other side and eat our lunch out of that. Black–eyed peas and some fatback. We had that, and we'd go cross on the other side. The other children didn't have that, but we had that ourselves, me and my brother. [The other children] I guess they had apples and peanut butter, I guess. We went over the other side. The schoolhouse was on a—go up the hill, and on the other side was a place where you can go over there and eat your lunch, just like a park. Just like a park. I guess we were so ashamed because we brought those jugs with black–eyed peas, and we didn't want anybody to look at us.

My mother, she worked, did day work. I had a paper route, the *Washington Post*. I'd fold it up and throw it in the doors. They give you so much papers to deliver, and the bag. I remember that. And then after that, then I worked at a grocery store and carried groceries to people's doors on a bicycle. I remember that. That's a long memory. [What did you do with your money—keep it, give part to parents?] I went to movies, bought donuts, something like that, cakes. A guy used to come around selling gingerbread on one of them trucks. No, I didn't make that much. I didn't make a whole lot of big money. CC Camp. We was in the CC Camp, in the Washington, D. C., CC Camp. I guess I was in my teens then. We were getting a dollar a day, $30 a month. We had three C's on the shoulder, a green uniform. I remember that. [WPA?] I can't recall now, because it's been a long time. They died out. I can't remember them. They [worked on roads] digging ditches and stuff like that. It was kind of hard times up in Washington during that time, because they wasn't paying too much in Washington when I was up there. A long time they wasn't paying like now they're paying. They might be paying just a little bit, but your food—your food was cheap, you know. Why you could get fatback for five cents a pound, when it was during that time in Washington. [In CCC] I lived in a barracks, worked on the roadway with a pick and shovel. We didn't live at home, and we had to go from there out in Maryland, way out there. A roadway, I remember that. But after...what happened after that...during that time I was in the CC Camp when I got out of school, I was about seventeen, and I went in the service in the Navy.

## Clifton Boyd

I was born in Oxford, North Carolina, Granville County, 1909. Oh, yeah, I remember right much [of the Depression]. Only thing was, my Daddy was a mail carrier, so we didn't have to worry too much about income, you know. I worked in a grocery store at the time, made about $6 a week, and it was good money then. I always lived on Main Street. We had a radio, yeah, had a Philco, ain't that what the name of them was? We had one of them. [Roosevelt's fireside chats?] No, I can't remember much about that. I can't tell you what we listened to. No, I didn't have any trouble finding a job, just like I told you, I had this job in the grocery store. People had to eat, you know. My Dad was half owner in the store, you know. That's the reason I had the job. And I worked there, let's see, I worked there about six years. And I got married in 1934. My wife's been dead since 1981, and one lady, I went with her for eight years, and she died in 1989. I got another lady, and I been going with her nine years. I been in Carrboro since 1943. I moved to Carrboro from Bynum, North Carolina, between here and Pittsboro. I lived there about nine months.

During the war, I worked at Camp Butner, during the war. [Wasn't in the army.] No, I was a 4–F. The doctor said I had heart trouble. I went to the doctor, and he said, "Ain't anything in the world wrong with your heart." I went to the doctor after this, you know. But what I...I was scared to death, that's what was wrong with me. I was so shook up. And I was a 4–F, and I went to work at Camp Butner during the war, worked down there 'til they closed up.

[CCC and WPA] Yeah, I remember them, yeah. I didn't have to [be in them], because of the grocery store. That's what my life was, grocery store. I worked in a food store in Chapel Hill twenty–five years, and I retired in 1972.

## James Farrington

No, I ain't lived here all my life, but I was raised here. I lived in New Jersey for a good number of years. I was born here, I was born in 1920. [When the Depression started], I was in school. Lived in Orange County. Lived on a farm. Raised mostly all of everything we eat. We raised chickens. We had plenty to eat. [We hunted] for rabbits, squirrels, 'possums, birds. [Went to school] in Orange county. [School buses?] No, not at the beginning. Later on they got buses. We had to walk, I'd say about three miles. It didn't seem far. We'd get out there, what I mean, we'd ...there'd be a bunch of us, you know.

We didn't have any electricity, just oil lamps. Later on, we got electricity. No, we didn't have no indoor plumbing. We had to use the outhouse. No, we didn't have no pump, we had a well, let the bucket down in the well, crank it up. We had a big bucket, oh, I reckon about three gallons of water at a time. It was pretty hard to pull up. We had fireplaces and a wood stove in the kitchen. We had a—what do you call it—a heater in the living room, one of those pot–bellied stoves. [ Wood.] Had to chop wood, yeah. We had it pretty good.

•••••

**Lucy Rodgers Watkins**, of Chapel Hill, has worked for thirty–two years in non–profit education and community and human development programs. Her poems have appeared in *South Today*, *Echoes*, and the *UNC–Greensboro Alumni Magazine*.

# The Uncertainty of Life on a South Carolina Farm

## Elizabeth W. Tandy Pinckney

After the Great Depression ended, we often dated our remarks by saying "Before the Depression"—"During the Depression"—or "After the Depression." But once it was over, the easy flow of my life had been changed forever.

In the 1920's my father was a successful cotton farmer in mid–South Carolina. His father had been a successful cotton farmer, as had his grandfather and his great grandfather. In 1918 he had married a local school teacher and right away began to build his dream house. It was a large colonial style brick house with tall white columns, located back from the highway in a beautiful grove of oaks. The $10,000 mortgage seemed insignificant at the time.

As we four children came along, my father always enjoyed doing things to make our lives richer. For instance, one day a man appeared at our farm driving a wagon pulled by a big mule beside a little donkey. My younger brothers and younger sister and I were charmed; we had never seen a donkey. Melting before our enthusiasm, Father brought out his prize–winning sow, "Lady Watson," and traded her for the donkey. I'm sure the former donkey owner was amazed at his good fortune as he drove off with that enormous, dignified hog, crated, in his wagon.

Then Father had our blacksmith reduce a regular sized buggy to fit the donkey. On the back of the buggy the blacksmith fitted a rumble seat. We children would harness the donkey and call Mary and Bo, our colored playmates who lived in the grove. Somehow we all fitted into the buggy and away we would go, but at a donkey pace. We quickly found we could get a little speed if we scraped a piece of tin on the wheel.

Another of Father's wonderful ideas was to have a small log cabin built among the trees near the house. It was to be our play–house. There was a roofed porch and a regular fireplace with a rock chimney. The builders finished the construction on Christmas Eve. On Christmas morning we were taken out to the playhouse. Inside, stood the Christmas tree fully decorated. There were curtains at the windows and a table with four chairs. The table was set with little plates, cups and saucers, and Santa had left one of his sleigh bells for our dinner bell. We enjoyed the playhouse for many years, finally using it to store our bikes.

In the summers we would go to the North Carolina mountains and camp for a week. In the early days there were no paved roads in the mountains and no camp grounds or conveniences along the way. We had to carry all our supplies, including many blankets, as there were no sleeping bags then. When he was six months old, Mike, the baby, was bedded down in the car on the seat.

All this called for more physical labor than my father enjoyed. So, behind our car was a second car loaded with all the supplies and driven by two of our men from the farm. Bennie, our Negro overseer, was the driver and cook. He made pancakes and fried sweet potatoes over the campfire, and even today when I smell bacon frying, I think of Bennie's wonderful breakfasts. In our lead car rode Mama, Father, four children, and Bennie's younger sister, Lizzie, to help out.

In those days life for my mother was pleasant. I'm glad she was not able to look ahead at what was to come. She had a big vegetable garden and a beautiful flower garden. There was always a strong man she could call from the barn for heavy work. There was a cook in the kitchen and someone to do the laundry. She would go calling in the afternoon after rest time, or she would entertain callers. I remember going calling with her; when she found the friend absent, she would take out her silver card case and leave her engraved card.

Mama would take us on long lazy walks down in the woods behind the fields where we would make a little fire and toast marshmallows. She was active in our Methodist Church and she took great pleasure in her ladies' study club. In 1932 it fell her turn to entertain when they celebrated the 100th year of George Washington's birth. The ladies all came in costume with powdered hair. I watched from upstairs, peeping through the bannister rails.

In the late twenties the price of cotton was going higher. Word was it would probably reach forty cents a pound. Then why sell at thirty cents? And so my father began to store the bales and wait. The price began to go down. Surely it would recover. But no. When he was finally forced to sell, it was five cents a pound. That was in 1929. The slow, easy life of our small town suddenly began to change.

In 1933 the banks closed. That day my aunt, a young widow with two small children, was visiting us. I remember when she heard the news of the banks' closing, she said, "There goes my last $32.00." Our town, unable to pay cash to its school teachers, hired local women with teaching experience and paid them with certificates to be cashed later. My mother became one of those teachers.

On the farm we grew our own food, but there was no cash for clothing and other necessities. Five families of color lived on the farm. They needed to be paid with cash.

My father took a job with the Federal government in the Farm Credit Administration. This took him away from home for the first time. Most of that time he was in Kentucky. We saw him twice a year on his two–week vacation.

My mother knew little of farming. There was asparagus to be gathered, packed, and shipped. There was wheat and corn to be gathered, and our new peach orchard was approaching its fifth year—the year the peach trees bore enough fruit to ship. Mama and Bennie set up a peach–packing house, hired extra labor, and learned the business from the ground up. She had all this along with her new teaching job and four children under the age of twelve—all in public school.

I was the oldest child, so Mama took me with her to the Grange meetings. They were night meetings with a small group of grave–faced farmers, who talked about serious matters I didn't understand. I suppose Mama felt this experience might contribute to her training as a farmer.

She wrote my father every day but didn't want to burden him with her difficulties—after all, he was doing the best he could. So she unburdened her problems to me. At the age of twelve, I could provide very few solutions. I can remember thinking over and over, "Oh, if she would only hush."

True, there was lots of gloom and doom around us, but we had fun, too. There was the radio with Amos and Andy, Edgar Bergen and Charlie McArthy, Kate Smith, H. V. Kaltenborn, Major Bowles, Kay Kyser, Fibber McGee and Molly, George Burns and Gracie Allen, and Bing Crosby.

There were jigsaw puzzles and we played lots and lots of card games.

In those days our family didn't go to the movies often, although the cost was only thirty-five cents. But across the highway lived an aunt who liked to go to the movies several times a week. A movie was shown every Monday and Tuesday, another on Wednesday, then a new one for Thursday and Friday and a Western on Saturday. For reasons no one knew, my aunt didn't speak to most people in town, including my mother and father, but she chose to take me along for company on the eight-mile trip. I remember the news reels showing the breadlines over the country, the relief programs, the migrants, and the unemployed men selling apples on the streets of New York City.

I don't seem to remember scenes like that in our town. We all knew each other, and I think sometimes we were too proud to admit our difficulties. A close friend says he remembers accompanying his father when he went to the local bootlegger, not for liquor, but to borrow five dollars to put food on the family's table for a week. "Then," he added proudly, "I also accompanied him when he returned to pay the debt."

When we saw someone in need, we tried to help in some way. About two miles away, another aunt, a "grass widow," lived with her two children and my crippled grandmother. They didn't have a garden so my mother would share her vegetables and pork when we butchered a hog. Aunt Chloe decided she might be able to make extra money by raising turkeys. But she had much to learn about those stupid birds.

The turkeys should have been happy; they were contained in a nice, grassy grove of big pecan trees. But as they grew, they would fly up into the tall trees—then just sit there with no idea how to get back down. They were a constant source of trouble for Aunt Chloe, and I must say my lack of respect for a turkey has lasted 'til this day.

We often saw hoboes peeping from the doors of freight trains and occasionally they would knock at our back door. When they saw the big house set back among the oaks, I suppose it looked like a promising spot for a meal. They were always very polite; my mother never turned them away. She would fix a meal, then find a comfortable place outside for them to eat. If the weather was bad, she would direct them to the playhouse.

One day a charming little Irish lady knocked at the front door; she was selling Irish lace. Seeing someone from another country was a real treat. My mother was enchanted. When the lady finally left and Mama realized she had paid one hundred dollars of our scarce money for a table cloth, she was horrified and begged me not to tell Father. Of course I didn't, but I was stunned to hear her ask me not to tell Father; we never kept anything from him. Now that I think of it, I never saw that lace table cloth again. I have no idea what happened to it.

There was one other thing I think Mama kept from Father during those difficult days. Our house mortgage was held by a bank in Greenwood, forty miles away. By this time the house was twelve years old, so the $10,000 loan had been reduced somewhat. My mother finally found it impossible to make the payments. One day as she turned into our long drive, there, nailed to a tree, was a notice saying our house was to be sold by the bank. She got out of the car and tore the notice off the tree.

Her only hope was Uncle George, the husband of my father's sister. They lived just across the highway, but as I have written, our families were not close. Uncle George had money—he owned and operated the only cotton gin in the area. Mama put her pride in her pocket and walked over and told him her problem. She wept as she told me later how he opened his wallet and peeled off one hundred dollar bills.

My mother had beautiful brown, wavy hair. As long as she lived, it was never cut short. She washed it in the kitchen sink and used a vinegar rinse. After drying in the sun, it was combed and twisted into a bun and worn at the nape of her neck. We had no beauty shops, only Mr. Long, the lonely barber. Occasionally, my mother felt her hair needed thinning. She would take elaborate steps to be assured Mr. Long would alone in his shop. Heaven forbid if a man should walk in and see her with her hair down on her shoulders! That would be immodest, she thought.

Prices in those days were quite different from those of today. Gas was nine cents a gallon, meat twenty cents to thirty cents a pound. A pound of potatoes was two cents, a wool dress was $1.95. Silk stockings were sixty–nine cents and leather shoes $1.79.

Speaking of clothes, my mother had six younger unmarried sisters. They passed their hand–me–downs on to me, the oldest granddaughter. Under the circumstances, we didn't sneeze at hand–me–downs, but in my case there was a problem: the aunts were all slender and attractive; I was tall, chubby, and awkward. The clothes would fit me but they were too mature. The aunts would dress me up and laugh hysterically. I'll never forget the saddle oxfords. Saddle oxfords were very popular in those days, but unfortunately these turned up at the toes. I never discovered what caused this, but I was willing to give it a try, thinking surely they would straighten out after I wore them a while. They never did.

We had church activities and school activities. The citizens of the town attended and supported our school plays, ball games, and May Day celebrations, and they taught us in Sunday School. When they met us on the street, they always expressed pleasure and pride in our performances. Somehow, we all seemed to have remained cheerful. Maybe living in a small town during the Great Depression wasn't so bad after all. I've never read Mrs. Clinton's little book, but each time I hear the title *It Takes A Village To Raise A Child*, I think of Ridge Spring.

•••••

**Elizabeth Tandy Pinckney** was born in Ridge Spring, South Carolina, and studied journalism at the University of South Carolina. She has published in *Home Life* and in various newspapers. She has recently written a children's novel and is working on another. She very recently married Gaillard Pinckney and resides in Beaufort, South Carolina.

# Yesterday's Brooklyn

## Carolyn Rashti

It was so cold in February, 1935. We lived near the shoreline in Brooklyn surrounded by potato farms and estuaries (we called them swamps then) with tall wheat–colored winter grasses that flowed gracefully under the icy winds from Jamaica Bay, chilling winds that invaded the crevices of our little bungalow. I was five years old, and my mother was very pregnant. My father was out of work again, and our meals consisted mainly of potatoes with a gravy Mama made from boiling soup bones and onions.

My mother was a fine pianist; she didn't like to cook. She told me romantic stories of informal concerts she gave at the Brooklyn Museum and the Brooklyn Academy of Music, and the wonderful restaurants she went to when she was single in the days before the crash. She worked as a teller at the Bank of America in Manhattan. Mr. Gianinni, the bank president and a recent American, was a generous employer and very fair to women, rather revolutionary for a man born in Europe and during the 1920's. Mother was determined to be an emancipated woman, to free herself from the endless work of the lives of her immigrant parents. She earned a generous salary, loved the arts and gourmet cuisine. She bought beautiful things for her parent's home and glamorous clothing for her semi–professional concerts, but never failed to set a significant amount of money aside in a savings account in addition to purchasing stocks offered to the bank's employees. In only a few years she managed to collect an impressive nest egg. During one of her vacations, she sailed to the newly–developing vacation land of southern Florida (only ships traveled there then) with Rose and Erwin, her sister and brother–in–law, a free trip in exchange for her caring for their two little boys. Florida's billowing clouds in clear, blue skies, palm trees, and warm sea breezes were a breathtaking contrast to the chilling winds and depressing gray skies of Brooklyn winters. She decided to stay in this fantasy land after Rose and Erwin returned home, and would make her life in this beautiful clime and where the arts abounded. With a new job, an apartment, and her savings transferred to Palm Beach, she bought a car—a convertible, an extraordinary feat for a woman then and a symbol of her independence. And then it happened. The market crashed. Every bank was bombarded by depositors withdrawing their accounts. There were only two people ahead of her in the line when the bank ran out of money. Her job and her funds were gone, and she was in a strange place feeling defeated and scared. Rose and Erwin sent her passage money home. But returning to the depressive weather of the North made the economy's depression even greater, and fear can often defeat courage and diminish dreams. Thoughts of independence faded, and falling in love could be easy, even practical. The idea of a team of two trodding together through the terrible times offered some consolation. And so she did. And so I was conceived.

In 1935 mother's second unborn baby was as hungry as all of us. Bernard McFadden, a guru of organic nutrition, minimally processed foods, and the "You are what you eat" originator, proclaimed tomato juice to be an all–round food; and since it was cheap, it became a major component of our diet, except for father's. Other McFadden favored foods as mushrooms, potatoes, and onions were often available as volunteer gifts of the earth in our backyard, and so added their nutrition to our humble but tasty meals, and especially with Mama's soup bone gravy. In spite of a complete lack of any dining formality, it was my daily responsibility to find some kind of flowers for our humble table. Delicate chamomile daisies were waiting in spring, and somewhere through the winter months there were always gray and tan twigs with red berries to be found, and red and yellow leaves in the fall, perfect for a small bouquet for the center of our table. Esthetics seemed one of Mama's core values.

Daddy was no fisherman, but he would walk the mile or so with the neighborhood men—there wasn't much else to do during the day—who fished on the pier in the Bay and shared their excess catch, which added protein to our meager diets. Buying ice for an icebox in winter was a terrible extravagance, so perishables were kept in a wire cage on a northeast window ledge that got little, if any, sun. For badly needed extra money, Mama gave piano lessons on our old, but beautiful, upright piano; and when lessons were over, she would play for me and we would sing wonderful songs together and laugh.

That was a very stormy winter, and after one particularly long night of snow and fierce winds, our front door was completely snowed over and unopenable. Mama climbed out the back window with a shovel to free the doors and windows from under what seemed like an avalanche. Not surprisingly, her labor pains began. She gathered her things, took me next door to our beloved teenage neighbor, and, with her galoshes and umbrella, crunched through the deep snow to the street corner to wait for the trolley that chugged along behind the snow plow and took Mama to hospital. The baby was born two months prematurely and was very tiny; Mama said he floated out in all that tomato juice. He had to stay in hospital for over two weeks. Of course, at Kings County Hospital there were no medical fees for those of us, most of us, in poverty. When the baby finally did come home, he weighed only four–and–a–half pounds. We put him in my doll's carriage and called him "Tiny" and played with him on the porch so he could get as much sun as possible in the short days of winter. Mama thought the sun's vitamin D would help make him strong. He developed quite a tan. In later years, she blamed herself for his poor vision; she had not protected his eyes from the sun.

Spring brought the promise of a new garden in the back yard, some early vegetables, and the occasional trip to the village. Mother always seemed to find places where she could get clothing, household articles, and even a few toys for next to nothing. Very cheap articles were readily found, but the word was out not to buy them if they were made in Japan. No one really understood quite why. Almost all of the neighbors were in the same state of poverty, except for those whose wives found work when the husbands could not. Women were cheaper labor than men.

Before the summer was over, we were dispossessed, from our bungalow because my father, still out or work, could not pay the rent. The lack of a roof over our heads brought much anxiety to Mother and seemed to energize Father to find any kind of employment to get enough money to, at least, pay for the rental deposit at some new location. And so we moved into a two–family house in which the owners lived upstairs. In the process of moving, our wonderful piano was dropped and could not be repaired. It was a devastating blow to my mother, and she grieved ever after. The landlord and his wife were an elderly couple with several grown children and grandchildren, all of whom came for their Sabbath dinner every Friday night. Every week the house was filled with wonderful cooking smells and sounds of endless chopping for gefilte fish and nuts for halvah, and as their family arrived, there was lots of shouting and laughing and singing. It was ten years before my parents realized that these happy people had just escaped from the Nazis. They always seemed to cook more food than they could consume, and so Saturday night we were the joyful beneficiaries of the ample leftovers. Strange and delicious foods along with breads and cakes provided us a banquet, and with Mother's ability to stretch foodstuffs, our feast often would last for several days.

My mother never considered getting a job outside the home; that would have betrayed her concept of the responsibilities of motherhood. She was always concerned with her children, where they were, what they were doing, who they were with. "Juvenile delinquents" was the phrase used then regarding children from broken homes who got into trouble; and this terrified Mama, for there was much tension between her and her husband, and our home always seemed on the verge of being broken. Two years later a third child was born, adding to our family's financial burdens and exacerbating my parents' strained relationship.

Father seemed in a constant cycle of losing his job, becoming depressed, drinking, and coming home in a dreadful temper. He became more and more abusive to my mother, and she made sure her children were out of sight when he arrived home. Late at night when I couldn't sleep after listening to my parents' awful shouting and my mother crying, she would come into my room and sing softly to me:

> *"Please mister, take me in your car;*
> *I want to see Mama;*

*They say she lives in heaven—*
*Is that very far?*
*My new Mama she's very cross,*
*She scolds me every day;*
*They say she does not love me,*
*for I'm always in the way,*
*Always in the way,*
*I can never play.*
*I wonder why they don't kiss me*
*Just the way with sister Dee*
*Always in the way......I'm always in the way......"*

and we cried together.

We lived in the house with our Jewish neighbors for over a year by the grace of their compassion and patience in collecting rent that was always several months behind. My mother's fear of her husband's continuing abuse and her depression convinced her to pack our few things and take her children to live in her mother's and father's house. I don't remember where Father stayed. We lived in Grandma's and Grandpa's house for almost two years, much to their financial strain. Their house was in Germantown in the city part of Brooklyn. It was brick and stuck together to the houses on either side of it, and all the backyards were stuck together too. In my Grandma's yard was a magnolia tree that amazed the neighborhood surviving the winters. Grandma said it was because the brick gathered heat from the sun and shared it with the tree. She grew all her flowers from seed and was continually scolded by Grandpa for watering them daily—after all, water was very costly. These two immigrants came to America with nothing but a baby and a dream. It took them a lifetime of baking and selling bread, first from out of their tiny apartment, and then from their own home purchased literally by years of saving pennies (there were no mortgages then).

As the world struggled with the depression and Hitler turned Germany into a threat to humankind, our country seemed poised in a state of suspension. And so did my family.

Upon the urging of Father, who had finally found a bakery job that he managed to keep for over a year, we moved, once again, to live together in another little rented house back in the farm country of Brooklyn near the Bay. It took a long time to catch up financially, to rebuild the basics of a home, to restart a life in a new neighborhood, and to tackle the challenges of a new school. And once again that winter was terribly cold, and with Father's minimal salary, the fuel bill was left unpaid. On many frigid nights, the temperature in the house was so low Mama was compelled to find a safe shelter for her children. She gathered us up with warm clothes for "an adventure." We took the last trolley of the night into the city so we could sleep in the warmth of the subway. Subways were clean and safe then.

Though his wages were limited, Father's bakery job provided the family with the most wonderful breads and cakes. My favorite was a German honey cake baked in a loaf pan, dark brown from honey and molasses and covered with slivered almonds. Sliced, still warm from the oven and buttered, it was a gift from the gods and Father.

One day the bakery owner planned a birthday party for himself, his friends, and staff. Father, in lieu of a gift, painted a portrait of his employer in varied shades of chocolate and vanilla on a large sheet cake. It was a great and beautiful surprise and astonished everyone. The newly–elected leader of the baker's union was a guest at the party and was most impressed by the likeness and artistry of the portrait, and word quickly spread through the unions of this talented baker. Father's art became in great demand for banquets and parties of the newly developing unions and increased his limited income so that, within a few years, there was even enough money to buy a small house.

And then another devastation happened. Japan attacked Hawaii, and America became part of the dreaded war raging throughout most of the world. With the majority of the country's men gone off to the armed services, those left behind, including women, found job opportunities everywhere, and wages were suddenly and shockingly high. At last the basic comforts of life became attainable, like real beds instead of cots and store–bought clothes that fit and were pretty instead of used clothing from community stores. Father even bought a beautiful car—a used Cadillac! Oh, it was so impressive and we were so proud! But the time he spent in it did not include his family, and the car quickly lost its luster.

Those long, hard years took an enormous toll on my parent' marriage that never seemed to be reconciled. The relationship between them continued to erode, and the terrible tension in our home was finally relieved by separation and divorce. As we grew toward adulthood, each of us carried the scars of the wounds that imprisonment in poverty inflict not just on the body but in the heart as well.

Mother finally had to take a job. She paid the bills, helped each of us through college, and managed in only a few years to accomplish an extraordinary feat—she paid off the mortgage. At long last, independence, a dream finally attained through the courage to survive, to sustain the dreams, long ago dreams, at such a price.

**Carolyn Rashti** has a master's degree in counseling psychology and spent twenty–seven years in the world of dance. Her most rewarding years were in Connecticut raising her daughter. In North Carolina her creativity is expressed through acting in community theater and writing. She looks forward to retiring in the Southwest soon, to write and swim in the sun among God's mountain sculptures.

# Recollections

## Nell Ferrell White

Being the youngest and the only girl in the family, I was not as aware of the deprivations as the boys were. I did not have to wear hand–me–downs. My three brothers worked some. My oldest brother had a job at a clothing store. The two younger ones made a little cash by doing odd jobs for people, like mowing grass. I really don't remember much about the Depression. I was the baby of the family and taken care of by all the others.

Things were cheap then. One of the things I remember was the two–cent stamp. My mother would send me to the Post Office with two letters and a nickel. I got to keep the penny. I knew how to get lots for my money. I bought those suckers with a ball of candy on each end. I could buy two of those with my penny.

Before World War II, Clinton, North Carolina, where we lived had the largest variety produce market in the world. My father worked for a cotton and produce broker. When the produce market fell in New York, local farmers were glad to see corn, beans, peas, and such for fifteen or twenty cents a basket or crate. At that price, they were careful to keep their crates for use the next year. So, my father kept a gunny sack at the market and frequently brought it home filled with whatever was cheap that day. Tomatoes ran from one dollar and a half to a dollar and ninety a bushel. But my mother would not can tomatoes that cost her more than one dollar a bushel.

My mother could do more with a five–pound hen than anyone I have ever known. The first day, we would have baked chicken, with dressing, rice, and gravy. Then we would have chicken in pastry. Finally, from that same hen she would feed us chicken and rice soup.

I never heard any talk that I remember about the Depression in my family. I do not know much about what was happening beyond our front door. That's the truth.

●●●●●

**Nell White** was born in Clinton, North Carolina. She is a widow and has three children and three grandchildren. Nell has completed one children's novel and is working on another.

# Remembering Knecht Drive

## Margaret Valiquette

I moved away from Knecht Drive when I was nine. How is it then, that my memories of it are so much stronger than of any of the other places I've lived and left throughout my life? Is it possible we are imprinted at birth—as birds are—so that, no matter where we go, we will never forget the place from where we came?

I've returned a number of times over the years—usually passing by on Main Street where trolley cars once rattled and clanged on their way to and from downtown. Occasionally, I'd make the turn onto the side street with one or another of my children or grandchildren in order to point out the bungalow where I was born.

But this time is different. This time, I stop the car and get out. Silence streams toward me like a slowly cresting wave, engulfing the maple trees and neat frame houses that line the street, in its passing wake, and it is 1935 again. I am in front of Kleinfelder's Candy Store where I spent my hard–earned pennies on Tootsie Rolls and Mary Janes, and my brother Bob swapped bubble gum cards and pop bottle caps with his friends.

A child stands beside me. Shadows stretch out from the soles of our shoes and lie in body shapes on the pavement before us. *"My name is Margie,"* she says. *"I'm seven years old."* *She takes my hand, and her eyes meet mine. They are my eyes. She is me.*

*Clip, clop, clip, clop.* A closed wagon pulled by an aging horse passes by. The driver hops out at the first house and reaches back for a carrier filled with bottles of milk.

They rattle as he hurries up the steps and onto the porch to exchange them for empties from the day before.

*"Strawb-e-r-r-ies!"* A high–pitched voice calls from a produce–laden farm truck. A woman leaves her kitchen with a baby on her hip to bargain with the farmer and gossip with his wife.

A slat–sided truck, dripping watery polka dots in its wake, rolls to a stop at the curb. The driver climbs out of the cab and comes toward the rear of the truck. A leather apron covers his protruding belly, and another strip of leather is strapped across his shoulder. His mouth, mostly hidden behind an imposing handlebar mustache, assumes a stern expression. Tongs in hand, he reaches into a canvas–covered cave to grasp a block of ice and pull it to the edge of the truck. With a wink in our direction, he wields his pick so precisely that crystal clear slivers of ice fall into Margie's waiting hands and mine.

The shadows at our feet are shorter by the time we reach the place half–way down the block where the street curves on its way to the river not far beyond. Margie stops as if restrained by an invisible fence. We have come to the boundary of her world.

We turn, instead, into a vacant lot with a neatly cultivated vegetable garden bordered by towering pink hollyhocks. In their shade, a small boy wields a toy shovel in a knee–deep hole. His name is Jackie. *"I'm going to dig all the way to China,"* he says.

In the next yard, an older boy tosses a tennis ball against the garage. He comes to the fence to retrieve a missed throw and pauses to watch the excavation. I recognize him without hesitation. Augie—the next–door neighbor who taught me to walk and had a photograph to prove it, who rescued me from a fall during a re-enactment of a *Lone Ranger* radio adventure, who snapped my arm with a rubber band as we walked home from a Saturday matinee, who—some years later—gave me my first kiss and wrote me love letters from his Army barracks.

*"That hole's getting pretty deep, Jackie."* His voice is as I remember. *"Better be sure to cover it up before you go in for supper, or we'll have Chinamen all over the neighborhood by morning."* Laughing, he returns to his solitary game.

An advancing chorus of mother–calls empties the sidewalk and yards in the late afternoon. The daily adventures of *Jack Armstrong, the All–American Boy* crackle across the airwaves into family radios.

After supper, laughter spills from the open kitchen window of Margie's house as she dries dishes and shares tales of the day's escapades with her mother. Her brother Tommy plays with a toy truck on the floor nearby. Dickie, the baby, slumps in his high chair and rubs his eyes, longing for his bed.

One by one, the doors of the houses open, and the children gather again, marking time, waiting for the evening's action to begin. Swinging his roller skates by their straps, Augie leaves his porch and continues up the sidewalk towards Main Street.

Bob and his friends form a circle on the terrace steps, each with a cardboard box in front of his Indian–crossed legs. *"I'll give two Barq's Root Beers for one Vernor's Ginger Ale,"* Bob calls then drops the bottle caps into a hand containing the desired trade.

A warning whoop from the top of the hill brings the trading to a halt, and the boys join the others at the base of the streetlight by the vacant lot. Margie makes room for me beside her on the curb. Squinting, I follow her gaze to where Augie stands with an arm stretched over his head like a scruffy Statue of Liberty. He rakes a shock of sun–bleached hair from his eyes and tugs at the drooping leg of his knickers. Squatting, he snaps the innertube bands that encircle his toes to hold the front of his roller skates onto his hightop gym shoes and checks the buckles on the leather straps that circle his ankles. Excitement mounts as the trolley rattles by on the street behind him on its way to the loop at the amusement park at the edge of town. As if on cue, the conductor clangs the trolley's polished brass bell, and Augie cups his hands at each side of his mouth. With all the force of his twelve-year old voice, he shouts, *"Ollie, Ollie Outs in Free!"*

Bending his knees, he braces his hands against the pavement and pushes forward. Rising like the mast of a schooner running before a storm, he begins his descent. Passing the Babe Ruth sign on the side of the candy store, he jumps—his legs pressed tight together—to miss the grate that opens into its cellar. His arms fly out like wings as he crosses the slanting apron where the alley enters the street. His knees bent and his body collapsing against his heels, he skims across the smooth concrete humming beneath him. Each time he comes to newer, coarser pavement, he explodes like a geyser to his full height, flails his arms above his head and howls, joining the din that has engulfed him in his flight. Slowing as he approaches his waiting fans, he accepts their applause with a bow.

While Augie removes his skates, Margie places an empty green bean can she has rescued from her mother's kitchen in the center of the street and returns to explain the boundaries of the game to me.

*"The boys like to hide behind the bushes around Mrs. Spiers' house,"* she says, *"but I don't. Sometimes she comes out and shakes her broom and hollers that she's going to call the police."*

With a quick round of *"One Potato, Two Potato,"* to decide who will be *it*, the game begins.

*"Five, ten, fifteen, twenty. . .!"* the counter calls, covering his eyes and slowly circling the can. Deepening shadows cloak the players as they move noiselessly down walkways between houses or hide behind the trees that border the street. *".... .ninety–five, one hundred! Here I come, ready or not!"*

The shout echoes through the apparently deserted neighborhood, and the search begins. The first person defeated in his race to kick the can before being caught becomes *it*, and the counting begins again.

As night creeps closer, the only remaining illumination radiates from the street light high above us and encircles the now–ravaged bean can. One by one, porch lights flicker up and down the street. A final shout of *"Ollie, Ollie Outs in Free!"* signals the end of the game, and the players fade into the darkness.

Ripples of silence follow us across the street, grow to a wave that laps over the curb and against the terrace as Margie climbs the steps to her porch, turns, and peers back toward the circle of light.

*"Goodbye,"* I call, knowing she will not hear.

The silence crashes against the screen door closing behind her and recedes into the darkness.

•••••

**Margaret Valiquette** was born, grew up, and raised seven children in Dayton, Ohio. Since moving to North Carolina, following a fifteen–year career in newspaper publishing, she has edited a newspaper for older adults.

# Life in the Grocery Business

## Marjorie Svoboda

As a child I felt loved and safe. I have my parents and a large extended family to thank for that. I didn't feel any effects of the stock market crash, nor did I know what it meant. I was only eight years old.

I always was well dressed—had school clothes and Sunday clothes, all of which were made by my mother and mostly made over from hand–me–downs. I didn't own many items of clothing, but then, if one had too many, there weren't large enough closets in homes to store them. Our family didn't own a car, nor did we know many who did. There was no TV or radio to keep the airways spewing forth the news of the day, and I, as a child, was uninformed that doomsday was ahead. Parents at that time didn't discuss problems with their children, but did feel a need to protect them.

One day when I went home from school for lunch, there was a man in rather old, frayed clothes sitting on a step in our back hall with a plate of food on his lap. He was a hobo who rode the rails stopping in cities to ask for handouts. This was a common occurrence. Apparently, there was a communication system among hoboes who would identify houses where the inhabitants would provide one with a good meal, since once one fed a hobo, others would appear expecting the same treatment.

During my whole childhood we lived in Racine, Wisconsin, which was an industrial town, the home of J. I. Case, Johnson Wax, Horlick's Malted Milk, and Hamilton Beach companies, to name a few. The majority of our neighbors and store customers were factory workers. The children who were my classmates were children of factory workers, and many of them were immigrants. The Great Depression or effects of the stock market crash were not discussed with children at home, nor were they topics discussed in elementary school.

For years I begged to be allowed to work in our grocery store—I thought it would be fun—and years later when I really was needed, my enthusiasm for the task had waned. In the store was where I learned about the Depression and its effects on people. Men would come in the store and pound their fists on the counter accompanied by the words in a loud voice, "The government ought to do something about it!" The daily newspaper would carry cartoons satirizing the present human condition, such as a character peering around the corner of a building with the caption, "Prosperity is just around the corner." Talk about a bummer, Hoover won the presidential election in the same year as the stock market crashed. His famous utopian promise was a chicken in every pot or lunch pail and a car in every garage, conditions never realized during his tenure.

When people bought groceries, they bought only as much as the money in a little purse would allow, and many times not enough to feed their family. It was a time of credit customers. A record book with carbon copies which could be removed took the place of the credit card of today. People were more self–sufficient than most are today. They had gardens and yards, which boasted of fruit trees, both of which enabled the woman of the house to can vegetables and fruits and make jams and jellies for the coming winter months. In the store I was made aware of the fact that because of the Great Depression, many bread earners had lost their jobs as factories and businesses had shut down or downsized. In one case, the Nash car company completely moved out of our city because the workers went on strike and refused to take any company offer. Finally, the company carried out its threat and moved its whole Racine operation in one night to Milwaukee—just twenty–two miles north—to join another of the Nash–Kelvinator operations, which proves the old adage that a bird in the hand is worth two in the bush.

One of my jobs in the store was to help package food items for "relief" orders. "Relief" was a form of welfare, a city program whereby those in need would apply for "relief," which was in the form of groceries. There were specific items, such as spaghetti, rice, flour, sugar, coffee, oatmeal, laundry and facial soap, toilet paper, and some canned items such as peas, corn, and tomatoes. There was a standard order based on the size of the family. This would be delivered to the recipients once a week. Providing relief orders was one of the things that helped my father keep the store and not be forced into bankruptcy. Business was very slow. Sometimes only a few customers would present themselves in a day.

I overheard a man tell my father that he felt very ashamed that he was forced to apply for relief. Even with good credentials, he had been unable to secure work after he lost his good paying job.

Men who were jobless had a difficult time filling their days. They were accustomed to working five and one–half, ten–hour days a week with only Sunday as their day of rest. Now, the days were endless and very depressing. As time went on, they lost their feelings of self worth. On the other hand, the women still had the regular household tasks to do, jobs or no jobs. The wife had to be ingenious about stretching the food and patching and mending their already scant supply of clothing. At the same time, she tried to help her husband to retain his self esteem.

A customer I often waited on was a little woman in her 90's by the name of Grandma Castile. She asked for (this was before the day of the self–serve super market) a number of items such as a half–dozen eggs and enough other items to fill a peck bag. She always tried to spend at least a dollar and apologized when it totaled less. When Grandma had a big birthday party for her one–hundredth year, Mom baked her a huge, beautiful Lady Baltimore cake from scratch—this was before cake mixes—and it had one hundred candles on it.

I don't remember that anyone I knew was evicted from a rental property for the lack of full payment. Apparently, the mortgage institutions too were rather forgiving. I did know that my father cashed in his life insurance policy to make mortgage payments on our home.

Times were tough. My father had not made the wisest choice in the purchase of a store. The previous owner who also owned the building had charged a maximum price for the store fixtures and other items. It took my father a number of years as the Great Depression deepened to realize that the business was a "no win" proposition. After much deliberation and planning, he and my mother decided that there was a possible solution. There was a large, bright unrented store on a corner only a half–block from the present location. It had a large defunct beer hall across the back of the store and extended behind the adjacent store, making it three times the size of the bakery in the old store. Dad was able to rent the building for less and found a good supply of used counters, display cases, scales, meat slicers, and other items at very reasonable prices, such as $10 for the candy case, and comparable prices for the bakery cases and for oven and bakery pans. The cases had to be scrubbed and painted in white, instead of the dark oak of the ones in the old store. Dad and others helped install shelving and painted it white. Then came the real problem—how to move all the inventory to the new store without the knowledge of the previous building owners who lived above the old store. Dad feared that they would try to stop them and confiscate some of the merchandise for his breaking the lease. Neither my brother nor I knew what the plans were. All we knew was that we were to stay with the grandparents that whole Sunday. We found out later that all our adult relatives descended on High Street—the location of the new and old stores—along with any means of conveyance, such as cars, wagons, and even wheelbarrows and baby buggies, to carry merchandise from the old to the new store, a distance of only half a city block. Needless to say, there were many sore backs and legs at the end of the day—that day in 1933. This was a turning point in the success of the business. The old baker who came with the old store remained there, and a Danish baker was hired for the new store. He was a wonderful baker in the truest Danish tradition. This helped business, along with the introduction of my mother's angel food and sunshine cakes. The bakery items and the cakes were also sold by some of the members of the group of stores to which my father belonged. This, too, helped the coffers. The oven in the bakery was never shut down, since it was coal fired. After the regular baking was done by the Danish baker, it was freed up for other uses. My mother used these times to bake pies, cupcakes, and her famous sunshine cake, and cookies.

She also baked hams and turkeys for customers at twenty–five cents and fifty cents respectively. These quarters and half–dollars were for my mother to keep. After she had accumulated enough, she would buy items for the house or items of clothing.

During this time, some people had to part with the silver dollars saved as mementos in earlier years. A single dollar could purchase a meal for a family. As these and Indian head pennies found their way into the cash register, my father would remove them and save them. From time to time, other old coins would appear, which he also saved. I have a Monarch Teeny Weeny Peanut Butter can full of the Indian head pennies. They were used by my father instead of poker chips in gambling card games. My mother was the recipient of the silver dollars. When she had accumulated enough of them, secured in a couple of my father's shoes in their closet, she would carry them down town and use them to purchase a new dress.

1933 was also the year of the beginning of the end of the Great Depression, starting with the "bank holiday" instituted by our new president, Franklin Delano Roosevelt. The WPA (Works Progress Administration), which was part of the NRA (National Recovery Act), along with many other administrations, was instituted to get people back to work. These new acts and administrations introduced acronyms into our language. The street which ran in front of our store was paved with brick. This was one of the streets to profit from the WPA—by men pulling up bricks and again resetting them. There were always too many men for a job. (Have you seen street patchers on Chapel Hill streets? They still are practicing the lessons learned in the Great Depression.) The street didn't improve and was the butt of many a joke, but those lucky men had a place to go to work and earn a meager income, which was the purpose of the WPA. They could hold their heads a little higher in spite of all the jokes.

Ingenious methods of survival surfaced during the Depression. A man who lived near our neighborhood contracted to buy a goodly number of geese which he planned to raise to sell for holiday meals. One night, as our family sat in the living room doing our homework or reading and listening to the radio, there was a noise in the front of the house. When my father investigated, he found a goose was batting the outside of the porch with its wings. Dad picked it up and took it into the basement and secured it in the wood bin. For the next week, we tried to find the owner of the goose. There were a couple of small farms near our home, but none had lost a goose; and my father decided we'd have goose for Thanksgiving dinner. He invested in fencing and built a "Goose House" so the goose could live outside, and bought feed for the beast. On an evening a few days before Thanksgiving, there was a pounding at our front door by a man who accused us of stealing his goose and demanded its return. My father explained that he had attempted to find the owner of the "lost" goose to no avail, and that he had incurred expenses fattening the goose. It fell on deaf ears. Dad was subjected to the accusations of the Goose man that we had stolen his property. This man was well aware when the goose found its way to our house. I had told all the kids on the way to school, including this man's older son, who was a rude and crude kid. There is no way that the owner didn't know we had his goose. He was just waiting until it was fat enough and he didn't have to pay for its food. I don't remember what we had for Thanksgiving dinner, but it wasn't goose.

On two different occasions, I was witness to the business of making or selling "moonshine." On my way to a music lesson after school, I passed through an immigrant neighborhood. I witnessed law men smashing equipment used to make moonshine and carrying out kegs of liquor. On the other occasion, some friends and I had gone to a factory pond in our neighborhood to skate on the ice. This was after supper and was still very early in the evening. On our way home, we saw candles burning in the windows of an empty factory building. We felt like Nancy Drew and her friends as we tried to peer into the building. We were scared away when someone came out and yelled at us. We made a hasty retreat. The next day the newspaper reported that a factory with a still had been raided later that night after we were there. Obviously, these enterprising people found they didn't have the luck of Al Capone.

My Uncle Harold, my Godfather, had a good responsible job with a manufacturer of candy molds. The company had to close its doors, since the candy industry was adversely affected by the Great Depression. Uncle Harold worked in the business office as a bookkeeper and was well aware of this eventuality and began to investigate the possibility of starting his own business. He contacted an employee skilled in the manufacture of molds, and together they decided that a two–man operation, one in the manufacturing end and the other in the business end, could survive on the decreased needs of the candy manufacturers. They set up shop in the second floor of a carriage house that had been in Harold's family for years, and which had an ideal amount of space. In a short time, they were in operation, and the needs of their two families were well met with the profits.

Another uncle, Art, my mother's brother, was a very intelligent man. It seemed that he had an eye for schemes in which he had to invest little time to allow for his favorite pastime, bridge, and, at the same time, to provide a good living for his family of a wife and six boys. Earlier, he had met a man with similar habits and desires by the name of Baron Von Stronsdorf. Together, they contrived an addendum to the "Bank Night" instituted by movie theaters in our town to increase attendance to week–night movies. These were on Thursday nights and would be worth $100 to the holder of the winning ticket. To receive the money when your number was called, you had to be present. Most often the movie offerings were either B or C movies. Art and the baron conceived the idea to offer a Bank Night Guarantee for a quarter, the same price as a theater ticket. The winning ticket holder would receive from the guarantor the equivalent amount to the award offered by the theater if his number was drawn, whether or not the holder was present in the theater. These tickets could be purchased from almost every store in town. The business thrived and extended to most major cities in Wisconsin, Michigan, and Illinois. They had it made. They had employees who collected the receipts from the ticket sellers and had the task of paying the lucky ticket holder. There were many weeks when the award was not claimed. Of course, this was too good to last. After a couple of good years, some law makers in one of the state legislatures questioned the legality of the guarantee and found it illegal. After the first state had found that the practice was illegal, the others followed, and Uncle Art had to find another source of easy income, which was pinball machine rentals.

Another scheme instituted by the movie theaters was "dish night." The purchaser of a ticket was entitled to a dish item. Many of our relatives as well as my family had a mixture of china patterns for everyday use, so this was a way to obtain a new set of dishes that were all the same pattern. The movie goers were presented with the dish item as they entered the theater. The items were held in laps of the customers, and when he or she got up to visit the rest rooms or at the end of the movie, many would have forgotten their coveted lap items, which would then crash to the floor.

Some women belonged to a "Larkin" club. The women would meet for an afternoon in the home of one of the members. They would have refreshments and be shown Larkin products, which were primarily home furnishings including furniture, accessories, drapes, and such. These items were purchased through an easy payment plan by paying a small sum each month until the purchase price was met, after which the item would be delivered. Many households were able to afford the price of household items using this plan, and also to enjoy fellowship with friends. The gatherings ended the afternoon with a few games of "bunco," a dice game. Today, Larkin furniture items are deemed to be desirable antiques.

The Olsen Rug Co. enabled families to replace their worn rugs with new ones at bargain prices. All one had to do was send woolen items such as old rugs, suits, and coats, which were then reclaimed and fashioned into rugs of various sizes, designs, and colors at much less than the price of new rugs. Not only were they a bargain, but they were reversible too. Olsen rugs covered the floors of my childhood home for many years.

Signs of the Great Depression appeared in homes. There was the constant presence of men who had time on their hands. Most men didn't have hobbies at that time, and if they did, they didn't have the money to pursue them, just the time. Gold fish appeared in bowls. These were pretty orange ones with fanning tails which could be watched to while away the time. They cost very little and could be fed bits of bread, or the food could be bought with pennies. Another thing that appeared in some homes was a chemical garden made with a base of a piece of coal over which a solution of salt, ammonia, and bluing would be poured. All these were common household items—nothing to buy. Here was another thing to watch, to see these base materials transform into a beautiful winter scene of salt crystals with a blue tinge.

The family card table became a resident of the living room to hold the ever–present jigsaw puzzle in an uncompleted form. We only had one puzzle. The early ones were made of wood, as was ours. When the feat was accomplished and we all had time to admire the beautiful picture, it would be returned to the box, and the whole process would start over. One might be lucky to find another family with whom to trade puzzles so that the challenge of putting one's own puzzle together didn't get boring.

Board games were popular, especially a new game called Monopoly. One not only enjoyed handling play money in huge amounts, but also had the opportunity of purchasing utilities, streets, and houses and hotels. Ah, fantasy land!

Churches helped people in various ways. They still had ice cream socials, pot luck suppers, bazaars, picnics, and activities for the youth, to name a few.

In an attempt to get people involved in a new activity, a few instrumentalists in our congregation invited others to join them in forming a band. For years instruments of many former musicians were abandoned in closets and attics. Some of these were dusted off and found new life in the new little band composed of both young and old, novice and the more accomplished. After many hours of rehearsals and many more of individual practicing, St. Paul Harmony Band was finally prepared to perform during young people's plays, dinners, ice cream socials, and other activities. Our efforts were appreciated, even though it wasn't always harmonious.

A couple of pastimes emerged to add a spice of life that was sadly lacking—the pole sitters and the marathon dancers. The newspapers kept the public informed of the status of each on a daily basis. Our town had a pole sitter. It was a challenge to the daring souls to see how long they could last sitting on a platform on top of a pole. It required ingenuity to plan the platform, how food and other items could be sent up to the sitter, what items were necessary for life, a means of communication, and a means of securing the individual on the platform so that he didn't fall off, especially while he slept. A pole sitter wasn't given recess and allowed to descend at times. Once a descent was made, the contest was over.

There were contests in the marathon dance in different parts of the country. The progress of the dancers was followed by radio and newsreels at the movies. I just remember seeing the tired souls trying to conserve their energies leaning on each other and still moving sufficiently not to be disqualified. It was a grueling way to while the time away and attempt to make a few bucks.

I believe the Great Depression made people tougher, more self–reliant, and prepared them for the bigger trial which was yet to be introduced to the people of the free world, World War II.

•••••

Before **Marjorie Svoboda** retired, she taught college chemistry and was a research professor at the UNC Chapel Hill School of Medicine. She authored numerous articles and published in professional journals and two book chapters. Recently, her writing has been of family memoirs, including a biography of her mother, and editing the memories of her grandfather's early life in America, which were written in German and translated by her daughter.

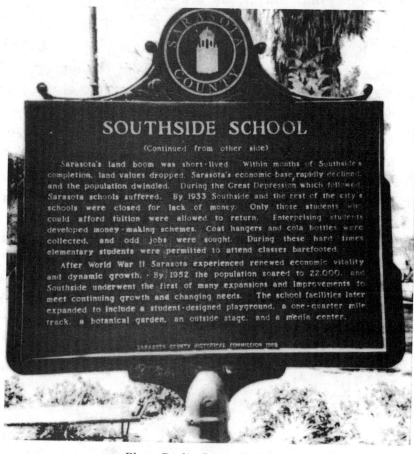

Photo Credit: James C. Huber

# Married Children

## Marjorie Kaplan

### i

The omens were good for the move. Jenny's father was forty, her mother thirty–five, and Jenny was ten. They were all divisible by five, except for their car, a 1929 Chrysler. Jenny could divide 1929 by three and by 643 and nothing else, but she kept trying all the way South. The year, however, was 1932, and Jenny thought that it would be hard to find a duller number to divide.

It was like a vacation. The family was not one for games, but they did have a wishing game which they played when they stopped for their picnic lunches at the side of the road. Their wishes were different from their wants, and Jenny knew the difference. Jenny *wished* to fly around the world with Amelia Earhart or to spend a week with Charles Beebe in a bathysphere at the bottom of the ocean. But she *wanted* a boy's imitation leather coat, sheepskin lined with a big collar, like her cousin Billy's, and a helmet with isinglass goggles like an aviator's.

Her mother had *wanted* to go to Chicago to live when they had finally sold the drug store in Mt. Lincoln. But she always wished for good things like milk for all the babies in the world, or Christmas trees for all the orphans, or flowers for all the graves on Decoration Day.

Her father's wishes were always funny, a giraffe to trim the tops of trees, an elephant to water the garden, a watchskunk who could tell friends from enemies. But he had *wanted* to go South after he sold his store, back to his boyhood home.

"The house has just been standing there empty for more than a year," he said, "everything in it, Jenny, just as it was when your grandmother died. And the land will take care of us. You won't need that aviator's coat in the South – you'll sit in your overalls under a pecan tree in the woods right behind the house, and shoot us a squirrel for supper at night. Why, when I was your age, I'd go out barefooted with a rifle and fishing pole and camp by the Tangipohoa River for a week at a time. Every few days Mama'd send your Aunt Bernice out on a horse to see if I was okay. Sometimes there would be ten to twenty cottonmouths squirming around out there on the ground."

Jenny always wore shoes. Her mother was afraid that invisible slivers of glass might enter into Jenny's bloodstream through the soles of her feet, or that she might step on a stubble and die of lockjaw.

She doubted very much if she would be allowed to go barefoot into the swamp, but she enjoyed her father's stories. Her father had rarely spoken before he sold his store. He called it "getting out from under," "little more than breaking even." In fact, while he owned the store he had hardly been home. During the day he sat waiting for customers at the little round ice–cream table in the back of the store. He played chess with men who, Jenny's mother said, didn't have enough to do. They sat in the store and exchanged little blue pamphlets which her father said were "real literature" and her mother thought were trash. On Saturday nights the men played poker and drank whiskey at the American Legion hall and slept right through the church bells Sunday morning.

174

"No one can blame a man for not working in these times," her mother would say after returning from dusting the showcases at the store, "but they act so doggone smart about it. And they have such dirty mouths on them. Every woman that passes by, she can be a grandmother. They still have something to say."

But on the trip Jenny's father talked to her all the time, especially when her mother would rest in back to give Jenny a chance to sit in the front seat. Jenny would listen and at the same time look out the car window and count the four–legged animals on one hand (mostly dogs, horses, and cows) and the two–legged animals, (birds, people and chickens) on the other, making secret bets as to which would win. Her father would bounce along, his straw hat almost hitting the ceiling of the car. "Care for a fried chicken dinner?" he'd say, and veer the car a little, pretending he was aiming at a chicken. His Southern accent, which until now had just softened his speech, became so pronounced that he sounded like one of the men in the minstrel show the American Legion put on.

"Your Mother would have liked us to take care of your grandfather's apartment building in Chicago. I could have worked Friday and Saturday in one of your uncle's grocery stores, and we'd wait this depression thing out. I'd give in before it did, Jenny. No, sir. All those people in Chicago are warped," he said, never even bothering to exclude her mother's family.

They drove for three days, stayed at tourist homes at night. The highway was sandwiched between the Illinois Central Railroad on one side and strung–out towns, where men in overalls sat under the tin awnings of stores, on the other. When their car going South met a train going North to Chicago, the train men hung out of the window and waved at them and Jenny's family would wave back. Sometimes the engineer would reach up and toot his whistle. The last night they traveled through the Mississippi swamp. There were deep ditches filled with water on either side. Jenny's mother slept in the back and Jenny sat high on the front seat bouncing as it bounced, her feet dangling above the floor, while her father told her stories.

"I went North to pharmacy school, Jenny, when I was just seventeen years old. After my first year I took the Illinois Central back home for the summer. When I got a whiff of this swamp I leaned out the train window and tried to breathe it all in at once. It was all I could do to keep myself from pulling the emergency cord and jumping off the train."

Jenny inhaled deeply. A train came by and blinked its light at them and her father blinked his car lights back.

They arrived on a bright, rainy, yellow–green evening in early September. Jenny and her father got out of the car, and stood under a live oak and looked at the house, the last one on the street. Beyond it were the woods. The leaves deflected most of the rain, and only warm drops of water fell on them. The unpainted house and fence post looked and smelled waterlogged. The rain sounded as if it fell on wet things. Even the scraping of the gate against the bricks sounded wet. The high grass poked through the fence and lay sodden across the front walk.

A thin dog with large feet came out from under the sagging porch to meet them. His hair was rain–grayed and plastered against his sides.

"Look, Jenny, you have a dog already. Hiya, Pooch." Her father put the suitcase down to scratch behind the dog's ears.

"I think I'll call him *S and B*," Jenny said. "Short for *Skin and Bones*."

She loved the sound of initials. "Isn't it a nice dog, Mom?"

Her mother was still sitting in the car and didn't seem to hear the question. She had her hand against her cheek as if she were waiting for her husband to check the address. Wouldn't he know the house he grew up in?

Although it rained almost every day in the fall, Jenny still felt that they were on vacation. The trees, grass, and rain hugged the house and seemed to make it a part of the outside even when the doors and windows were closed. The days were the colors of southern rivers and lakes, blue green, gray, and yellow–brown. There were none of the sharply etched pink and white days of Mt. Lincoln when Jenny longed to be an aviatrix. Here the sky and tops of trees seemed to blend together with a mist that came all the way down to the ground. When Jenny played in the high grass, she pretended that she was a deep–sea diver at the bottom of the ocean. She got along well at school. She learned to jump double dutch, to whistle a tune blowing both in and out, and to whistle though her thumb knuckles with her hands clasped together. She and Dolly Jane were the best spellers in the fifth grade. They were always picked to be captains in spelling bees.

Her father and mother had no friends. Her father didn't want to return the calls of his old classmates. He said it would cost too much money to keep up with them.

"They were too nice," her mother said to Jenny. "He wouldn't have returned their calls if we were the wealthiest people in the parish."

They had put aside enough money for the strawberry plants they were going to set out in December, the fall and spring vegetable gardens, and the chickens. If they would do without a telephone, new clothes, the car, movies, marcels, friends, they figured they had enough money to last them the nine months of the school year. By that time something was bound to happen. It seemed like a lifetime away for Jenny, but once in a while she did wonder what it was that was going to happen. Her mother suggested that during the winter when there was no gardening her husband might get a job repairing streets with the WPA, or that perhaps they would accept her family's offer in Chicago if nothing better came up by June. But Jenny's father said, "I'm sure of two things in this world. I don't want to go on relief, and I'll never go North again."

One time when Jenny was with him in the Central Drug Store, he had said to the owner, "If you're ever in a pinch for a pharmacist, let me know. I may be able to help you out." But other than that he did not look for work.

He went hunting with S and B, who, the rest of the time, lay under things (the car, the house, the shed), and was not a pet at all. They brought back pheasant and quail, and Jenny's father showed her mother how to cook them. He taught her how to cook grits, gumbo, red beans and rice, how to fix turnip greens and bake corn bread. He chopped wood from the swamp to burn in the cookstove. It was Jenny's job to fill the saucers under the legs of the table with water to keep the ants from crawling up.

As the days became shorter and colder, they'd sit around the kitchen table after supper, while the fire burned out. The rain would drip down the dark bare kitchen windows distorting the glass. Jenny sitting at her place would absent–mindedly kick at a square of tin nailed over a knothole in the wideboard floor. It was then the house felt just like a vacation cottage.

But the thing than bothered Jenny's mother most was the high grass in the front yard. They didn't own a lawnmower. At first, they had hired Charlie, a colored man, to mow their lawn once a week for twenty–five cents. He had come over with his sad horse Grover who pulled a little wooden cart with lawn tools inside. Grover had a lumpy pink–gray body that looked like a bag of rocks slung between his front and back legs. He had a bony head and always looked sad while he chewed the weeds at the side of the road.

Jenny was sure that he preferred fresh, tender grass and she would offer him handfuls of clippings. But even while he ate the grass out of her hand, he looked sad. After a few weeks, her father discovered they could no longer afford Charlie. They had not allowed enough money for their strawberry plants, and two of the chickens had died.

"I'll keep stopping by," Charlie said. "Something's bound to happen."

"I'll have to borrow a mower and do the grass myself," her father said.

But he had never mowed a lawn, and he hated to borrow things, and the grass grew higher.

"Borrow a mower!" her mother said. "I'll mow the lawn."

But by that time it needed a sickle.

"Borrow a sickle! Borrow a sickle!"

But Jenny's father, who hated to borrow things, now found himself safely past the necessity to borrow a mower. He waited, and sure enough winter came, and the grass stopped growing.

Winter came late one afternoon. Her father had been setting out strawberry plants all day. It was almost night when he came in.

"It got dark so fast," he said. "I could watch it settle over the ground." From then on, the days were a steel gray color. There was no garden work to do. Jenny's father set up another little stove in the living room that he had to keep supplied with wood. They were always cold, and at night all three of them brought their chairs around the stove. Her father went less far into the swamp and often came back with wood not only wet but also green. Even when Jenny couldn't see the smoke, she could feel the heaviness of the air she breathed and a smarting in her eyes. At bedtime she'd escape upstairs, at first refreshed by the clean air and then chilled by dampness of her pajamas and the blankets, and lie in bed counting the times her teeth chattered, and worrying about a Christmas tree. Her father, although he was always home, had stopped talking very much. He spent his days moving chess pieces around a board and reading through a set of Sir Walter Scott he had found in an upstairs bookcase. The pages were still uncut when he brought them down and silver moths crawled around the bindings.

Like her father, Jenny had not worried about the grass. She had let her classmates know from the beginning that her living arrangements were temporary, that her family owned a lawnmower in the north, that it was foolish to connect a telephone to call strangers, that the town was so small they didn't need a car to go around in. She kept the fact that they used oleo and skimmed milk a secret. Although they might not have any money, they were not *poor people*. But when winter came, Jenny began to worry about a Christmas tree. She was sure that they had not set aside any money for a tree, and she knew her grandfather's Christmas check had to go for shoes. It was clear to her that the only people who did not have Christmas trees were *poor people*. Her whole family might even become somebody's Christmas project. A whole Sunday School class might turn up Christmas Eve with a box of canned goods, a bag of oranges, and a toy Christmas tree. Jenny could become the poor girl in her school room and sit curved sideways in her seat, smell like stale graham crackers, never know the answers, cry easily, and wipe her nose on the hem of her dress. She'd have to stand by herself at recess and chew on a strand of her hair. Of course, there *were* poor children who swore and broke windows, but without question Jenny was fated to be one who cried easily and chewed on a strand of her hair.

Her poor–girl thoughts worried her so much that when she caught flu the first week in December, she was glad to stay home and do nothing but sleep. But one evening when her fever was high, she dreamed that she was trying to count to the end of numbers and there wasn't any end. She woke up crying. "There isn't any end to numbers. I can't count to it."

Her mother was leaning over her. "You've had a bad dream. Try to go back to sleep."

She was afraid to go back to sleep. But while she was lying awake in her bed there was no rest either. She pictured a whole Sunday School class crowding into the living room. Dolly Jane carried a little tree. She was so restless her mother finally wrapped her in a blanket and took her down to sit by the stove. Her father felt her forehead. "Another day to run its course is my guess."

Jenny just sat there. If they weren't going to have a tree, she didn't care if she never got well. Her mother seemed to read her mind.

"You have to get well by Christmas, Jenny."

She felt too weak to keep her worries secret any longer. "What are we going to do about a tree?" she wailed.

Her mother pulled the blanket around Jenny and glanced at her husband. "I've been thinking Jenny, that we'll have a pioneer Christmas. We'll do just what the pioneers did. Daddy will chop a tree from the swamp and you'll make colored paper chains and we'll pop corn in the evenings and string it and sing Christmas carols."

"Will you, Daddy?" Jenny said. "Will you chop a tree from the woods?"

"Sure thing," her father said.

"And when you grow up," her mother said, "you'll tell your children about your pioneer Christmas."

"If I had known earlier," her father said, "I could have chopped all the trees in the swamp and put them in the house, and we could have put all our furniture in the woods."

"And maybe," her mother said, "On Christmas Day we'll all go to a movie!"

She said it as if it were Jenny who was the movie fan. The truth was, Jenny hadn't missed movies at all, and her father hated them.

"What was the name of that movie the pioneers saw?" her father said. "It was probably a cowboy and Indian movie called *Christmas Massacre*, the only three–dimensional movie in history. The only trouble was those forefathers of ours found themselves with the leading roles of the whole production."

Jenny laughed as if this was a good joke, although she knew that her father really didn't care for her mother's suggestion about a movie. Even after her mother told her to stop, she felt little gulps of laughter keep coming up, she was so relieved that they were going to have a Christmas tree. The next day, as her father had guessed, she began to get better. Her poor girl thoughts vanished as if they'd never existed, once she began to think about the tree. She had always played outdoors in front of their house because the swamp at the edge of their back yard had frightened her with its dark and jumbled look. But now it seemed like a giant storehouse of tall cone–shaped Christmas trees protected by the strong sky, which often during the winter was as dark as their iron stove. She decided that when spring came, she and her friend, Annie Lucille, would find a hide–away place in the woods and bring out crates to sit on and maybe a few dishes. But for the winter Jenny had to amuse herself indoors. She worked every night on paper chains. She colored tablet paper with crayons and cut it into strips three inches long and a half–inch wide, and she brought red and green scraps of construction paper home from school to use for the chains. She went to bed with flour and water paste hardened on her fingers to lie and think about the tall tree blocking out a dark green triangle in the corner of their living room. She hoped that there would be room between the tree and the ceiling for the gold foil star she had made at school.

"When will we sing Christmas carols, Daddy?" she asked a week before Christmas.

"Christmas Eve is time enough," he said.

"Tell me about the trees you had when you were a little boy," Jenny said.

"I can't remember," her father said. "That's you mother's department. One Christmas tree is the same as another to me."

Her mother remembered every Christmas tree she ever had. She put down her sewing, took a deep breath and smiled. It was a glazed smile that aimed between Jenny and her father, past the stove and into the wall.

"I remember the Christmas when I was five years old," she said. "We still had real candles on our tree. We little children, my brothers and I, had to stand outside the sliding oak doors of the parlor while the candles were burning, and Pa sat next to the tree in his leather chair with a bucket of water and a bucket of sand at his feet. After ten minutes, he and Ma and my older sisters blew the candles, out and then I took George and Royal by the hand—they were hardly more than babies—and we went up to the tree to look at the decorations. Our tree was always as high as the ceiling."

"When are you going to chop down our tree?" Jenny asked her father.

"When it stops raining and I have time," he said.

It rained all week, but finally two days before Christmas at supper, her father said, "I got your tree." She started to get up. "Finish your supper," he said. "The tree will keep." Then he began to dawdle over his red beans and rice.

"Did I ever tell you about the Christmas I spent in France during the World War?"

"Yes, I believe you did." Jenny said.

He should have been finished eating, but he picked up another slice of cornbread, and he cut it through the middle perfectly even and spread oleo over each of the smooth surfaces all the way to the edges.

"You're only ten years old, Jenny, and already my life is almost played out for you." He took a bite of cornbread. "Did I ever recite *Horatius at the Bridge* for you, Jenny?" He lifted his water glass. It was almost empty. The hanging white glass lampshade was reflected in the pupils of his eyes and in each of the facets of the cut glass. The inch of water left in his glass rocked back and forth reflecting a jumble of colors.

> *Lars porsena of Clusium*
> *By the nine Gods he swore...*

"Oh, Daddy," Jenny said. "That one lasts forever."

> *...The great house of Tarquin*
> *Should suffer wrong no more.*

"Cut it out," her mother broke in. She took his plate from in front of him. "Stop teasing her. Go and bring in the tree."

Her father put his glass down and covered his thin face and long nose with his hand and laughed in little hiccups, and his forehead turned as red as if he had pulled a great

185

joke. "Oh, Lordy, Lordy," he said. Then he swung around in his chair, got up and went out the door, all in one swoop. He came back carrying the tree. He'd buried the trunk of the tree in a big round cracker can. The bottom of the can was all Jenny could see. It'll never hold, she thought, with all the decorations. She ran ahead of him into the living room and pointed to the corner. Her father stepped forward and set down the tree.

She knew right away the tree was wrong. But maybe her father was still joking. The cracker can was big enough all right; the whole trunk was buried in it. It was more a bush than a tree, no real shape, wider than tall. The branches were sparse and uneven with a few long needles poking out randomly. Jenny looked at her father to see if he was teasing, but he had his closed face, and then she looked at her mother's face and saw there the same expression she felt in her own. The same pull under her chin, the stiffening of the skin on her cheeks. The tree seemed to draw her eyes until each eyeball focused into one sharp dot of disappointment.

An anger pushed up in Jenny's head against her ears. "That's no Christmas tree," Jenny said. "I hate it. Throw it out. It's a bush not a tree."

"Why, Jenny," her father said, surprised. "It's only a Christmas tree." He glanced over at her mother.

Our faces feel the same, Jenny thought.

"Okay," he said. He was mad. He picked the tree up, put it under his arm and walked past her mother, the smell of pine trailing after him. He carried the tree through the hall. The can bumped against the wall once and the branches scraped the wallpaper. He stamped through the kitchen, slammed the screen door, and from the porch he pitched the

186

tree into the yard. Jenny could hear the needles shiver when the tree hit the ground.

Jenny ran upstairs and threw herself on the white bedspread. She was careful to keep her feet off it. The rain was breaking into sudsy splashes against the dark window. Even though it seemed cold enough for Christmas in Illinois, she knew the rain wouldn't turn to snow. She thought of her last Christmas in Illinois and the road and train track that ran together all the way up North . . . She looked at the pile of colored paper chains in the corner. Her father could have stopped her at the first hundred links, not let her make 589 and say, "Fine fine," when she told him. But at least her father's face was either calm or closed, not like her mother's, whose eyes, cheeks, nose, and throat wrinkled and tightened and bobbed up and down making everyone have to feel what she was feeling. If her mother had said, "Jenny, this must be the kind of tree the pioneers brought in when the Indians were right behind them," Jenny would have gone along; and if her father hadn't got mad and had said, "I baptize thee Christmas tree, Little Bush," she would have laughed. She caught her breath. What if Dolly Jane asked, "Did you have a Christmas tree?" She would have to say, "No;" and if Dolly Jane did not ask, the tree would become another secret like oleo and skimmed milk. Her world would fill up with secrets until she could not remember them all. She would have to keep counting them, and there was no end to numbers.

When people had too many secrets to count, they became poor people. She jumped up and sat on the side of her bed, afraid to lie there any longer. She looked out toward the swamp with its shaggy uneven tops of trees separating the deep black of the woods from the cloudy black in the sky. The woods, through the rain, looked like the shadow of a restless buffalo herd, with, now and then, a tall tree, whose lowest branches were higher than the house, rising above it. The past few weeks, she'd pictured the swamp outside her bedroom window as a dark row of points, as if all the trees were shaped like upside–down ice cream cones at a soda fountain. Now she knew that even if it hadn't been raining when her father cut the tree down, and even if her father had gone out and hired a world famous Christmas tree expert to search for forty–seven days in the swamp, he wouldn't have found a real Christmas tree, no matter how hard she and her mother wished.

Jenny got up and stood at her mirror. She put her hair behind her ears, and stared at her profile, tilting her chin. When I grow up, I will learn to hold my face still. She walked to the stairs and decided to count by twos going down. In order to make it fair she took two steps at a time.

"We really have lovely ornaments in Illinois," she would say to Dolly Jane," but they are imported and my mother was afraid they would break." Then she went down to ask her father to bring back the Christmas tree.


ii


When Jenny went back to school after Christmas vacation, she began to feel strange. She wanted to let her hair grow to her shoulders. She would go up to her mother's room and stand by the dresser smelling Evening in Paris perfume. Her mother was kept busy making over old clothes because Jenny grew so fast. It was lucky her mother had saved Grandpa's Christmas check for shoes. Her parents treated her as though she had grown older. When she and her friend, Annie Lucille, collected eggs one day, they left the gate to the chicken yard open, and three hens got into the strawberry patch. No one scolded her, but her mother told her to be careful in a way that made her feel that she was trying to hide the seriousness of the act from her. Jenny stopped counting things. She never wished anymore that she'd wake up in the morning and find that she was really a boy, and had only dreamed that she was a girl. She no longer wanted to go out to play wearing her cousin Billy's outgrown knickers. That made it even harder for her to understand why she made such a stupid wish the night before the freeze.

She and her mother and father were sitting around the stove. It made a sizzling sound as the water boiled out of the wood, and smoke rose up from around the lids. It looked like an Aladdin's lamp.

"I wish, I wish," Jenny said, thinking of the Aladdin's lamp.

"What do you wish?" her mother asked. They hadn't played the wishing game since fall.

Both the bathysphere and the airplane sounded too cold, worse even than going out into the cold hall and into her damp bed. She tried to think of a comfortable wish.

"I wish I had a boy's imitation leather coat, sheepskin lined, with a big collar," she said out of habit and she laughed at her silliness giving an old, outgrown want for a wish.

"You're cold all the time, aren't you, Jenny?" her mother said. She glanced over at her husband with an expression that reminded Jenny of Dolly Jane. Dolly Jane had looked the same way when Jenny had put only one *m* in *accommodate* and had to sit down. Jenny was surprised that grownups remembered the spelling bee look. Jenny had wrinkled her nose and stuck her tongue out at Dolly Jane. She looked over at her father. He had his box turtle look, all closed up. His face seemed to snap shut from hinges in his cheekbones.

"I wish," her mother said, "I wish I was sitting in one of Pa's steam–heated flats. Some tenants say he keeps them too warm, and they open their windows at night to let cold air in. "I can't heat the whole of Diversey Boulevard," Pa complains. But still he keeps it warm. I'd like to sit by a radiator and let the heat soak through my skin and bones. There's one little cold spot inside me that just won't get warm. It's almost like the beginning of death."

What had happened to her mother, Jenny wondered. Nothing was ever *like* anything else to her mother except in old sayings. "Poor as churchmice," "green as grass." Now her lifeless hair was pulled back, her skin unrouged; even her blue eyes seemed covered with little tan transparent discs. Jenny had been thinking of her all year with brown marcelled hair, pink cheeks, and blue eyes, the way she had looked last Decoration Day when she was the mother who walked along with the fourth grade in the parade of children carrying flowers to the graveyard.

"It's just like the temperature of Mammoth Cave inside me," her mother went on. "It never changes."

Her mother's wish was stupider if anything than Jenny's. But Jenny felt responsible for having started on the wrong foot.

"What do you wish, Daddy?"

He got up from where he was sitting and opened the door of the stove. He pushed in a big log. There was a hiss as the wet wood touched embers. The log sent bright red sparks out, more than Jenny could believe were there. White edged ashes drifted up, and the fire was dead.

"I wish," said her father, "I wish I had enough money to tell everybody in this whole goddammed world to go to hell." Without even bothering to exclude his own family, he slammed the door behind him.

That was a wish, all right, Jenny thought. But it wasn't very funny. It must have been the wrong night for the wishing game.

That night the temperature went down to fifteen degrees. The frost did their strawberries some damage. Jenny almost felt that her father didn't care. It would soon be spring, and there was no sign of the thing that was bound to happen.

Spring came in all at once in Louisiana just as winter had, instead of coming in one sign at a time as it did in Illinois. In March it was there. Jenny had become shy. If she saw a teacher from school or a boy in her grade coming toward her now, she crossed the street so she wouldn't have to speak to them. If it was unavoidable, she'd mutter, "Hey," while looking at the ground, and then run all the way home through a path in the woods to wear off the excess energy the meeting had generated. A year ago when she ran, her body was all one piece, but now her legs seemed to move on their own from her hips. She wondered at what age she would begin to run stiff–legged like grownups.

The strawberries came in about the middle of the month. Her father and mother picked them, and after school she helped cull and pack them in boxes. They filled the bottom of each box with the smaller ones, and placed the big ones carefully across the top. She went down with her father with the first load. The man took a box and poured all the strawberries across a table. "Class B," he said. Jenny wondered if it had been because of the frost or the chickens she'd let in the garden, or whether she'd packed the strawberries in the wrong way.

It was hardly worth picking them and buying the boxes her father said, as they walked home from the railroad. Jenny felt as if the man had classified *her* as Class B.

But they weren't cold any longer. The yard was filled with amaryllis at Eastertime, and they picked bouquets for the whole house. Her mother sent some to Chicago. She filled the hollow stems with water and stuffed the ends with cotton. Only Jenny's father didn't seem to know that spring had come. He hardly left the house. It was her mother who weeded the garden. Her father moved chess pieces around on the red and black board. He started to read the Leatherstocking series.

But as the garden and flowers grew, the grass grew too. Her mother asked her father once to borrow a lawn mower. He looked up from *The Prairie*. "When I have time," he said. But with the spring rains and warm days, the grass needed a sickle before he finished the book. Her mother stopped sitting on the screen porch in the spring twilight after supper to say, "Good evening" to the occasional passer–by. Instead she sat out on the back porch on a wooden kitchen chair, or played solitaire in her room behind closed doors, looking guilty and gathering the cards together if Jenny stopped in to ask her something. One Saturday morning, she left the dishes and went out into the shed and rummaged among the old farm tools, and came back with a rusty sickle. She went to the highest grass. It merely bent over at the touch of the dull blade. She kept swishing it back and forth until the grass lay over on the ground and stayed there.

Nobody every thought of that one," Jenny's father said. "Just wear the grass out until it lies down."

Her mother didn't smile.

"Maybe I can sharpen it when I have time." Her father said. He laid the sickle down on the back porch where it was rained on during the night.

Sunday morning after church was always her mother's worst time. Before church was fine. She wore her white gloves and her hat with the little veil over her eyes. She laid out Jenny's best clothes. She didn't really make any friends at church, but she enjoyed returning the gracious smiles of the elderly well–dressed parishioners, and the handshake of the pink–faced minister in the vestibule of the church after services. She even seemed to enjoy threading her way through the shiny parked cars, on her way home. But once they turned down their own block, she'd become short with Jenny. The day after she found the sickle, as soon as they got home, she walked straight through the house to the back porch. She still wore her hat with the little veil down over her eyes. She stooped with her white gloves and lifted the sickle and walked to the edge of the swamp and hurled it into the underbrush. She came back and got out cold green beans. The gloves removed, her hat still on her head, the veil tilting over her eyes, she put out turnip greens, a bottle of vinegar, some cold corn bread, and sorghum— throwing all this on the table—among a jumble of knives and forks, she called to her husband, "Get your grub, such as it is," and went upstairs slamming the staircase door behind her.

Jenny and her father sat down, Jenny stiff with embarrassment, her father tight–jawed, and they made a little meal in near silence.

"Women get nervous sometimes for no reason. Just their nature," her father said. But he hated it when she used words like grub, Jenny knew. He never was especially clean or neat and cared nothing about his appearance, but he would cringe at words like grub, or B.O., or jokes about outhouses.

Whenever her mother had a nervous spell, she became extra calm and loving. In an hour she came down and hugged Jenny, brought them a dish of pecans and a pitcher of cold water to the porch.

"Tonight I'll fix our supper on plates and we'll sit in the living room and listen to Eddie Cantor."

She used glass plates and china cups and white napkins. They all listened to Eddie Cantor's jokes and to Rubinoff on his violin. Eddie Cantor sang a song that Jenny liked.

> *Potatoes are cheaper,*
> *Tomatoes are cheaper,*
> *Now's the time to fall in love.*

After the program they sat on the screened porch. The grass and trees were gray and silky in the dark.

"If our neighbors don't like our grass, they can lump it," her mother said.

But that night when it rained again, and Jenny got up to go to the bathroom, she found her mother standing by the hall window. Jenny half–asleep said, "Why are you standing there, Mom?"

"I'm watching the rain," she said. "Sometimes I think it rains to spite me, to make the grass grow faster."

Jenny remembered her own nighttime fears about numbers. In the morning Mom would say, "What a silly idea to have about the rain," Jenny thought sleepily as she stumbled into the bathroom and back to her bed.

The night before her birthday, April twenty–seventh, Jenny was allowed two cups of sugar to make pecan brittle. On the morning of her birthday, she went right out to the screened porch to see if her candy has hardened. The color of the day was pale green. Raindrops clung to the screen and dripped onto the table. The pecan brittle hadn't hardened but instead there was a sticky, shiny brown glob in the middle of the plate surrounded by murky water with little pieces of pecans, like rocks, anchored in it. Jenny put her arm on the porch ledge that held the screen and let drops come down and cling to the light curved hairs on her arm. She put her forehead on her arm, and thought of all the good words she knew, fate, love, hope, crystal, infinity. She sort of breathed a blur between them and gave the thoughts rhythm from the back of her throat. She was sure if she had the time to bring all the blurs out of her mind and into words, it would make a beautiful poem. She heard her mother open the oven door in the kitchen, and she could smell the cornbread.

"I wish you'd do something about the grass today. I promised Jenny she could have two girls over after school for her birthday," her mother said.

"Okay," her father said, "I'll see about it when I have time."

"Not when you have time," her mother said sharply, "not when you have time. It'll never get mowed. Do it today.

Today's the day she's having friends over. The other way we can wait forever. Do something today."

Her father hated to have people talk to him in a sharp voice.

"I told you I'd take care of it. I don't know why you carry on so about it," he said, "It's only grass for Christ's sake, not our life's blood."

Her mother's voice rose. "It could be," she said, "and you wouldn't lift a finger. We could be starving. The house could fall down, and you'd go on reading books. My father used to get up at three o'clock every morning and take the wagon down to South Water Street to get his produce. Other men don't have time to read books or play checkers."

"It's chess," her father said. "Just be quiet. I'll take care of it today."

Jenny was shocked at the word *today*. She ran into the kitchen, but her father had his box turtle look.

Jenny didn't ask any girls home that day. That had been her mother's idea, not hers. She dawdled on the way home, wondering if there would be a cake. She tried not to step in any cracks. With the slanted bricks of the walk it meant fitting her foot in sideways, and once she tried to take too large a step and she lost her balance. Her foot came down hard on an anthill between cracks. She stooped down and tried to push the sand together into another hill, but the ants ran out in all directions. I'm too old to worry about ants and cracks any more, she thought.

She looked toward her house. There was a dark figure in the yard that blocked out the light. It was Grover, the sad horse, who looked even lumpier and lower slung than he had last fall. He must have broken away from the cart and gone into the yard to get fresh grass while Charlie was working in back. She laughed and pushed down on the bar that latched the gate, then stopped to close it again. The sound of the iron latch and its pieces hitting together and the wet iron smell made her stop. Tom Mix's horse, Tony, could nose open a latch. She looked at Grover. He wasn't even aware anyone had come. He chewed and his tail swished the tops of the grass behind him. The grass practically hid his legs and feet and almost touched his sagging middle. Grover wasn't like Tony, who could unlatch gates. Grover barely shifted his eyes sideways as she passed. Someone had let him inside the yard. He acted, Jenny thought, as if he had more right than she to be there. She'd never give him clippings again.

When she came into the living room, her father was moving pieces around the chessboard. "What's that horse doing in our yard?" she asked.

Her father looked up. "He's eating the grass, Jenny. Your mother wanted something done about the grass, so Charlie and I made a deal. We both benefit. While Charlie's working in town, Grover's here eating our grass, getting fed at the same time, and it doesn't cost either of us one red cent."

He moved his black knight and took a white pawn and then he put the two pieces back to their original position. He looked up at Jenny. "If you have a problem, Jenny, stick with nature, not with people. Just tuck yourself in with nature, Jenny. Remember that."

Jenny went out to the kitchen. Her mother was crying and stirring a cake for Jenny's birthday. With each stir the back of the wooden spoon hit the side of the bowl, "Why are you crying?" Jenny asked.

"I was just thinking about the day you were born," her mother said. "You were such a cute baby."

"There are a lot of cute babies in the world," Jenny said. "I don't think that's anything to cry about."

## iii

On May thirtieth, the night of Decoration Day, Jenny lay in bed in her grandfather's flat and listened carefully to the clang of the Lincoln Avenue streetcars. The train ride, her aunts and uncles at the station were an exciting blur, but the persistent clang of the streetcars across the otherwise quiet night always placed every bit of Jenny in Chicago.

It was hard to believe that only the night before, she and her mother and father had walked to the train station. The suitcase her father carried had hit her bare legs. They had waited inside the station under a dirty yellow light. Jenny watched her face in the narrow mirror of the gum machine. When they heard the train whistle, her father bent over to kiss Jenny goodbye. She pulled away. He seemed not to know what to say to her.

"I'm going to miss my helper here," he said. "But even grownups can't have everything they want, Jenny."

In the little mirror Jenny saw her face snap shut. So that's how it happened. At eleven years old, the closing up muscles in your cheeks started to work. How old she looked! Almost old enough to explain to her father what she had finally understood about grownup wants, and how really it was the things that *he* wanted, or didn't want, that decided what happened to their family.

They went out to the platform and stood in the drizzle while the train adjusted itself on the track. Her mother cried, and Jenny stared into the dining car windows.

Her aunts and uncles met them at the station in Chicago. They exclaimed at how lanky Jenny had become and how terrible her mother looked. The whole family went with them to her grandfather's apartment. Jenny's aunts made coffee and set out summer sausage, rye bread and butter, dill pickles, leiderkranz cheese, and chocolate eclairs; and they all sat around the kitchen table and talked. The many different tastes struck Jenny as foreign and luxurious, and yet she was filled quickly and couldn't finish her éclair. Absentmindedly, with one finger, she spread out rays from the wet circle that her glass of milk had left on the oilcloth. The adults all seemed to be talking at once. Her aunts and uncles asked her mother about the house, the cold, the food, Jenny's father. But her mother kept coming back to Grover.

"He wasn't like those smooth horses you see eating grass behind white fences," she said. Then later, "He wasn't like the horse that pulls the wagon that delivers newspapers to the Russian on Lincoln Avenue."

Finally her youngest brother unwound his feet from the legs of his chair. He touched his wife's arm. "Okay, okay. We get the idea. It was a nag, ready for the glue factory." He got up. "But it wasn't the horse. It was the whole lousy set—up. That's the way you have to look at it." He glanced at Jenny. "I'll talk to you tomorrow," he said to her mother.

They all left soon after that. Billy's mother handed a bag to Jenny.

"It's old," she said. "Billy outgrew it, but remembered how crazy you were to have one. You can wear it to play in."

Jenny took refuge in an almost forgotten childlike act. She yawned and rubbed her eyes as if sleepiness and tired eyes were her only concern. She could not open the bag. She had not only outgrown her boyish desires, she was sure that her sleepy wish on that cold night for an imitation leather coat had somehow or another set up a whole chain of things happening that she couldn't stop.

Her mother grabbed the bag and pulled out the coat. "What you've always wanted, Jenny. Try it on!"

But her grandfather, who had been checking the thermometer on the living room wall, turned to the two lingering women impatiently.

"Can't you see the child is dead tired, riding all day and night on the train. She can try the coat on in the morning."

Her mother's oldest sister, whose husband traveled, stayed overnight with them and slept in the next bedroom with Jenny's mother. Jenny decided she would try the coat on to please, but that she would never, never wear it as long as she lived, even if she froze to death. Each time she woke up during the night she could hear the streetcars and the muffled droning voices of her mother and aunt in the next room. Toward morning when she woke up she heard the hollow sounds of horses' hooves on Diversey Boulevard, and the clink of milk bottles. She thought that she was the only one in the flat awake. Then she heard her mother.

"It wasn't like the milkman's horse either," her mother said.

As Jenny fell back to sleep she pictured Grover in the front yard and her father in the living room sitting by a telephone with a big book of names in front of him. The swamp in back was moving forward encompassing the shed, and gray moss covered the back porch. With no one to fill the saucers with water, crowds of ants crawled up the legs on to the kitchen table; and the floor, without new tin patches, rotted away, and vines grew up into the kitchen and entwined the wood stove, and went all the way up the walls. Her father didn't notice, or perhaps he welcomed the blending of the inside and the outside and the land taking over. He grew older and quieter, reading and moving chess pieces, and calling people up on the telephone. He called each person and said, "Go to hell," and checked off their names with a little gold pencil. He made no exceptions even when he came to Jenny's grandfather, her uncles and her aunts, even her mother. When he came to Jenny's name, she held her breath. He stared at the book for a whole minute without moving, and then he called and checked her off.

## Note:

Jenny had no prophetic insight. The swamp never took over the house, but as times improved, a developer bought the swamp from Jenny's father, filled it in and built small plantation–style houses on it. Her father took the swamp money and opened a country drug store where he prescribed, just like a doctor. He became prosperous and married a young girl. They raised hunting dogs for a hobby and bought a boat to fish in the Gulf. Her mother became pretty again, but would never risk remarriage or leaving Chicago, as if once having learned a lesson, she had no need to learn it again. Jenny, at first, tried to change back to the person she was before she went South. Failing that, she tried to change forward, but she never succeeded completely. It turned out that the things that she thought were forever, like the swamp or her parents' marriage, could vanish in a few years, leaving barely a trace. While the ragtail ends, the little unwanted scraps of childhood can last the rest of a life.

•••••

**Marjorie Kaplan** was born in Gary, Indiana. She has published two children's books and a short story collection.

# Living in South Carolina in the Thirties

## Martha Stribling Smith

In 1929 I was five years old—just beginning to notice the world outside home and extended family. For the next thirteen years, until I went away to college in 1942, I was a participant in the hard times of the Great Depression. But I remember those years not as "hard" so much as changing. I had nothing to measure them by, and I think I was by nature an optimist, watching for promising new experiences. School and after school recreation filled most of my hours. Skating with friends, sometimes on the sidewalk, but mostly on the asphalt (smooth) paved streets, was exciting, especially at night. Traffic was much lighter in those days. Later the city decided to close off a long block of boulevard/divided road on Saturday nights for skaters. My first "dates" were with Bobby, who played trumpet in the high school band. We met at the skating "street" after my brother had escorted me there.

Learning to ride a bicycle, even a second–hand one, was a great thrill. My brother learned first, and since we could only afford one, there were unavoidable arguments over who got it when. On one occasion, he and I were going to the same party, and he took me, sitting on the crossbar. I was so nervous because he went too fast ( I thought). I grabbed the handlebar and made us fall into a shrub.

My mother, a home economics graduate of Winthrop College, had worked as Cherokee County home demonstration agent before she married my father, the county agricultural agent. He often said, "We couldn't keep a home demonstration agent because they kept leaving to get married. So I married Ethel and kept her."

Mother did not work after they married, at least not after my brother and I arrived on the scene. At that time, many jobs had nepotism rules. Some even had rules against married women working. Since my mother was very competent and active, she held a variety of community and church volunteer jobs. She continued her volunteerism all her life, even into her eighties.

She was a good cook, giving us nutritious meals, using vegetables from my father's garden and chicken and eggs from our chicken yard. One of my early chores was to scatter grain and bread crumbs for the chickens and to gather the eggs. A more exciting job was gathering figs from our trees, which were taller than the roof of our garage. We were permitted to climb up on the roof and into the trees. We ate some of the fruit on the spot, but Mother made fig preserves with most of them. In later years when I had been widowed, I had a house near the college where I taught. My father brought a fig tree from his yard so that I could enjoy the same sweet, brown figs.

I also climbed up our pecan trees, which were sturdier trees than the fig trees were. From them, I got wonderful views of the neighborhood and beyond.

We seldom had meat other than chicken, bacon, and sausage, but the beans, corn, cabbage, squash, beets, peas, limas/butter beans, and tomatoes were good. I protested vehemently when faced with asparagus or okra, however. Not until I was grown did I really discover the pleasure of those fresh treats.

Since my father was a government employee—state and federal, we had a steady, but limited income. I remember hearing my parents talking seriously about the decision by South Carolina and/or Washington to cut salaries of government workers. My memory is that my father would be reduced to two hundred dollars a month. But my brother and I were never hungry, and the house we lived in belonged to us, with a mortgage that I was never aware of being in danger. There was always money for "worthwhile" things like visits to a specialist for my eye problems, for violin lessons for my brother and piano lessons for me, for tickets to plays and concerts at Limestone College near where we lived. I especially loved plays. We children would always sit on the front row if we could. When the lights would go out during a mystery, we would shriek with delicious horror. The College art department presented a May Day festival in their woodsy amphitheater. They recruited town children to be the elves and fairies. One year I encountered what remains a hazard for me in the outdoors—poison ivy. I sat under a tree in my abbreviated costume waiting for my cue to enter. You can imagine the unpleasant results.

We did not take family vacations to the beach or mountains. We spent Christmas and time in the summer with our two sets of grandparents, fifty and a hundred miles away in South Carolina. My extended family included uncles, aunts, and cousins. Some of them are still important people in my life. Most of the uncles and aunts had attended South Carolina state colleges: Winthrop College for women and Clemson for men. There was no question about money when the time came for college for my brother, nor for me. We followed the family tradition.

The Depression years in South Carolina had a devastating effect on the farmers, whose return from cotton dropped to five cents a pound. Since helping farmers was my father's job, he was very troubled by this. Even I sensed his concern. He encouraged them to diversify by planting fruit and vegetables.

One year he identified melons—cantaloupe and watermelon—as good cash crops. Many of the farmers raised good stands of these, and when their crops were ready to market, my father had to come up with a plan. He sent out fliers to truckers and truck stops. Soon he was getting calls—at all hours—for directions to farms with melons for sale. I think he did not do it this way the next summer, however.

Another plan he organized was a fresh market. This provided my first job. I became the treasurer of the Farmer's Market. From eight until eleven every Saturday morning I sat in the small building with a cash box. My responsibilities were to make change for the sellers, mostly women, and to collect ten percent of their sale proceeds at the end of the morning. For this I was paid seventy–five cents—pretty good for a thirteen year old in the middle of the Depression. I loved it.

In the late thirties and early forties , my father arranged to do a radio program from Spartanburg, twenty miles away from the nearest radio station. He gave information about the proper fertilizers; which varieties of seed were best; how to do contour plowing to retain water and avoid erosion; and what prices were predicted for cotton, grains, hogs, various vegetables, and fruit. I confess, I did not listen to this program after the first time or two. But it was a popular service for the farmers.

Another project of the late Depression was the encouragement of peach growing in Cherokee County. The climate was favorable, land was cheap due to the bad economic times, and my father located growers in New Jersey who were interested. One family that came south is still there and prospering. Look for Farmer Dom's Market when you go through Cherokee County on I-85. Their peaches are the best!

About this time, my father was offered a state–level job at Clemson as editor of the South Carolina Extension Service, in my opinion, a recognition of the creativity and energy he had been putting into a difficult job.

Incidentally, when my parents sold our house, the buyer was the Farmer Dom Family. A Clemson classmate of my father later gave prominence to the place of peaches in the economy by giving a water tower shaped like a giant peach and painted very realistically. It is known as the "Peachoid," and is very visible beside I-85.

My memories of the Depression years are colored by the books I read during the thirties. Then and always I have been a reader. The big books for me were *The Good Earth*, *Gone With The Wind*, and *The Grapes Of Wrath*.

I was interested in Pearl Buck's book. She was part of a Presbyterian missionary family in China, the Sydenstickers, and my mother took me to many Women's Auxiliary meeting at the church when missionaries spoke and the mission study books were discussed. Therefore, I knew something about China, as well as, Japan, Korea, Mexico, Brazil, and where other Presbyterian missions were located.

I remember, particularly, reading *Gone With The Wind* with my mother and brother, who was in bed with the mumps. Mother and I sat on his bed and took turns reading, laughing at the humor and crying together at the sad parts. We mourned the burning of Atlanta and cheered Scarlett's coping skills. All these novels gave me ways to think about these experiences of economic hardship in South Carolina and the rest of the world. I credit these writers with giving me a social conscience and sense of direction for my life.

•••••

**Martha Smith** has retired from teaching English at Elon College, Elon College, North Carolina.

# On March 13th, 1934, Dillinger Robbed the First National Bank in Mason City, Iowa

## Lila S. Azhari

It was 3:00 p.m., and I'd been reading at the library. Dad, a doctor who had his office on the fourth floor of the bank, usually left for home about 4:00 p.m. The bank was near the library, so I often stopped at the office and walked home with him.

When I got across the street from the bank, I noticed a well–dressed man with a tripod. He said to me, "We are photographing the bank, young lady. Please don't cross the street that way. Cross over there."

"All right," I said, and did as I was told.

As I crossed the street the way he asked me to, I saw another very presentable–appearing man with a tripod. He was also "photographing" the bank. I saw Dad looking out of his window at the scene below. Some people walking by paused to look. I heard someone whisper, "That's John Dillinger. He's robbing the bank. Those aren't cameras. They're machine guns! Let's go to the park and watch this from the underground restrooms. We'll be safe there."

I went over to the park and watched, too. Only our heads could be seen, but we knew they couldn't really see us.

Pretty soon we heard shooting. No one had a gun, so no one shot back. After awhile a car with running boards drove up and stopped by the bank. I saw my father looking out of an office window as two hostages were brought out and placed on the running boards. I prayed Dad would be safe up there on the fourth floor. The men in the car had guns, and they drove off with their hostages. No one got hurt in that robbery, it seemed.

I was afraid to go near Dad's office. I took a safer route home, but as soon as he got home, I told him what I had seen and how worried I was about him.

"I saw a man speaking to you," he said, "but I wasn't worried about you. It seemed very casual until I heard someone out in the hall shout, 'John Dillinger is robbing our bank'."

He said to me, "I spent a sleepless night last night. Not due to any particular reason or finances, but just felt I could not bring myself to undergo sleep. I was answering a letter from one of my patients when I heard, 'BOOM, boom, boom.' I smelled some sharp smoke and gas coming into my office. I didn't know whether it came from outside, through a window, or the inside office door."

"I glanced out the window," he continued. "The corner of State Street and Federal Avenue was jammed with humanity. It looked like a circus parade crowd in the center of town. There on the south side of the bank were four men with guns in their hands. They were shouting and shooting. Gas was filling my office. My eyes were watering. I couldn't see to write. I took one drink, then another, not caring for anything but that human herd moving and minding orders from the gunmen. I wondered where you were, Sister."

"I was watching from the park, Dad," I said.

Then he continued, "If I had had a rifle, I could easily have picked off two fellows shouting orders and shooting as easily as the drink I had had or the cigar I had been smoking, but I lacked the rifle—not the marksmanship or the bravery, for I was provided with both. It seemed to me how clever are the law makers of this country! The law breakers are armed, but the law–abiding people appeared disarmed. The thing looked so easy. It's a wonder every bank isn't held up illegally."

"Are the people cowards? Oh, no! Only no one seemed to care in the least. They just stood watching the show. Unlawful ones robbing the lawful ones. It was force used against force. One upheld by the nation, the navy, the police, and the law, and the other by seven fearless men. The sad part is—the seven won."

•••••

**Lila S. Azhari** of Chapel Hill is a native of Iowa and taught primary grades in Chicago Public Schools for eighteen years. She studied writing at the University of Iowa and Michigan State University, and is now working on a history of her father's life.

# Skimping and Saving

## Betty Kichline Gerow

I was born in 1917 and my husband Jim in 1911, so we were both the right age to have a hand–shaking acquaintance with the "Great Depression" years. We were among the more fortunate, however, because both our families had steady incomes, such as they were, after the 1929 stock market crash.

Jim's father, a railroad engineer, was killed in 1921 by an engine explosion. His mother, along with three other plaintiffs, successfully sued the railroad. She took the money to set up trusts for her two children and to build a roomy two–story house with a fully equipped apartment on the second floor, which she always managed to rent.

My own father was a meteorologist, a federal employee with an office in Raleigh. Although his peak salary had not gone beyond three thousand a year at the time of his death, in the early forties, he earned some extra money by keeping the books for the largest drug store in Raleigh. Both our families skimped and maneuvered none–the–less in order to have even the basics.

Jim, who became my husband, worked at odd jobs from the time he was fourteen years old. By playing in a dance band, he managed to get himself through college and do graduate studies at Columbia and Duke.

I went without finery of any sort and enjoyed precious little paid entertainment, such as movies. There was no extra money.

I still have vivid memories of scenes: the soup and bread lines; beggars; my mother always managing to scrape up plates of food for the daily hobos that came from the rail line near our house in Boylan Heights, where we moved when I was fourteen years old; my total shame and sort of heart break when some of my girlfriends asked me when I was going to get some new shoes; my first job after graduation from Meredith College as a high school teacher in Raleigh for less than one thousand dollars a year (1937–1938); the times when teachers' salaries could not even be paid; the frightening runs on the banks; the unemployed man next door who continually shouted to the world that President Hoover was the cause of all his ills.

To illustrate how so many of us tried to manage, let me tell three brief stories.

My parents were determined that my sister and I would go to college, so mother decided to add to the education fund in her own way. We lived in a typical wooden duplex, just two blocks from the Capitol. We had a regular living room, dining room, kitchen, two small bedrooms, one very small bath, and a long back porch with lattice siding. Mother decided to rent her daughters' bedroom to two young men working in my father's office and did so, moving Mildred and me to the back porch! She found a cheap iron double bedstead for us and wrote her sister to send her one of the down comforters they had made at their Pennsylvania–Dutch farm home. The bed was next to the lattice and more than once on a winter morning there was snow on our cover. I assume that the experience contributed to my good health.

My first year teaching I earned less than one thousand for the year, but I lived at home, paid nominal room and board, walked to and from school most of the time—three miles—and still managed to save enough for summer school at the University of North Carolina to start my graduate studies.

For that first summer in Chapel Hill, I put aside in my budget all of seventy–five cents a day for food, but in our group of four girls who studied together, one girl had only twenty–five cents for daily bread. How do we three come to the rescue?

There was a popular drug store on Franklin Street with the typical little round tables and small wrought iron chairs. In the middle of each table was a ketchup bottle and some saltine crackers. The four of us would go there of an afternoon. Three of us splurged for a nickel coke each and shared sips with our friend with only a quarter a day to spend, while she ate crackers with ketchup! We all managed to pass our final exams on slim diets.

In 1932 my husband took his first job teaching, coaching, and directing band in a town east of Raleigh, where he found a place to get room and board for twelve dollars a month. One problem, however, came the last two months of the school year when the county did not have enough money to pay teachers at all. (The county did honor its commitment four months later—the teachers had actually come back.)

The other problem that we can laugh at now: the woman who ran the boarding house, a very large home place, filled the rooms to capacity for her much–needed income. My husband happened to be the sole male among the other teachers, six women. There was only one bath. The women had arranged signals so they could use the bath, one after another, without interruption. My husband had to leave extra early for school each morning to have time to tend to his toilet.

Amongst all the sad tales and even horror stories from those trying years, I must admit to some positive characteristics. First, there was order and discipline in most of our lives, as well as those values that we keep saying are missing now. In addition, we tend to forget that there was relativity. All things were reasonable in cost, as they had to be—ten cents for a loaf of bread, thirty cents for a pound of coffee, thirty–five dollars a month for our first apartment as a married couple (1939–1940), which was a brand new, well–built, two–bedroom apartment with all the amenities of the day. Of course, I still did my wash on my knees by the bathtub, using a dime store washboard. I sent only sheets to the laundry.

All these musings represent only a part of my memories of the Depression years.

A very permanent series of images they are!

●●●●●

**Betty Gerow** resides in Burlington, North Carolina. Before she retired she taught English at Elon College, Elon College, North Carolina.

# New Shoes

## Marie P. Spinner

November, 1935

It started out like any Friday morning at P. S. 21, my elementary school in the Bronx, New York. Miss Spencer, my fifth grade teacher, was patiently waiting for us to settle down after returning from Assembly.

"Class, turn to page ninety–two in your geography books. We'll continue with the countries of Europe and their capitals." Rolling down the multi–colored map of Europe, Miss Spencer tapped the pointer for attention. Just then a messenger walked into the room and handed the teacher a note.

"Maria, please report to the principal's office."

Placing my book on the desk, I stood up and glanced at my teacher who waved me towards the door.

Now what? I thought. Did my younger brother misbehave? I walked quickly to the office and knocked.

"Come in, come in," called Mrs. Caterson. There were five other students in her office.

"Fine. Please form a line and follow me," she said crisply.

Marching down the hall like six wooden soldiers behind their commander, not daring to whisper, we entered Room 111. A dozen other children were standing at attention, among them my brother, Joseph, and my sister, Tina. Seeing me, Tina waved and called out excitedly, "We're getting new shoes!"

"New shoes?" I asked and glanced toward the principal.

"Yes, it's true. You children were especially selected," Mrs. Caterson assured us, smiling brightly, and gestured to a tall, rugged man in overalls. "We have Mr. Bruno here from the Home Relief Bureau. He'll take your foot measurements for the new shoes, which will be delivered to the school in two weeks."

With the end of that speech, she left Mr. Bruno to do his job. One after another, in strict precision, Mr. Bruno measured our feet with something like a slide rule, putting our name, size, and class on a list, then dismissed us.

All the way home from school, Joseph and Tina chattered about the new shoes.

Joseph said, "I hope mine are dark brown hiking boots like the Boy Scouts."

"Mine just have to be black, shiny Mary–Janes with bows," said my very fashion–conscious, six–year–old sister.

They turned to me, "What about you?"

"Me?" I was recalling the whole incident at school. The Home Relief was where once a month Mama and Papa went for provisions. They took the trolley to the Depot where the Government Surplus Food was distributed. Lining up with so many other families, they received their allotment of flour, corn meal, canned goods, and sometimes clothing. I remembered how tired my parents would be after the trip carrying the food in sacks from the trolley stop, then the five long blocks to our apartment house. And now the Home Relief was giving shoes to selected students at school? We must be poor.

Tina persisted shaking my arm. "Maria, what about you?"

"Oh, I don't know what kind of shoes we'll be given. Sturdy ones, I'm sure."

After supper I was alone in the kitchen with Mama and blurted out, "Mama, are we poor?"

"Poor is a strong word. Why?"

"Well, I've been thinking, ever since Mr. Bruno from the Home Relief came to our school to measure feet for new shoes to just a select group of children. Poor children. I never thought we were poor. Are we?"

My mother put her hands on my shoulders and gently spoke to me for the first time as an adult.

"Maria, we are going through hard times. A Depression. The whole country is hurting, some families worse than others. We're lucky that our government gives us assistance with food and clothing and work for your father on the WPA. That's the Works Project Administration. We have our health, are happy, and love each other. Don't we?" I nodded. "So you see, we may be needy, but we're not destitute and are blessed in so many ways. Now give me a hug, and go finish your homework."

Two weeks later the shoes arrived. I was summoned to the office to receive my new shoes. Mrs. Caterson was on hand to supervise. Removing my brown, buckled shoes, which were hand–me–downs from cousin Josie, I slipped on my new shoes. They were a pair of dull, black, wing–tipped oxfords that laced up and looked like boys' shoes. I was so disappointed that tears formed on my eyelids. I felt so humiliated! No fifth–grade girl would wear shoes like mine. They were ugly and clumsy. I hated them! Hiding them from Mrs. Caterson was impossible, for she insisted I wear my *new shoes* back to class and pick up my other shoes after school.

Walking back to my classroom was like walking the last mile of a doomed prisoner. My footsteps, loud and heavy, echoed in the quiet hall. No way could I muffle the unbearable squeaks.

How I arrived at my desk with everyone looking and pointing to my shoes, I have no idea. How I lived through the day until the three o'clock bell is another mystery. I was the last to leave.

"Maria," called Miss Spencer.

"Yes," I replied hesitantly.

"Can you stay a minute?"

"I suppose so."

"So, tell me about your new shoes."

I looked at her horrified. How could she! I stammered, "New shoes?"

"Yes. New shoes." She laughed and pointed to my shoes.

I looked down at those painfully, unattractive, boy–shoes and then at Miss Spencer.

"They *are* ugly, aren't they?" she said this time with a giggle.

"You really think so," I said, crestfallen.

"I think they're funny. Look again," she said.

I did. The shoes did look funny on my feet. What ten–year–old girl with long narrow feet like mine would be seen with them? They were a joke. I had to smile.

"Good for you. Don't worry about the shoes. You'll get used to them. Pretend they're your magic shoes and wearing them every day will be a challenge."

They surely were strange looking boy–shoes, but if I attached red tassels, they would be rather colorful and distinctive!

"Thank you, Miss Spencer. I hope I can cheer up my little sister. She was looking forward to black, shiny, Mary Janes with bows."

My new shoes lived up to their reputation. They wore like iron and were part of my wardrobe until I entered Junior High. When my brother inherited the "Depression Shoes," he removed the tassels and thought the black oxfords were swell for a boy.

Which they were. Hadn't I thought so all along?

●●●●●

**Marie Spinner**, of Chapel Hill, formerly of New York, a retired elementary school librarian, has studied writing at "Life Time Learners" at Norwalk Community College.

# A Childhood Memory

## Robert Seymour

I was four years old in 1929 when the stock market crashed, and so I grew up as a child of the Great Depression. I was among the fortunate, however, for I never felt deprived of anything, even though my parents may have had cause to wonder how they would survive.

My father was a public school teacher, and the only anxiety I ever heard expressed was when he came home month after month and complained to my mother about not being paid. I was too young to comprehend the seriousness of the crisis.

We lived next door to my grandfather whose large frame house was surrounded by a farm. Because he had a huge vegetable garden and livestock, there was always plenty of food on our table even when money was scarce.

I do recall, however, that during those years we sometimes feasted on rabbit, something I have seldom eaten since. Grandfather had a faithful African–American hired man who built rabbit traps and placed them in the nearby woods. His name was Clifford, and he became my friend. I liked nothing better than following him around as he did his chores and especially tromping through the woods each day to check the rabbit traps. It was an exciting adventure for a little boy.

One day Clifford asked me if I would like to have a rabbit box for my very own. I was ecstatic at the thought. When he brought it to our back door, I admired it as my finest treasure and immediately began to consider where it should be placed to have the best chance of catching a rabbit.

My parents suggested that the grassy plot behind our garage might be an ideal location, and that is where I put it. Subsequently, every morning thereafter I would leap out of bed and race outside to see if there was a rabbit in the trap. Over and over I returned disappointed, but each morning my hope was renewed.

Then one day, vividly etched in my memory, I approached the trap, and much to my delight, the trap door had sprung! Sure enough, I had a rabbit! With great pride, I raced back to the house to share the exciting news. I boasted to everyone in the neighborhood about the rabbit I had caught.

Not until I graduated from college did I learn the truth. My parents had conspired with Clifford to put the rabbit in the trap! They could not endure the pain of seeing me check the rabbit box morning after morning and return crest–fallen. So much did they love me!

•••••

**Robert Seymour** is Minister Emeritus of Binkley Baptist Church and currently serves as president of Friends of the Chapel Hill Senior Center.

# A Trilogy

## A little Jewish girl lives in the Ghetto

### Libby Lefkowitz

#### The Mitzvah

Hanging on to momma's skirt
as up she climbed the dingy,
scrunched–in stairs.
The steps were steep–
tight even for a little girl

It was dark
and way past eight.
Street lamps turned low
in a rundown neighborhood
Historic, yet ghetto.
Home only to the Jew,
Trenton of nineteen hundred thirty–two.

Momma is carrying our one good pot
next door
to the old two
who have the flu
Watched over by Si with dignified air.

Their teacher son is barely there.
He's tipsy.
His test papers strewn
Upon the unswept floor.

Up we climb to the top
I remember well
that sour smell.
The Siets are quiet
Cold in bed,
tattered cover pulled up.

They spoke only in
that foreign tongue.
Zshe hut geh coomen
"She has come."
They eat.
Hot soup needs no language
Momma, lady bountiful,
Mother Teresa of Lamberton Street.


### The Cakes

I was cleaning out the burners
of my stove the other day.
It smelled of spongecake baking.
You know, when the batter starts to boil over
and caramelize and the edges begin to brown.
It's got a special smell.

Back in momma's kitchen on Lamberton Street
I had spelled momma:
she beat the eggs golden, a hundred strokes.
I follow after, our electric mixer, a flat metal paddle,
of meshwork coils with a wooden handle

Every now and then I stick my little finger in the stiff
meringue. It even tastes good raw.

We carry the filled pans down to Market Street.
To Mr. Kohn's Bakery. Momma doesn't trust our coal
stove.
The panettiere is a big fat man who always pinches both
my cheeks
when the cakes are done at five cents a loaf.

They're steaming when they come out of the huge ovens.
"No", momma says, "You mayn't have any now.
Wait until they cool. You don't want a belly ache."
Back in the kitchen she turns out the sponge
on a clean dish towel. My mouth is watering so
I can hardly stand it.

I help momma wash and put away the big yellow mixing
bowl
that once was Grandma Ida's. I sweep the floor.
It's covered with special Passover white cake flour,
and with a clean used toothbrush dust out the big
box–like sieve
that has a red crankhandle,
anything to keep busy until it's time to taste the cake.

"Momma, this is the best ever. The best you've ever
made."
Momma gives me her answer:
"Nonsense, child, you say that each and every Passover."


Trenton

Loaded branches of flowering apple
touch the ground
at Stacy Park.

Momma sits
dozing on the wood bench
her wavy black
braids all undone.
I'd stolen the pins,
arranging her hair
like the movie stars
in sister's *Photoplay*.

Gone is winter,
Sun glinting off
the once snowbound
river.

Time when the *General*
fired his rattle–wheeled
two ton stanchion.
The broad cast
cannon's target—
hidden Hession
across and icy
no man's land.

I let my kid brother,
Joey, be Washington.
Ancient gray stone
barracks stand
watching,
as we shinny up
the mounted fusil.

*Fire*, my brother shouts into the quiet air.
Sound reverberating on the gurgling Delaware.
A masonry wall protects us from the treacherous currents.

**Libby C. Lefkowitz**, whose husband was a physicist, writes romance novels. She is an environmental activist and joined the North Carolina Society for Ethical Culture early in its formation.

# Bench Dwellers

## Sam R. Marks

To look at him, you would hardly classify him as the average bum that makes the benches of Central Park his lodgings.

He was unshaven, his clothes were unpressed, his shoes worn and filthy—yet there was a certain something about him, perhaps that strange expression on his face or the deliberate manner in which he smoked his pipe, that seemed to raise him above the army of homeless New Yorkers who, with the close of day, return wearily to the benches in Central Park.

Take the man sitting beside him. Now there was a true specimen of the "Bench Dwellers." His clothes were perhaps less worn, his face less in need of a shave, and his shoes less dusty; yet there was nothing about him to make you think he did not belong where he was.

They had been sitting there for more than an hour but neither had spoken a single word. The strange individual sat there moodily smoking his pipe and staring straight ahead, as motionless as the lamp above by whose light the other man was just beginning to read a newspaper. He shifted about restlessly as he opened the pages of the paper.

"Paper?" he inquired of his companion.

No answer from the smoker.

The restless one shrugged his shoulders. The paper interested him, perhaps because it was almost six months old. He had found it while rummaging about in a rubbish pile, still in good shape. He opened it at the comic page, characteristic of most bench dwellers. It produced no smile. He then turned to the front page. His eyes took on an interested expression. He folded the paper so as to obliterate everything except what he was reading. The expression changed to a look of hate.

"Crooks!" he growled between his teeth.

He was gazing at big headlines that fairly shouted all about the Sloane Investment Company going bankrupt.

"Crooks!" he repeated venemously.

"Would you believe it," he addressed the silent one who gave no sign of listening, "when this paper was printed I had my own home and all necessary comforts? Look at me now—a plain bum, and why? Here, read this and see why. 'Sloane Investment Company Fails! Samuel Sloane Announces His Firm is Bankrupt.' That's why you see me here, broke and ruined. Bankrupt, he said. Robbery, I say, plain, down–right robbery. Sure they investigated him but they found nothing. They wouldn't; he's too slick for them. Thieves, damn thieves! That's what I call them. Here I am without a home or a cent to my name, and where do you suppose Mr. Samuel Sloane is now? Sitting on a park bench broke like me? No, not a chance. He'll have plenty of money—my money or some other sucker's life savings—living a life of ease and luxury."

He slammed the paper viciously down to the ground.

"Crooks, all of them," he went on bitterly. "Why— — — why, man, what's the matter with you? Are you sick?"

The smoker had stopped smoking; the color had drained from his face. His hands were shaking as if with ague and his body trembled. Slowly he arose, and the creaking of his aged bones was audible in the stillness of the night. Still trembling, his hand went to the pocket of his ragged coat. It fumbled there momentarily and finally came out with a card.

Bending low in a bow, he handed his card to his astonished companion.

"My calling card, sir, my last one," he said in a proud voice, and with all the dignity he could muster he stiffly walked out of the circle of light cast by the lamp above them. The other's eyes followed him until he was out of sight, then he turned his eyes to the card in his hand. It was old and dirty, the edges bent and torn. On it, engraved in delicate handiwork, was the name "Samuel S. Sloane."

•••••

**Sam Marks** was born in Russia and emigrated to Cleveland, Ohio, with his family in 1923. After retiring in 1981, he moved with his wife Ann to Chapel Hill. His memoirs of life between two world wars numbers over one hundred stories, one of which has been published in his army division's book of war stories.

# A Virginia County Memory

## Mitchell Forrest Lyman

Roughly, the period of the Great Depression for the United States, began with the stock market crash in 1929 when Herbert Hoover was president. It extended until 1942 and the beginning of the second World War.

That event, indirectly, caused the death of my Great Uncle John Mitchell, the inventor of a pipe coupling which had made him the wealthiest member of our family. However, after the stock market plunge, he became very depressed. He was one of those who could not "take it." Uncle John put a gun to his head and pulled the trigger. His death was a strong lesson for the rest of us. The lesson we learned is that character with endurance and perseverance is the best wealth after all. Confidence in one's own ability to endure gives hope and power to survive.

After Franklin Delano Roosevelt's election to that office, he started government programs which gave thousands of unemployed people jobs to do, therefore, an income. Jobs helped these people have pride in achievement, a certain independence, and some hope of being able to find "life, liberty and happiness." It is *damned* hard to be happy when your stomach and the stomachs of your dependents are growling with hunger; when inadequate diet is promoting malnourishment for them; and you and they are about to be evicted for non–payment of rent.

That remark reminds me of an old song titled "Bill Bailey," I think that's its name. Part of the lyrics make a plea: "Won't you come home, Bill Bailey? I need your money. I'm all alone."

There must have been many women feeling those lyrics, because thousands (or was it millions?) of men took to the road, thumbing rides with anybody who would stop for them, trying to get to some place where they could find work, at least two meals a day, and a bed for the night. Oh, yes, that place should have a post office from which they could send money home. Or, it might be at residence of one of their in–laws, where their wives and children had, in desperation, already moved.

Many women made the clothes for their families. They salvaged good material from large–size garment to fashion clothes for smaller individuals. Besides that, an intricate, carefully calculated system existed whereby wardrobes were passed from one child in the family to another. A child who got the *new* garment caused considerable envy to the ones who did not, and much self pity for the last one on the "totem pole," who eventually received it.

There were occasional clothing drives—*bottom line or last ditch*—by churches. These were shipped to the "heathens" through their mission programs.

The never–ending accumulation of small pieces of fabric were stitched into quilts. Once tops were assembled, they were filled with cotton batting, backed, and mounted on a quilting frame. Invitations were sent to friends to come help. The event, known as a "Quilting Bee," was a popular social gathering of the time. Possibly every community had some version of it. In the 1930's little round pieces of fabric, gathered into yo–yos, as they were called, were used to make colorful quilts, spreads, pillow covers, and even lady's jackets. The craze spread all over the country.

When I was in my early teens, my double bed had a yo–yo spread. I would lie on top of it, put a finger on first one and then another yo–yo and reminisce. *Where had I worn the garment from which that scrap came? Who had been with me?*

Precious fabric came from another source, too, for us countryfolk. Every sack which held chopped grain to feed the chickens that came to us could be used. Some "genius" in the bag industry decided to print the cloth in many different patterns—plaids, stripes, *"millefleurs."* Lots of swapping helped us accumulate enough matching fabric for our planned projects.

My close family lived in the country and grew most of our food. We had no threat of starvation. However, cash money was hard to come by, and there were things we could not grow, like sugar, salt, and thread. My grandmother traded eggs for these. We did not have to buy gas. We rode in a buggy pulled by the plow horse.

When I was ready for college, my mother and I secured three scholarships. These came from DuPonts, from percentage of orders sent to Montgomery Ward on my Scholarship Blanks, and from the National Youth Administration—a work fund set up by Franklin D. Roosevelt.

Several years later we were deeply into WW II and it is said that it lifted the economy out of the Depression. What an irony!

•••••

**Mitchell Forest Lyman** of Chapel Hill was born April 1, 1918. A member of the North Carolina Poetry Society, the North Carolina Haiku Society, the North Carolina Writers' Network, and the Friday Noon Poets, she has one book of poetry; *"Kaleidoscope,"* published, and has published in various anthologies and won one first in a poetry competition.

# Cousin Walt

## Joan F. Long

Walter Hayes, better known as Walt, was my Mother's cousin on her Mother's side of the family tree.

He was a handsome man. Tall, with wavy black hair and deep blue eyes. Always dressed in a suit, even if it was not very clean, a dirty white shirt, and a faded necktie.

I recall him coming to our house late in the evening, just in time to eat supper and spend the night. He never owned a home, a horse and buggy, or an automobile. He must have learned early in life how to get by without working. My Father said that he was the laziest man that he had ever known.

However, Walt was a very talented person who could converse on any subject, whether it was politics, foreign trade, or the weather. I believe he was well educated, as he enjoyed using big words to impress people. We children loved to see him come, as he would teach us songs such as "Jimmy Cracked Corn, and I Don't Care." He would take newspaper and cut it somehow and pull it so it became a Jacob's ladder as mentioned in the Bible. He could cut paper that became a long string of dolls, each perfect and looking as if they were holding hands. His hands were adept at making things with string. As hard as I would try, I never could master Job's coffin and other things he would create. His penmanship was truly excellent. Many people asked him to write in their Bibles. I still have the Hayes Family Bible that has names in it written by him.

He would spend the night in any home that would ask him in and sometimes where he was not very welcome. One lady in the community told of his spending the night in her home. In two or three days after he was gone, she smelled an odor coming from one of her bureau drawers in the room where he had slept. Thinking perhaps it was a dead rat, she cautiously opened the drawer. This was before most country folk had indoor plumbing. However, Walt had invented a commode out of the ladies large bowl that was part of her antique bowl and pitcher set, by urinating in it and closing it up in the drawer. He was even too lazy to pour it outside.

Walt Hayes was one of the sophisticated "street people" as we would refer to him now. He had life all figured out without putting out much effort, and because he was family, our door was always open. Growing up in Randolph County, North Carolina, during the days of the Great Depression was an interesting experience when one had cousins of his caliber that visited two or three times a year

●●●●●

**Joan Fields Long** was brought up in Randolph County, North Carolina, but has lived with her husband Cecil in Chapel Hill, North Carolina, for forty years. Mother of two and grandmother of six, she has been writing since she was a little girl. She is a member of the Christian Writers Group.

# The Trip Home

## Libby Lefkowitz

*We climbed the stairs to the second balcony, Poppa and I—to the cheap seats where it was dark and scary. But I loved watching Charlie Chaplin eating his leather shoe because he was so hungry. The scene where the cabin is tottering over a snowy cliff makes me laugh.*

• • • •

It was almost dark by the time Uncle Yancy and Booth checked out of the Town and Country Motor Inn. In the lobby Booth hugged Elvira and shook hands with Asbury.

Sue Ellen and Bill had already left for Greensboro. Uncle Robert, with daughter Janey and her two little girls, were well on their way to Philadelphia in the Plymouth Voyager. Freidel could tell, by the way Booth touched the car, that he coveted the navy blue van—wished it were his to haul around his keyboard and sound system from gig to gig.

Aunt Zilda showed signs of nervousness. She was anxious to get on the road. She didn't like Yancy's having to drive at night, especially on an interstate.

Admittedly, he had had a big weekend, but at two o'clock he went back to their room and took a nap.

"You turn right here, Uncle Yancy."

Booth was directing him to the same highway they had used to reach the motel. By now, the inside of Yancy's car felt like a home from which there was no escape.

"Yeah, Bubba, I recognize that car lot."

At the intersection a block–long Ford dealership shone with colored pennants flapping along a taut high wire.

A tolerable stillness fell over the auto, except for an occasional yawn, as they sat together less anxious now because Booth knew the way.

Headlights from oncoming traffic flickered on and off their faces as the Dodge sped along.

The intermittent lumination triggered memories— other times, in other automobiles; perhaps Mary, Zilda and Yancy were thinking of their own marriages.

Freidel sat on Booth's lap, reminded of her childhood, her place in the hierarchy of the Katz family. Sitting in a moving vehicle, for an extended time, was hypnotic, encouraging this pastime of remembering.

• • • •

It was hard to separate fact from fiction, but she knew at an early age that Poppa was no earthshaker. He had been worn out by his bad business deals and tragedy in his personal life. She knew Momma had turned her heart away from him long before her own birth.

She can still remember Poppa's face when he came home sick with fatigue. He had left the house at dawn—working with a gang of men shoveling rocks onto roadbeds in Roosevelt, New Jersey. Roosevelt was a new town, not far from Trenton, named after the president voted into office on the New Deal, a platform meant to pull the country out of the Depression. The work detail was known as WPA. Freidel knew well what the letters represented.

Did her adolescent behavior now have anything to do with the hard times? Or was it that she was a middle child, or did it have to do with Momma's disappointments?

Momma had a beautiful home on Center Street when she first married Poppa, who had one of the first Model T Fords in their neighborhood. Poppa was prosperous. He bought cattle at farm auctions and sold the animals to the *schlechthaus* in Trenton where a rabbi, trained in ritual slaughter, recited a blessing or prayer over each creature he put to death.

When farmers raised fewer cattle and when meat packing companies emerged and swallowed up little businesses like Poppa's, he could no longer make the mortgage payments. Armour, Swift, Eckrich, Hormel, and Smithfield Packing Company had won out. Poppa moved the family to a rental that had no heat except a coal stove in the kitchen.

Freidel wanted answers.

Momma and Poppa had had four children. The oldest died on his eighth birthday, a few months into the Depression. Each blamed the other for his death that began as a cold in the ear. Momma said it was because Arthur was delicate and needed to sleep in a warm room, especially in winter when it was snowing. Poppa said Momma needed to take better care of their children, that she had been neglectful and was not smart enough to raise children. Freidel remembers that he took over the chore of bathing them when they were sent home with lice. Unfortunately, there was never enough hot water because coal was expensive. About then the family moved in with Grandma Katz, Momma's mother, to save money on rent. Grandma

Katz owned her own home. Grandma helped with the cooking too.

When Freidel was born, Lakey became the older child. Big sister, Momma, and Poppa had wanted a boy. Freidel was meant to be the son to replace Arthur.

One night when Freidel was little, Poppa had taken her with him in his dump truck to Atlantic City to pick up a set of scales he had bought from Axelrod's brother. How happy she was to be alone with Poppa! He was pleased because he could sell the scales in Trenton for a profit.

Axelrod was the Katz family's friend who drove a laundry truck. Every other Friday, Freidel remembered seeing him come to the door with a brown paper parcel. He would pick up Grandma Katz's bundle of dirty linen. A large, clean, white, cotton bag with a drawstring was always included in the parcel. Mr. Axelrod would coo at Freidel, pinch her cheek, while Grandma counted out money she owed. He would pick up the net sack, wave, and be off again.

Grandma was the *baleboosteh* of the household. She knew how to deal with the wet wash. Maybe that's what bothered Momma—living with Grandma, doing what Grandma said.

Momma kept on crying for Arthur. She wanted a baby boy and Poppa finally relented. Three years later Joey was born. With Joey in his wicker carriage, with her and Lakey holding onto its sides, Momma hurried down many streets to a big office. This they knew to be the *Relief Building*, where they stood in a long line waiting to be given chits to be used at the bakery, the butcher shop, and the produce store on Market Street.

Momma took them shopping with her, and she handed the storekeeper the piece of paper while he filled a grocery bag. Sometimes Mr. Kohn took out a big ledger and wrote Momma's name on a page lined with numbers and dollars and cents signs.

Poppa was always angry. He'd come home from his WPA job on the roads, covered with gravel dust, and be so tired he'd fall asleep on the living room rug. He kept an old calfskin moneybag filled with a few coins in the back part of the bedroom closet, and he would yell like crazy if Momma took out a few pennies to buy candy for them.

*"Vas has tu getun mit de gelt?"* he would shriek, and he wouldn't stop hollering until Momma would lie down on their bed in a dead faint. He would grab her nose and pull hard while we children looked on and cried for him to stop.

One day as Momma was washing curtains in the upstairs bathtub, Poppa got into a big fight with a neighbor—a colored man worse off than Poppa. Mr. Jefferson drank so he wouldn't have to notice how unhappy and hungry his children were. Momma said his oldest child was more than unhappy. Claude was angry. Claude was the reason Poppa was out in the middle of the street taking a beating.

The boy had picked up bricks and hurled them into neighbors' houses. When he knocked out our living room window, Poppa went outside to settle the score. Freidel remembered running upstairs and begging Momma to rescue Poppa. Poppa was a small man. Mr. Jefferson was twice his size.

• • • •

Yancy interrupted Freidel's reverie. "Anybody have to go? Ah'm gonna get off here. All right, Ma?"

"Good idea, I do need to use the little girl's room, Yancy," Mary answered.

"You have your medicine with you, haven't you, Ma?" Yancy did not want to go back—once was enough.

"Indeed I have," she said.

Two hours had gone by and they were just a short distance from the town of Dillon and the North Carolina border. By the time they got back to the car, it was completely dark. Riding would be less tedious, since they had had a break.

Booth brushed the back of Freidel's neck with his lips and whispered, "Let me get Yancy on 95, then we can mess around a bit—it's gonna be a long night."

Both Zilda and Yancy stared beyond the windshield to the white line in the middle of the road, unaware of backseat shenanigans. One could not fool Mary, though; and not just because she was seated next to Booth and Freidel. The grandmother saw firsthand how much better Bubba was with Freidel around, tomfoolery or no.

"Now don't you fall asleep on me," said Zilda. She reached over, slapped Yancy's face. She heard muffled titters in the rear. Freidel had forgotten all about her dark thoughts.

"Ah, Lawd! He'll run off the road!" (It was Mary's voice).

"Zilda, ah'm not tired—relax—ah got hot coffee right here, where I can drink it if I need it."

Cutting loose was something Zilda could not do. She continued to watch Yancy and peer out into the blackness.

"There's 'South of the Border'." Mary was the first to spot the place. The stretch of road was so well lighted it looked like broad daylight. Booth and Freidel blinked at the madcap scene, their eyes adjusting to the brightness, as Yancy slowed up for a last look. They all rubbernecked as the graffiti on the pink buildings slid by. Mary wanted to say more.

"That was a lovely weddin'. That sure is a big Navy place Elmo's at in Charleston and I liked our guest room." She had shared the motel room with Yancy and Zilda.

"My bed was soft and comfy, and all that food, my, my—I hope Ruby Ann planned to get all that leftover food home. Didja see all the presents she got?"

Mary's grandchild had displayed her wedding gifts on a table at the Officer's Club.

"Sue Ellen brought them all back to Ruby Ann's—food and all, Ma." Zilda spoke up, eyes never leaving the road.

"Now don't you go worrying 'bout that, Ma" Yancy said.

"She got so many lovely dishes. They all had the same pattern, I do believe," Mary continued. "All those flowers in church, and weren't you clever to catch the bouquet, Freidel, 'n Bubba the garter? You and Bubba will be next!"

The last remark prompted Zilda to turn around, startled by the two laughing fit to burst.

"Don't know why you think that's so funny. You act like you're married already." Grandma couldn't help teasing her grandson.

Freidel looked toward her in the dark. She was truly a remarkable woman.

● ● ● ●

When Mary Wilkes's husband died unexpectedly from an aneurysm, the family was certain it was the result of carrying feedbags to put on trucks at the local Ralston Purina loading dock on Fowler Street. He started at 7 a.m. and finished at 7 p.m., six days a week.

Mary learned quickly in 1937 how to keep her family going. It was either that or starve. Mary took over. She was an excellent piano teacher, but now that so many folks had more pressing needs and could no longer afford the dollar she charged for lessons, she reduced her price to twenty–five cents. It meant she had to double up on the number of pupils she accepted. It also meant she had to find a second job.

Woolworth's Five–and–Ten hired her to play piano in the sheet music department. Zilda and Asbury would have to get their own dinners, but at least there was food on the table. Their little house on East Main Street was lit by kerosene lamps. Booth's father and Aunt Zilda would go to the hardware store together with a large tin can, filled with fuel, which they carried home in Asbury's *Radio Flyer*.

● ● ● ●

Freidel admired Mary. She had aged without a trace of self–pity, showed courage and resourcefulness in raising Zilda and Asbury, who treated her not unkindly, proud she had the interest to give back to her community, keep her sense of humor. She considered it her duty to God to play the piano in church, entertain the sick in nursing homes, the local hospital, and at senior centers in downtown

Durham. These things she did, but it was how she responded to people that made her so special—how she treated them.

Mary went over all that had happened during the last two days, chuckling softly to herself so as not to disturb the two lovebirds. "Asbury wasn't gonna make me take off mah coat if'n I didn't want to! That weddin' cake was so delicious."

Freidel could see that both Yancy and Booth, dressed in their best, liked Mary's recounting of the weekend's events that were a milestone in her long life. Mary's voice was soothing.

"Grandmom, how did you like the dancing?"

"I did. I meant to tell you what a good idea it was. I love you, Bubba." She leaned over and stroked his head. "Bubba, that music of yours made everyone so happy. Little Dee Dee just hung on to me for dear life. That sweet child danced my feet off."

She'd have to mark down and name all the family in her journal when she got home. It was a diary Mary kept on her bookshelf, starting from the time of the stock market crash.

Yancy had his coffee, found his way to Chapel Hill wide awake. Booth took Grandma's hand when they got to the Manning Drive intersection.

"Do you know where we are, Granny?" he said.

"Yes, son, we're almost home."

**Libby C. Lefkowitz**, whose husband was a physicist, writes romance novels. She is an environmental activist and joined the North Carolina Society for Ethical Culture early in its formation.

# Lean Years on a Wisconsin Truck Farm

## Violet Krall

I was the youngest of six children in the Lutz family. We lived on a family truck farm outside the city limits of Milwaukee, Wisconsin. My parents were second generation immigrants from Germany. My father learned the truck farming business from his father.

The farm, Wildrose Farm, occupied twenty acres, most of which was devoted to raising vegetables and the remainder for growing fodder for the animals—two cows, two Morgan horses, and chickens. Each spring my father would purchase two pigs. In January they were slaughtered and the meat was canned, smoked for ham and bacon, or made into various sausages: bratwurst, summer sausage, and blood sausage.

The horses were an integral part of the farm as they were used to plow the fields, pull the wagons, for family transportation, for pulling the wagon to peddle the produce and to convey it to the market in Milwaukee. In later years, the horses gave way to a Ford truck for delivering vegetables, but my father continued to plow the fields with his horses until he retired.

Life was never easy. Everyone in the family had to work in the fields and do his or her part. My first chore was to gather eggs, a cash crop which sold for about twenty–five cents a dozen. I had to reach under the setting hen's warm feathers for the egg. All went well unless the hen objected and would peck my fingers. I felt proud that I was being productive and a help to the family.

Later, there were other tasks such as churning butter. My mother would pour the milk into a bowl and ladle off the cream. The churn we used required a cranking motion, not the type that used an up–and–down plunger. This was a tiresome job which lasted for about half an hour to one hour for butter to form. The final product was shaped into eight to ten one–pound bricks, wrapped in parchment paper and sold for about twenty–five cents a pound.

Later, I was able to seed onions, a difficult job, to shuck the dried corn cobs to be stored in the corn crib, and to take the dried corn off the cobs for the chicken feed. Another of my jobs was to carry buckets of water from the pump into the house, for we did not have water piped into the house until after I had left home when I married. Of course, that meant we did not have an indoor bathroom until that time either. One other task falling to me was carrying firewood into the house from the woodshed.

During the growing season, Monday and Tuesdays were devoted to gathering the vegetables and getting them ready for the Milwaukee wholesale market on Wednesdays and Fridays, where the produce was purchased by grocery stores and restaurants. Sometimes, I had to stay home from school to help get the vegetables ready for market. This made me very unhappy because I liked school. The rest of the produce was sold to city customers when my father would go through the streets selling vegetables, butter, eggs, buttermilk, chickens, and flowers we raised, such as gladioli.

The business was going well until the effect of the Depression came. I remember one incident which announced the appearance of the Great Depression. I was seven or eight at the time. One of my brothers and I prepared green onions for the market, involving washing all the dirt off the onions and bunching them. That day when my father returned from the market, he first stopped and threw the unsold onions on the manure pile—all he had taken to the market except two bunches. I wanted to cry. All that work, and no one wanted to buy them.

My father then made the decision that he could not afford to take his produce to the market, since he had to pay a fee for a booth and spend two days a week to sell to a shrinking market. He changed his retail route to include a more affluent area of Milwaukee. This proved profitable. After a while, he had good, reliable customers, and it did not require his going from house to house. When I was fourteen years old, I accompanied my father on the truck and went to the homes of the customers to take their orders.

During the summer, we also sold berries which were in season. Vegetables were sold by the piece, such as tomatoes, three for five cents, or a bushel for fifty cents or three bushels for a dollar. Carrots were five to ten cents a bunch and radishes, three bunches for ten cents. A small cabbage sold for five cents, cucumbers for five cents a piece; small gherkins for pickles went for one hundred for a dollar.

There were still many times when the production of the farm was greater than the sales, and in such cases the family had to eat what was left. The chickens did not know there was a Depression and would very often lay more eggs than would meet the needs of our customers and our own, so we ate a lot of eggs.

I took my lunch to school and was joined by classmates who lived at a distance too great to allow them to go home for lunch. Once, as I was beginning to eat my egg salad sandwich, the girl in the seat next to mine said, "You must be rich."

I asked her why she said that, and she said that they could not afford eggs. I offered to trade with her—her peanut butter and jelly sandwich for my egg salad. I thought it was a good trade, since we did not have enough cash to buy peanut butter. What a treat!

My city relatives often traded with my family. A number of them, forced to take relief from the city, received weekly allotments of nonperishable foods. They would trade some of them, which they had in excess, for fresh vegetables. Once in a while, we received peanut butter in exchange.

Naturally, we did not have a need for food, and my mother made over clothes for me. What we did not have was cash for our crops and to amass enough funds to pay the mortgage and the taxes. If the taxes were not paid, the county could take your property. If you did not make the mortgage payments, the bank could foreclose. This had happened to a number of local farmers. In two cases, there had been nothing left for the family.

When I was thirteen, I was trusted with a wad of bills, something over three hundred dollars, to take to the county court house in Milwaukee to pay the property taxes. I had to walk over a mile to the streetcar and then transfer twice to get there. When I proudly handed the wad to the teller, he made a comment to one of his fellow workers about the fact that my parents let a thirteen–year–old girl carry that amount of money through the city. I was rather insulted by that. Very helpful during the Great Depression was our being allowed to pay only the interest on the mortgage.

I do not remember that we had any great medical emergencies to require a doctor during that time. The Raleigh man would come to call on us at intervals to sell liniments, ointments (i.e., tar ointment), cough medicine, and Vick's Vaporub. If an accident involved cuts, cobwebs were used to bind the wound and lend their antiseptic marvels of healing. My grandmother had great knowledge of folk remedies that she shared with us. Even though she was of the Lutheran faith, she even resorted to Holy Water. She put some on my birthmark and said words that I did not understand. Eventually, the mark disappeared, and I often wondered if it disappeared because of the blessed water or on its own.

Yes, those were tough times, but there were some good times. Christmas was one. There were not many gifts, but the Christmas tree made up for that. We had a parlor which was not heated. During the winter, to conserve heat, it was closed off from the rest of the house with sliding doors. On Christmas Eve we all gathered in the dining room. Then my mother would open the doors to reveal a beautiful fir tree with a great many blazing candles, which transformed the room to a wonderland. Even the Great Depression could not take that from us.

Saturdays were a real pleasure—baking day! The house would be full of the wonderful aroma of baking bread and coffee cakes. My mother was a great baker. To eat her productions made any waiting worthwhile.

I had no close friends, so I had to entertain myself. That is when I began to keep a diary, which I have continued until this day and will continue as long as I am able.

I did many of the things children my age did, such as playing jacks and reading, and enjoying playing cards with friends. I even thought up a feeding experiment in which I offered various vegetables to our cows. They appeared to like whatever I fed them, except for the onions. Those they refused.

The years of the Great Depression taught many lessons which I remember well. I needed to put them into practice during the years of helping to put my husband through college and graduate school. They helped me in raising a family of five children.

•••••

**Violet Krall** is the mother of five and has grandchildren and great grandchildren. She was employed by the Department of Epidemiology, UNC: Chapel Hill. She retired to Chatham County where she continues to enjoy gardening.

# Hard Times

## Donald Elliott

"Times are really hard, right now, Mom," he said, sitting at her kitchen table, sipping a cup of coffee. "We have a long weekend at the plant, but I can't afford to take the family on a trip to the beach."

Anne looked at her son, Jerome, now thirty–five and the father of two. She lived on her pension and didn't have the money to give him. He wasn't really asking, she knew, but he would have taken it if somehow she had offered. "Hard times," she mused, thinking back to a time, half remembered, half recalled from stories she had been told later.....

Anne sat at the kitchen table in the cabin where she lived with her mother, father, and older brother. She was eating the last of the oatmeal, with a little milk from the old cow which they kept in a stable nearby. It was unusually cold for so early in November, but they were snug in their cabin, way back in a mountain cove, a cheery fire burning in the big fireplace. She was just five, a little pixie of a girl, her dark hair trimmed even with the bottom of her ears in back and cut in bangs just above her eyebrows in front. Her bright eyes looked out beneath them, like coals from the fireplace, her daddy said.

"Daddy's coming," she said quietly. "He's happy. He's singing about the pony."

Her mother, Dorothy, stopped her dusting and stood straight, listening for the first sounds of her husband's approach. Joe, her brother, stopped his whittling and listened, too. They didn't hear anything, but they knew that

Anne had ears as sharp as any animal; and if she heard him, he was coming. Grampa had always said that she had pixie ears and could hear something before it happened.

The little girl hummed the tune and then mouthed the words, along with her father:

"Go to sleep and rest, Dear Lad, for on the morrow
You will ride your pony."

Joe smiled because now he could hear his father too, and then Dorothy could. They looked out the window and saw him making his way up the hill, a sack slung over his shoulder, his old floppy hat almost hiding his face, the last words of the old Scottish ballad fading from his lips. As he neared the porch, they went out to meet him.

"Hello, Dorie," he said, "and Joe. And here's my little angel." Scooping Anne up in his free arm, he urged them all back inside, out of the cold. Putting down the sack and his daughter, he gave his wife a little hug, for he didn't believe in public displays of affection. Dorothy could see in his eyes that he was glad to see her, though.

"Well, I did real well," John said, as he took off his hat and coat and stood before the fire to warm his hands. "I got three days' work at the sawmill. Times are hard for many people, but we have what we need, for now". Walking over to the table, he opened the sack and took out the contents, one package at a time. "Dried beans," he said, "and some fat–back. Flour and salt, sugar and more oatmeal for Annie. Sweets for the sweet," as he handed small bags of peppermints to Joe and Anne, and an even smaller one of chocolates to his wife. "I stopped by the mill and got Alvin to grind a bushel of corn meal and send it up to us, so soon I want to smell that bread baking." He pulled out several more bags and cans; then he took out the last item and held it up.

"For you, Dorie, special," he said, as she looked at his prize, a large can of peaches, her favorite treat in the whole world. She went over to him and hugged him, as he watched her shyly.

"Yes, for some, times are hard, but we have all we need," he repeated softly as he smiled proudly at his little family.....

Anne came back to the present, humming a little tune which Jerome had heard so many times over the years, about the pony, and he knew that she was thinking about her father.

"I've got to go, Mom," he said, rising and putting on his coat. "Do you need anything?"

"No, Son," she said, softly. "For many, times are hard, but I have all that I need."

•••••

Born in November of 1932, **Donald Elliott** was aware only of the recovery from the Great Depression. He lived in several small towns in the Piedmont area of North Carolina, in six different homes before the age of ten. His life revolved around what was the major industry in North Carolina at that time: cotton manufacturing. He remembers the start of World War II, which brought an end to the Depression.

# Trap

## Beverly Chappel

We used to play in the old house. Our parents had warned us not to, of course, but in the devious ways of childhood we managed to slip over to the old Cranshaw place in the early afternoons when mothers were "resting" or in the delicious summer dusk when parents were relaxed and contented with the distant sound of childish voices.

The Cranshaw place sat on a block by itself. The Cranshaws had been well–to–do once and able to pay taxes on the entire block. Now high weeds and over–grown shubbery surrounded the house itself. So far as I knew, no one had any idea what had happened to the Cranshaws. The house has been empty for years. It was the depth of the Depression, and heaven knew who had the actual title to the land and the house.

The house had trap doors. It is the only house I was ever in which actually had trap doors, just like the trap doors in fiction. They were ingenious, hardly discernible in the broad planks of the flooring. Part of the game we played was to find them. They opened into closets on the floor below, or to spaces between walls. One space had a ladder which led down into darkness, below the house itself. None of us had the courage to explore that depth.

The house had been built before the Civil War, and the story was that the owner had abolitionist sympathies, and the trap doors had been used to hide run–away slaves. It must have been a beautiful house in its time. The entrance hall was wide and spacious, with a beautiful spiral stairway leading to the second story. Rooms on either side of the wall were gracious even in their barren desertion, with floor–length windows (panes now broken) looking out on what would have been a broad, green lawn at one time. There were many rooms, and the kitchen was tucked on the end of a long el at the back. There was a breezeway between the kitchen and the rest of the house, so I suppose the kitchen must have been a separate building at one time, in the traditional Old South manner.

Our parents were wary of our playing around the old house because it was rumored wandering tramps used the place as shelter now and then. One evening my father and I went over the house and explored it. We saw a pile of old blankets in a corner, and my father explained that they were probably used by tramps, and for this reason my friends and I better stay away. We didn't.

But actually, it isn't the house I wanted to tell you about. It's the Munroes. They came to live in the old Cranshaw place. One morning a decrepit truck turned into the over–grown drive; through the weeds we could see people milling about, hear children's shouts, furniture being unloaded. Our mothers were stunned. Little housework was done that morning. Women gathered on lawns to look and to surmise who in the world would try to live in that place. By night, flickering light from lamps (the place had never been wired for electricity) came from the block which had always been dark at night. Even fathers became curious about the new people.

The Munroes seem to consist of a faded, thin mother and five children—all with black hair and blue eyes. Myra Jean was the oldest. She was eighteen, and she had come to town to be a stenographer at the railroad station. Railroads were one business which seemed to be still operable during the Depression. The Munroes did not venture off their block, but they went to work on that old house as if they were a public works department in itself. Even the smallest child worked. They cut weeds with kitchen knives, since they had no other cuttings tools. It was odd that in that friendly community, no one offered them the loan of tools. People seemed to be just watching, getting used to the house being occupied, and wondering what kind of people would live there. In small towns there is, after all, a relentless—though intangible—caste system.

There was an old well on the place, and we could hear the creak of the pulley. When the weeds were cleared enough, we could see children going back and forth, and we knew why the people seemed to be using so much water. They carried pans, pails, buckets, and rags. They were scrubbing the inside of the house. The rest of that summer, people speculated but made no overtures. We children wondered if the new family had found the trap doors.

But when school started, the Munroes joined us as we passed their house. And in the inimitable way of children, the Munroes became part of our way of life. They were quiet children, but not stupid. After school, one by one, they would join us for a game of hopscotch on our driveway. Then as the days passed, we would drift over to their house and sit on the steps with the Munroes. Sometimes we played "tag" in and out of the ancient trees.

People in the neighborhood had been watching, listening, and of course, talking. Some conclusions had been drawn. Myra Jean was the sole support of the family. Mr. Munroe was a mystery unsolved. Men brought home news to their wives. So and so had been in the station, and the word was that Myra Jean was a good stenographer. Then a few men whose businesses were in no state to afford a stenographer of their own began to go to Myra Jean to get a letter or a contract typed. When she was not on duty, Myra Jean gradually became a public stenographer—not in a big way, but enough to give her a little extra money.

We saw Myra Jean only as she walked to and from work. She walked fast, with her head up, and she looked straight ahead. Our mothers were torn between admiring her for supporting her mother and the children and resenting her for being so "stuck up."

Still, no one called on Mrs. Munroe. It was as though the block that held the old Cranshaw place was an island, and none of the women in the neighborhood ventured to row across and say "hello." The Munroes were still questionable. We children understood this, in vague and devious ways. For instance, we asked the Munroe children if they had found trap doors. They only looked at us seriously with their wide blue eyes and said nothing. It was the silence that bothered us. If they knew, why not say so? If they didn't know what a trap door was, why not ask? Why keep so still about it? But in the face of that wide, serious stare, we found ourselves suddenly changing the subject, not knowing why... just feeling, suddenly, "different."

Then there was Mrs. Munroe. We never saw her except from a distance. When we were at their house, she stayed inside. Other mothers came and went when children congregated around a certain house. If children were on the steps, they were always being asked to move aside so a woman could get through as she carried a wastepaper basket out to trash can, or a load of washing to the line. Other mothers even brought drinks of water on request, or proffered crisp cookies right out of the oven. Mothers were just part and parcel of life. We never thought much about them, so long as they were around. It was the fact that Mrs.

Munroe was never around that gave us a slight feeling of uneasiness.

Myra Jean's salary, even supplemented by her public stenographer chores, had to go a long way. We heard our parents comment on this fact of economics time and again. It was obvious that there was a gap between the need and the fulfillment at the Munroe house. The "Depression" was an expression we were all familiar with. It was something parents worried about and fathers talked to other fathers about. It curtailed the movies we could see and the number of ice creams we could buy at Mr. Phillips' drugstore. It had something to do with the fact that I could not have a new outfit to wear when I appeared on a P.T.A. program. But we still had adequate clothes, food, and school supplies. It was soon obvious that the Munroes did not have these things in adequate amounts.

One late afternoon, I was sitting on the back step of the old Cranshaw house (it had never become, in neighborhood parlance, the Munroe house) with one of the Munroe girls when a voice called from the kitchen, "Susan, come get these potatoes and peel them for supper." Susan went into the house and came out with a pan of potatoes and a knife. Slowly, deliberately, without explanation, she began to peel. I watched with fascination. The peelings which fell into the pan were the thinnest I had ever seen. My mother had often berated me for wasting half the potato when I tried to help in the kitchen. But I was breathless with admiration as I watched Susan. "What are you having for supper?" I asked. "Potatoes," the dark-haired child answered. "What else?" I persisted. Susan lifted her eyes from the knife and looked at me with her wide, serious eyes. She said nothing.

That night at the dinner table I told my mother about the skill of Susan Munroe. My parents exchanged looks, and my mother's eyes were dark when she said, "Poor little thing. They have to learn not to waste a bit of food. I expect that is all they have for supper." I tried to imagine what it would be like to have only potatoes to eat. The Munroes sure were different.

When cold weather came, people audibly worried about what the Munroes would do for warmth. The old house had fireplaces aplenty, but no one knew how safe the chimneys were. A truck had delivered a load of cord wood, and we could see smoke spiraling from a chimney, and the women hoped the place wouldn't burn down, but I don't remember anyone actually doing anything about the situation. During the coldest weather one of the Munroe girls was always sick. As we walked to school we commented on this. Then one day I noticed that the coats the girls wore were always the same two coats, but they weren't always the same two Munroe girls in them. One day as we started to school, I saw the "sick" Munroe child at the window waving to her sisters as they left the house. She didn't look sick at all. And then I knew. The three Munroe school girls had only two winter coats between them. So one girl had to be sick in cold weather. When spring arrived, no one was sick any more at the Munroe house. I didn't feel like saying anything.

I'm not sure why I kept quiet about the girls and the coats. I must have been very proud to have figured it out, and my impulse was to tell. Yet I didn't. I guess I was just intimidated by the Munroe reaction to any remark which reflected on them personally: that wide, steady stare and absolute silence.

Reticence was not a quality confined to the younger Munroes. Myra Jean was reported to be as efficient as ever, but her quiet manner was causing speculation in town. She seemed to have no friends. She was cool and businesslike even to girls her own age. Young men who had been interested, as ever, in the "new girl in town" came away from the station uneasy, lacking confidence in their overtures. Myra Jean was never rude, but she was cool and silent. In a world adapted to noise, few people realize the effectiveness of silence. The Munroes did.

Then in the still, shimmering heat of a summer day, we saw old Doctor Yeoman's car stop at the Cranshaw place. He would make house calls when the young doctors were too busy. A short while after he left, Les Small came with this hearse which doubled as an ambulance, and took away a small form on a stretcher. The trouble with Les' vehicle was that it caused confusion: people never knew whether he was in the way to the hospital or to the morgue. This time he turned on West Street toward the hospital. One of the Munroe children had meningitis.

Our mothers brought us in and scrubbed us. They warned us to be sure to wash our hands before eating and told us we would have to get lots of sleep and that we were not to go near the Cranshaw place. For days we sat subdued and mumbled about meningitis which we understood not at all. Was it akin to a plague?

The Munroe boy was in the hospital a long time. Our parents wondered who would pay the bills. Myra Jean walked to and from work with her head high. The Munroe children did not leave their block. Then rumors started. Myra Jean had been seen in a neighboring town with Jim Hornbeck, who was a well–to–do "rounder" who owned a lot of bottom land. Would Hornbeck marry her? Not Jim, hooted our fathers. And why were they afraid to be seen in our own town, our mothers asked indignantly.

And then someone saw Myra Jean leave the station after dark one night and get into a parked car. Someone was sure it was Tom Woods' car, with Tom at the wheel. Someone else knew Myra Jean had been doing some work for Tom. But Tom had a wife and kids, everybody knew.

Then one man told his wife he had been hunting with Guy Smoke and by God, if old Guy didn't keep a roll of toilet paper in the trunk of this car. When he had teased Guy, asking what was the matter with a good broad leaf, Guy had grinned and said toilet paper had many uses, and girls weren't partial to leaves. When Guy's wife told this one, her eager listener remembered that she had passed the station a few weeks ago and seen Guy Smoke leaning over the desk of Myra Jean Munroe.

As winter approached, a stove was delivered to the old house, and a load of coal was dumped near the back door. None of the Munroe children were sick that winter, unless you counted the small meningitis victim who was still recuperating. Myra Jean still walked to and from work and was still reported to be just as efficient. But everyone knew now that Myra Jean had found a profitable side line.

In the spring, workmen came to replace broken window panes in the drafty house. They rebuilt the back steps, and there was pounding inside the house. Yard boys cut all the weeds down, so at last the entire house was visible. Susan Munroe didn't peel potatoes outside any more. The children grew as children will. They seemed to look neater, and their clothes were not so faded. We had heard our parents mention Myra Jean so much, and in such guarded tones, that as children we were highly curious about the older sister. But when we ventured some remark calculated to bring Myra Jean into the conversation, we were met invariably with the disquieting Munroe stare and silence.

The years went on, and once in a while people would call the old Cranshaw place the Munroe place. Somewhere in its depths, Mrs. Munroe worked and let out seams and turned coats and patched knees so that her growing children would be adequately clothed. Once, on the way home from school, we even went into the front room to see the little boy. We had been told that he was learning to draw, and his sisters had talked about his drawings so much that we were eager to see them. They were pinned to the walls and scattered over furniture. The room looked large with its high ceilings, but it had the feeling of being lived in, and we felt quite comfortable. We found we could not identify this room with the great barren chamber we used to explore.

When I was through high school, I left the town and went back only for visits. My mother wrote that Mrs. Munroe had died, but Myra Jean still seemed to manage the family. One time when I was back, I caught a glimpse of her at the station. She was pounding her typewriter. She raised her eyes—probably feeling my stare—and looked at me quietly. She still walked back and forth to work, with her gaze straight ahead. The town had grown used to the stories of her nightly activities. She was seen here and there with one man after another. "Everybody knows what she is!" spat out the women in wedded righteousness.

Finally, I was called back to my father's funeral. As my taxi pulled up to our house, I glanced west and saw a large brick and steel building, sitting amidst landscaped lawns, on the old Cranshaw block. When the chores of death were disposed of, I sat with my mother and commented on the change in the neighborhood. "Oh, yes," said mother, "that place was torn down last year just after your father got sick."

"But what happened to the Munroes?"

My mother looked concerned and then started talking in that tone which people always reserved for the Munroes. It must have been tone of voice, I reflected, that made me aware years ago that the Munroes were somehow questionable. It seems that the youngest child, through school, had left, and still Myra Jean was efficient at the station. Then one morning she did not come to work. Someone went to the house and could not get in. When she did not appear the next day, the constable was notified, and the authorities broke into the house and searched. Myra Jane was not there.

The bank which had owned the house through the Depression days sold the land to a farm cooperative. In due time, the house was razed and the new building put up. When the house was torn down, they found Myra Jean. Her skeleton was at the bottom of a shaft that ran from the second floor to a subterranean passageway, long caved in, which had once run from the main house to the kitchens. The sheriff said she must have fallen through a trap door, so clever the searchers had overlooked it. It was just as wide as the old floor boards, with the hinges underneath, and a small groove just big enough for finger tips. The groove was under the edge of a tattered rug—"Who could imagine such a thing," said my mother. Well, I thought, at least one of the Munroes knew about the trap door. I remember that one well. As children we had not dared explore its dark depths.

I remained silent.

•••••

Beverly Chappell holds a Masters in Education from Syracuse University and taught high school English for twenty years. In 1971 she spent a sabbatical year in England. She retired in 1980 and relocated to Durham, North Carolina.

# Who Am I?

## Madeline Lennert

During the Great Depression era, Thomas K. Lennert found that he was having difficulty making the monthly mortgage payments on his home. Through the Federal Housing Authority, it was possible to apply for permission to temporarily pay the monthly interest and defer the principal payments until a later date.

Thomas went down town to make the arrangements, filled out the necessary forms, and presented them to the interviewer, who asked him for identification. He did not drive a car and had no driver's license or any papers on his person which could identify him.

Suddenly, he had an inspiration. He rolled up his sleeve and showed the magnificent tattoo on the underside of his arm which included his full name. "Will this do?" he asked. The interviewer smiled and said, "That will do just fine." The paper work was quickly completed.

Thomas would never have dreamed that a tattoo he had put on his body on a dare when he was a young man would have helped him years later to keep his home for himself, his wife, and five children.

•••••

**Madeline Lennert** was born in Detroit. She has three children, six grandchildren and eight great–grandchildren. She enjoys writing poetry, fiction, and family stories.

# Life As Usual, Except.....

## Sybil Austin Skakle

Life in Hatteras, a small fishing village, where I lived with my mother and father, a brother, and three sisters during what is termed the Great Depression, seemed better in some ways than it had been before. Government decisions made during that time actually helped an area where the economy, dependent on fishing, was already depressed.

In 1936 my father and mother, with her sister and husband and two nieces, took a trip across country to California. When they came back, my father purchased a station wagon, planning to take our immediate family on that trip the following year.

Well, we never got to make that trip. I overheard something about that being due to "the Depression." At ten years, I did not know what they might mean, only that Daddy could not keep his promise to us. We never did make that trip to California as a family.

The worst economic period in United States history was between 1930 and 1940. I read in a resource book: "Depression Generation will be ages 65 or older." I fall in that age group. But it would take a history buff, versed in economics, to explain all the factors that caused it and the factors responsible for our nation's recovery. I am neither.

Daddy said our area felt the effects later than those in other areas. As a little girl, I trusted my intelligent father, who read the newspaper and listened to the radio.

As an adult, with some knowledge of economics, acquired while I was a pharmacy student at Carolina and garnered from living my life, I now understand that when people on the mainland had less and less money to buy fish, the price of fish must have gone down, and the demand for fish would have been depressed. Then our area began to feel the effects of the banks failing on October, 1929.

As I review those years, I expect the Great Depression accounts for gifts acquired with coupons for our Christmas gifts at some point and for my mother sewing doll clothes for all our dolls one year—a most memorable gift and a cherished memory for me, nevertheless.

Naturally, my father was affected in several ways. His nets brought less return, his freight boat carried fewer fish to market, and the fishermen who depended on credit from local merchants for food and other necessities would have had less money to keep their bills paid monthly in his store.

As a little girl, I observed there were many new young men on our island. There was a camp in Buxton where they lived with an older man as their superintendent. He directed their work as they erected sand fences and planted sea oats on our sandy beach to rebuild the shores. Never mind that it took away sand from the shore to cover those fences and build the dunes. Those dunes were leveled in 1936 when a mighty hurricane brought water in from the Pamlico Sound deeper than we had ever seen a tide. Many blamed those " d— sand fences" for keeping the water trapped, not allowing the tide to flow over the island from the Pamlico to the Atlantic Ocean, unhampered.

Older girls dated the boys, who married some of them and ended up staying to become part of our community. Leonard Gillikin married Neva Stowe.

The Civilian Conservation Corps helped a great many young men, some of them our own; Daniel Willis, who owns a dock at Hatteras, joined; Edward Midgett, now deceased, another area business man, served in the CCC for a number of years. There were many others who may have been CCC. I am not sure. Anyway, more money floated around, even though they received only thirty dollars a month.

While the CCC boys were young, between seventeen and twenty–three, and unmarried, the group that came later seemed older and some were married. Their camp was in Trent (later renamed Frisco) woods. Research reveals to me that these men were part of a relief program administered by the Works Project Administration begun in 1935. Men and women who benefited were known to us as WPA workers. Critics among us used to call road workers "shovel leaners," an unkind judgement and probably a bad evaluation of what was happening as they worked to improve roads and did other needed tasks. Some men from Hatteras and six other island villages joined the WPA, too. The work of the WPA benefited our state, from the coast to the Great Smoky Mountains.[1]

1    The New Deal of 1932 expanded work of Public Works
     Administration started under Hoover. The Blue Ridge
     Parkway had been proposed as a pleasure road by Joseph
     Hyde Pratt, University of North Carolina at Chapel Hill,
     as part of his role as supervisor of the North Carolina
     Geological Survey. ( See *The Blue Ridge Parkway* by
     Harley E. Jolly). Construction began in 1933 under the
     Emergency Relief Act as a Public Works Administration
     Project. In 1935 PWA seems to have been put under
     Works Progress Administration (WPA) with Federal
     Emergency Relief Administration and Civil Works
     Administration, when they were deemed unsatisfactory.

Photo Credit: *Visual Character of the Blue Ridge Parkway,*
National Park Service, 1997

Some of these men, too, found wives among our women.
One who became a respected, successful business man was
Scottie Gibson. He married Nettie Robinson and bought
Atlantic View Hotel. For years he and Nettie did most of the
hard work involved in that operation. Willie Newsome
married Nora Stowe, daughter of Nora Stowe, and
prospered as a business man at Hatteras, also. I remember
these two with a great deal of admiration.

Everyone owned his or her home debt free. That station
wagon? Chances are that my father paid cash for it. People
there lived that way. There were no mortgages. Store
owners, like my father, were ones to whom they were
indebted. I am sure that most debtors hated a debt as much
as my father did. They worked hard for what they earned
and were suspicious of government handouts and these
strange young men that benefited from programs Franklin
D. Roosevelt, that man up in the White House, had done
under something called the New Deal. And the Second New
Deal! Even Social Security, begun around 1935 and 1936,
came under their suspicion, deemed "another handout" and
a threat to one's self–respect and pride.

One program under Social Security provided welfare
grants for local distribution and included aid to dependent

children. How merciful that must have been for widowed women with young children. There were several in Hatteras village who would have benefited from that welfare grant section of Social Security. In years since, there have been billions who have received aid.

One innovation I enjoyed and appreciated was school lunches. I cannot remember seeing pinto beans before that. The only ones in Daddy's store were the big white lima beans and navy beans.

Mrs. Theresa Rollinson, whose name is on my birth certificate as a notary public, cooked for the lunch room, located in the back west room of the old school where I had attended first grade. Later Lucy Peele cooked. Cabbage, biscuits, beef stew, those pinto beans, and corn bread were so good and satisfying to my curious appetite, when I stayed to buy my lunch, even though our home was just across the dirt road from our school. The opportunity to work and earn instead of being forever at the mercy of chance and charity helped many among us.

Women like Nora Stowe and Vera Robinson were paid to go into homes to help with children or the ill. Some made mattresses over at the school house and/ or sewed dresses for needy folks. The village buzzed with activity.

Also, the first library was set up in Hatteras School under that program. Vera Robinson took care of the library. She was a widow whose husband had drowned, leaving her with a son and her mother, Mrs. Jean Scott, to care for as well.

I remember that summer I determined to read all the books in the library. As limited as the library must have been and as few volumes as it must have contained, I did not succeed. I took *The Adventures Of Robin Hood* with me when I went to visit my cousin in Wanchese. Many hours were needed for a little girl to read such a large book.

I will never forget Gene Stratton Porter's *A Girl Of The Limberlost*. Maybe that was all I managed that summer. No, I think I did better than that, for Mrs. Vera was a great encourager. To depend on a monthly income rather than sewing projects must have been a blessed relief to her. I can only guess. I was too young to be her confidante.

The "ill wind" that this era most surely seemed for our country and others brought money into our village, money that would not have been there except for the world–wide crisis, known as the Great Depression.

Many European countries had developed social security programs before World War I. While the New Deal ended in 1937, programs and agencies that were begun then still exist. These changed the relationship between the government and the people. We changed. For a little girl like me, the Great Depression seemed not so bad, except I had to be much older before I could afford to visit California.

●●●●●

**Sybil A. Skakle** has been writing prose and poetry since her retirement in 1990 as a hospital pharmacist. She has three sons and nine grandchildren. Her articles have been published in *Our State* and *The Island Breeze*. Her poems have appeared in various publications and anthologies and *Echoes*.

# How Uncle Harry Used the Depression

## Lucy Rodgers Watkins

Uncle Harry was round and jolly and always smiling. He was my grandmother's younger brother, and the only times I saw him were when he and Aunt Josie were visiting at her home in Virginia. Mississippi was too far away to visit. I don't remember their two sons, except for the stories that Harry, Jr., had once seen a man hanged; and Walter when he was ten years old wanted to be either a missionary or a prize fighter when he grew up. He became a scholar, poet, Rhodes scholar, and Princeton University professor, and some years later taught me in graduate school at Louisiana State University. Harry, Jr., moved west, becoming a conservationist, and lived at the base of Mount Shasta. Uncle Harry had to be an unusual man to have raised two such different sons.

Uncle Harry was superintendent of schools in Laurel, Mississippi. He saw to it that all children, black and white, came to school—he did the school census himself every summer—and he knew all of their names and their families. Latin was required of all children; and if they were proficient and had his permission, they were allowed to take Greek.

When the Depression struck the country and Laurel, Mississippi, people lost jobs, didn't have money, and, except for gardens, didn't have enough food. Uncle Harry looked around and assessed Laurel's resources—thick pine and hardwood forests and a broad streak of good, red clay—and figured out its needs—good school buildings and jobs. So he worked with the townspeople to set up a school building project. The red clay was made into bricks, the pines and hardwoods were cut to build interiors, and everybody who needed it had a job. I don't know where the money came from—perhaps the CCC and the WPA, and certainly there was a lot of bartering going on, and a lot of sharing—but when the Depression ended, Laurel, Mississippi, had some of the finest brick school buildings in the state or the South.

•••••

**Lucy Rodgers Watkins**, a native North Carolinian, has published poetry and worked for over thirty–two years in non–profit education and community development programs, at the U.S. Department of Labor, with the Ford Foundation, and as an education lobbyist in Washington.

# The Day I Met Bessie London

## Lila S. Azhari

One day, many years ago in Berkeley, California, I was in a restaurant having lunch with Andrew, my brother, when I mentioned a write–up I'd read in the paper. I was twenty. Andrew was eight years older.

"I didn't know Jack London lived around here, Andy," I said. "But I was reading about his wife, Bessie. It seems she lives in Piedmont. Is that anywhere around here?"

"Piedmont is practically next door," Andy said. "Why do you ask?"

"Because I'll never be able to take dissection next semester. I just cannot do it. I've decided against being an M.D. What I really want to be is a writer. I'm going to try to persuade Dad to let me switch to journalism instead of medicine."

"Well, good luck, Sis," he said. "I had to leave home to get out of studying medicine. People should let their children choose something for their life's work that makes them happy. That's my belief."

"Dad says I have a perfect hand for a surgeon," I said, showing him my hand. "I cringe every time he mentions it. I could never operate on anyone. I *want* to be a writer."

"Then that's what you *should* be," he said.

"I like Jack London's stories—especially the one about the dog. You know the one I mean?"

"Yes," he said, "I like *Call of the Wild*, too. Jack London was a very good writer."

"I'd give anything if I could meet his wife," I said.

"Then why don't you?"

"How would I get an introduction to her?"

"You don't need an introduction, Sis."

"I couldn't just barge in at her house and ask to speak to her, could I?"

"Why not? She might be honored to know how you feel about her husband's work. It might give her pleasure."

"You really think it might?"

"*I'd* be honored if *I* were in her place. If you want to talk with her, I'll drive you over there and drop you off. I'll circle around and pick you up later. It's worth a trip."

We got in his car and drove to Piedmont. We pulled up in front of a middle–class, attractive, frame house, halfway up a hill in a woodsy neighborhood.

"Good luck!" Andrew said as he drove off.

I walked up the hill and knocked on the door. A man in his early thirties opened the door.

"I'd like to speak to Bessie London," I said. "Is she at home?"

"I believe she is," he said. "I'm the caretaker. Just go around the house to the other door. That's where she lives."

So I circled around to the other door and knocked. A woman of medium height and weight with a friendly–looking face and gray hair opened the door. She was wearing a house dress that had little lavender flowers in the design. What I noticed most was that she wore black stockings and shoes. I thought she was the maid.

"I'd like to speak to Mrs. Jack London," I said.

"Would you?" she asked in a kindly way. "What about?"

"About how her husband got to be such a good writer," I said.

"I'm Jack's first wife, Bessie," she told me, ushering me into her living room and offering me a chair. "So you like Jack's work?"

"I love his stories."

"And you'd like to write, too?"

"Oh, yes," I said, " My father wants all four of us children to be M.D.'s because he is happy in that profession. But I am no good at sciences at all, and I dread the day when I will have to take dissection, or have to operate on someone. It makes me ill to see anyone cut, or even with a nosebleed. What I want to be is a writer, a *good* writer."

"Then you must write," she said. "What would you like me to tell you about Jack?"

"Everything," I said. "What was life like with him? How did you meet him? Just everything, if you will?"

"Well, I met Jack at a funeral."

"A funeral?"

"Yes, it was the funeral of a man I was engaged to marry. He was *Jack's* best friend. Until that *funeral*, we had never met. It was a sad day for each of us. We reminisced about my fiance that day, then Jack left the area. I didn't see him again until two years later when we happened to meet accidentally!"

"Was Jack living in this area then?"

"Yes, and we started seeing each other. He liked to write. I was a teacher. I taught math. After we were married, Jack wrote every day. He was not well educated, you know. I taught and supported us. In the evenings, I edited whatever he had written that day and prepared his manuscripts. It was three years before anything sold, but we didn't give up hope. We had confidence, you see."

"I'm surprised it took so long for any of his stories to be accepted."

"We were, too. But that's what life as a writer is like."

"*Call of the Wild* is a beautiful story," I said.

"Yes, I like it, too," she said.

"It must have been hard for you to teach and earn a living those three years, then come home, edit his work, and get it ready to send out every night."

"It was difficult, yes."

"Did Jack write from personal experience?"

"Sometimes he did. Have you read *Valley of the Moon*?"

"No, that's one I missed."

"That one was written about *us*, but after Jack's second marriage, he changed it and put his second wife in my place."

"I'm sorry."

"Yes. You see, it was *I* who was with him in *the early years*. We had two children, two girls. He loved those girls. One is in Los Angeles now, discussing possible movie rights or something."

"I hope she will be successful."

As I remember it, the living room had windows on its left side. At the far end was an upright piano with family pictures all over the top of it, giving an old–fashioned look to the room. On the right–hand side was a good–sized bookcase filled with books. Beyond the piano I seem to remember more windows.

As we stood together by the windows at the left side of the room, Bessie London pointed at a handsome, newer–looking house farther down the hill. A faraway look came into her eyes as she stood there. Finally, she turned to me. "You know, when I look down the hill, I don't *see* that new house at all. What I see is a big tree all leafed out on sunny days with Jack and his friend, Jack Spaulding, the poet, sitting beneath that tree writing."

We stood there awhile, then she took my elbow and guided me toward the piano. She told me about each family member in each of the photographs.

"It's kind of you to share all this with me—a stranger," I said.

"Well, you don't seem much like a stranger," she said.

We edged over to the bookcase on the right–hand wall. "These are all first editions of Jack's books," she said. "The publisher used to send me first editions. Jack signed them all. Would you like to see how he signed them?"

I opened several of the books. The autograph in each was the same. It said: "To dear, dear Mama Girl from Daddy Boy."

"He must have loved you and the children very much," I said.

"Yes," she said, "I know he did. But if you want to see the real showplace, Charlotte (I believe she called her Charlotte), Jack's second wife is the one who got everything."

"I'm not interested in her," I said. "You're the one who was with him in the beginning. It was you who helped him become the success he was."

I must tell you that my visit happened almost fifty years ago. But I believe Bessie said it was at a kind of woodsy place with rental log cottages, or something like that, while she and Jack were on vacation and Charlotte was renting a cottage near them that Jack and Charlotte met.

When they returned home, Jack asked for a divorce, which Bessie gave him. He married Charlotte, the one who now had the showplace and profits from his writings.

"I can't imagine him doing that," I said.

"No one could believe it," she said.

"What was it about her, I wonder?"

"Sheer animal attraction," she said. "There was nothing else that could have attracted him."

"Where did they live?"

"They lived in the Bay area. Jack used to come over every afternoon after they married to visit the girls and me.

He seemed to *need* us. When it started to turn dark outside, I would say to him, 'Jack, you'd better be getting home now,' but he'd linger on. It seemed as if he dreaded leaving me. Sometimes he stayed until ten o'clock at night."

"He must have been very lonesome," I said.

"Yes, he missed us and we missed him. Jack was the kind of person you'd miss."

"Are they still married?"

"No. They were vacationing in one of the islands. Jack came to visit us before they left. We also heard from him from that island. Later, we received a cable saying he was on his way home and had something wonderful to tell the girls and me—something we would be glad to hear—some wonderful news. His boat would dock at a certain time. He was anxious to see us as soon as he returned to give us the news, but we never found out what that good news was. You see, Jack died, mysteriously, before the boat returned to San Francisco."

•••••

**Lila S. Azhari** of Chapel Hill is a native of Iowa and taught primary grades in Chicago Public Schools for eighteen years. She studied writing at the University of Iowa and Michigan State University, and is now working on a history of her father's life.

# My Early Years

## Donald Elliot

The twentieth century event which affected more lives,
except for the four or five wars which we were involved in,
was the Great Depression. Three years after the stock
market crash, which heralded that event to the world, I was
born in Belmont, North Carolina. I have very few
independent memories of things which took place before
1938, so the recovery from the Depression was almost
completed before I was very aware of the world. From the
things that I do remember, and from some things which I
was told, I knew that people were affected in many different
ways, and it was hard to separate out the poverty caused by
the Depression and that coming from the ordinary life led
by the people I knew.

My father said on several occasions that he worked more
during the Depression than he did before it. He worked in
the cotton mills, and the necessities—food, clothing, and
shelter—people bought before anything else. The cotton
mills, at least those located where we lived, ran regularly;
we moved around to several different towns, as job
opportunities developed for my dad. As I recall some of the
events of my early childhood, I can tell how old I was when
they took place by where we were living at the time,
because we had lived in six different houses by the time I
was nine years old.

I remember once, in 1939, we lived in Gastonia, North
Carolina. I was listening to the radio with my older brother
(I called him Jake, although his legal name was the initials
J. C.), waiting for the Lone Ranger to come on. It was my
favorite program, and we had even sent off to join the Lone

Ranger Safety Club. I didn't know exactly how that worked, but I could hardly wait to get my club, so I could start pounding away at some of the things which needed to be hit. You can imagine my disappointment when it turned out to be a different kind of club, just a few pieces of paper, and I even had to promise to try to do things safely.

That day the announcer seemed to be more long winded than usual, and I ignored him completely, while waiting for the rousing strains of the theme music (the William Tell Overture, as everyone knows) and the hearty, "Hi yo Silver." When the announcer finished, my brother turned to me and said, "The war is over!"

"What's a war?" I asked, because I couldn't remember ever hearing that word before.

"That's where men stand in big holes and shoot at each other," he said by way of explanation. Visions of people standing in wells, at the tops of ladders, shooting away with guns which looked a lot like air rifles filled my head, because those were the things I was most familiar with. The wells I knew about were hand dug and were about four feet in diameter, and the well diggers used ladders to get in and out. Those would make great places to stand in and shoot at people. All of the older boys we knew and played with had air rifles, called BB guns by many of them, but not by language purists like my brother and me.

The war just ended was the Spanish Civil War, which brought Franco to power and fame to Ernest Hemingway, who wrote *For Whom the Bell Tolls* about the fighters in it. Many people believe that was Hitler's test field for his war machine, and it was actually the beginning of World War II. To a six–year–old boy, though, it was just something which delayed the beginning of The Lone Ranger.

One of the most interesting things to me was the arrival of the ice man. Most families had ice boxes, made of oak and lined with gray zinc metal. A pan on the floor underneath caught the water from the melting ice. A door on the top of the ice box let the iceman put in a block of ice, carried into the kitchen with big iron tongs. Food which had to be kept very cold could be put into this top compartment, but most things were kept in the lower compartment, reached through a door in the front of the ice box.

Every home had a sign to tell the ice man if any ice was needed, and if so, how much. That way, he could chip out a block of the correct size and bring it to the kitchen without making two trips. The sign had four triangles printed on the front, with the tips meeting in the center, and the numbers 5, 10, 25, and 50 printed in large characters around the outside, one number in each triangle. The sign had nail holes on each side and it was hung up in sight of the street with the number at the top giving the amount of ice needed that day.

We kids would follow the ice truck all the way down our block, because the ice from the ice house came in large blocks. The delivery man used an ice pick to break off the correct size block. There were always a lot of fist–sized slivers that broke off, spilling into the bed of the truck or out into the street. These little pieces of ice were fair game for us, and we almost got frost bite before the last of our chunks of clear ice had melted in our hot, little hands.

A lot of tradesmen came to our neighborhood. I never knew if that was caused by the Depression or if it was just the way people did things in those days. Once, a photographer with a pony came around, taking pictures of the kids, dressed in fur chaps and wearing red bandanas and sometimes a cowboy hat. I still remember pictures of me, my sister, and my brother, perched up on that pony.

Once a man who caned chair bottoms came to our house and my mother had him to do our chairs, the wooden straight chairs which were used in the kitchen. He was good natured about all of us nosy kids crowding around to watch that fascinating process, and he very quickly put new seats on our six chairs.

Our house in Gastonia was located beside a major highway, US 321, which runs from Tennessee, through Boone and Hickory, then through Gastonia on into South Carolina. In those days it was a major artery, and even today it is very busy. We were all warned about playing in the road, and to be very careful if we ever had to cross it. A little boy in our neighborhood ran out in front of a car one day and was hurt badly. About a week later, a neighbor lady took me to the hospital to visit him. The hospital was dark and cool inside, and had a strange odor from the antiseptics and disinfectants which they used. The little boy recovered and later was a kind of hero among the other kids in the neighborhood.

We did not have a car then, but my great uncle did. He let my dad use his car whenever we needed to go anywhere. The first car I remember riding in was a Chevrolet coupe, and it had a rumble seat. The enclosed part of the car had just one seat, but in the back, where the trunk is on most cars, there was a door which pulled open to reveal a seat, out in the open. Needless to say, we kids all wanted to ride there, with the wind in our faces, waving at everyone we passed. That didn't last long, though, because my uncle bought a larger car, a Chevrolet four–door sedan. The children, at least, missed the rumble seat.

Whenever anyone in a family would catch a communicable disease, the Public Health authorities would quarantine the house, posting a bright yellow sign beside the front door. Everyone was warned by this sign not to go into that house, for fear of catching whatever disease was there. My younger sister came down with polio, and we were quarantined for a long time. It must have been a mild case, because she was not paralyzed or crippled by it, but many other people who caught that dread disease were. Polio mostly struck young people, and in fact the common name for it was infantile paralysis. Up through my early teen years, there was a general quarantine for polio during several summers, and all of the kids had to stay home, or at least, away from large groups of people. Anyone who remembers those days can appreciate the Salk vaccine.

Most of my relatives lived in the mountains of North Carolina and Tennessee before and during the Depression. Based on the stories which they told at our family gatherings, I think that the Depression was actually an improvement for them. The poverty which was normal for the people living there was not made worse by the business reversals taking place in other parts of the country, for the government programs intended to help those who were out of work helped those poor people in Appalachia as well.

•••••

Born in November of 1932, **Donald Elliott** was aware only of the recovery from the Great Depression. He lived in several small towns in the Piedmont area of North Carolina, in six different homes before the age of ten. His life revolved around what was the major industry in North Carolina at that time: cotton manufacturing. He remembers the start of World War II, which brought an end to the Depression.

# A Southern Childhood

## Mary Ellen Priestley

I was born in Ashland City, Tennessee, a town near Nashville. My father, James H. Evans, was from Indiana where he had graduated from Purdue University in the sciences. He had moved south for the sake of his first wife's health, but she had died, leaving their son Fairfax, aged five. Not long afterwards, the rest of the family, including my grandfather and grandmother Evans, also moved south. Then my father's sister, her husband, and their two daughters moved to Tennessee, where they settled in Coffee County. Here the young teacher of piano, daughter of Dr. P.K. Carson, became the wife of James H. Evans. They settled in Ashland City where my father was appointed one of the first two county agriculture agents in the state. Eighteen months after I was born, I had a baby brother, James.

In the meantime, a group of Ashland City men who owned stores and other property, got together to buy a large plantation in Alabama along the Tallapoosa River. They persuaded our father to join them. We were packed up and moved by train to an area south of Wetumpka. We soon learned that most of the town and river names were derived from American Indian names. For example, Wetumpka, on the Coosa River, meant "falling waters." The river did run over large boulders before it ran into the Tallapoosa and on into the Alabama.

When the crash of Wall Street came in 1929, we were more fortunate than many, for we had home–grown vegetables, fruit, and meat. As garden vegetables matured and fruit ripened, our mother arranged glass jars and canned the produce for winter meals. Our father and a worker on the farm butchered hogs, and hams hung in the smokehouse.

Our mother, the pianist and teacher, learned to drive a car and took our Ford filled with vegetables and baked chicken, pies, and cakes to Montgomery, the state capital, where she joined others selling at the curb market. My brother James, aged twelve or thirteen, had learned to drive the car, and he was allowed to drive part of the way. This was before drivers had to have licenses. Upon getting to Montgomery, the state capital, and setting up the produce in the curb market, he remembers that he was given a dime to go see a movie.

Our school, the state Secondary Agricultural School, was probably the best in the state, for it offered two years of Latin and French, agriculture, home economics, and higher math. I was on the debate team which won the state championship, played my grandmother's violin in the orchestra, and sang in the chorus. While my girl friends were graduating and planning their weddings, I was considering scholarships in Alabama. Our father had already returned to Tennessee where he was employed by the Agriculture Department. He came back for my graduation and helped in packing up our household furnishings, selling the cattle, and moving to Hohenwald, Tennessee, the name being an English version of the German for "high woods." I accepted a scholarship at a junior college in Nashville, worked on the newspaper the first year, and edited it the second. I then attended Middle Tennessee State University where I obtained a bachelor's degree and experience editing the college newspaper as a senior. By 1938, news from Europe forecast US involvement in World War II.

**Mary Ellen Priestley** is a native of Tennessee, where she attended college. She had a double major in music and English, and she edited the college newspaper at Middle Tennessee State College. In World War II she served thirty months with the American Red Cross Club Service. She kept a journal which she is preparing for publication.

# Becoming a Doctor in Tight Times

## Donald K. McIntyre

In 1929 and 1930, a senior in high school, I knew nothing about stock. Nor do I have any recollection of the stock market crash occurring. Never rich, I learned in the next couple of years, as we all did, how people had put money on the line in hope of big profits.

One evening in the year after the crash, I was walking with my father in Central New York City when a gentleman approached us and requested change. I do not believe any words were exchanged as my father gave more than I would have expected, but he mentioned to me as we moved on that the needy one had known better days. It had been equally apparent to me, and I did not require more comment to fill in the rest of the story.

As I made my way to and from college classes in Philadelphia, I regularly saw—even purchased apples from—numerous vendors attempting to make ends meet , honorably, by selling apples from makeshift tables on street corners. It was a common but hopeless sight, obviously promoted by some anxious to help the victims of the Depression that followed the most widespread collapse of America's economy in the country's history.

Many unemployed, already more desperate and seemingly beyond hope, made any chance of helping them less likely to succeed by seeking relief from stress in the area around city hall drinking anything that smelled like alcohol.

The severe destruction of Germany at the end of World War II was dreadful. Physically, the landscape looked worse. There was less to work with and yet there was hope. The fact that, at least in Europe, the war had ended was positive. In the early picture during our Depression nothing positive was happening. Each month over the years, the trend was downhill, as if recovery would never begin.

My wife has often mentioned how fortunate she and her family were throughout those long years. Her father, earning a very modest income as an accountant with his firm in Camden, New Jersey, was in the minority of those who retained steady jobs. He was able to assist many less fortunate neighbors, who lacked jobs and, also, lacked adequate food. Such conditions were hardly temporary. They went on and on.

Leisure was spent enjoying times and pastimes with friends and neighbors. Money was not wasted on entertainment.

It is said that anyone who experienced the Depression never forgot it. The impressions were indelible because of the Depression's long duration.

In my own case, college took five years and ended with my owing the college four hundred dollars. This sounds like little today, yet was then nearly all one needed for a year's education while working. At graduation I was fortunate in obtaining a fellowship to study for a year in Germany, but it then took four years of teaching to pay my college debt and save enough to begin the study of medicine.

By 1942, my junior year in medical college, I had run out of money. The Depression was over, but not for me. I was again fortunate when the Army and Navy took over the expenses of medical college. Medical students were put in the military service with pay. I could finish school and start my internship at the Hartford Hospital, Hartford, Connecticut, at ten dollars a month.

Fortune smiled again when the day before my wedding, the mother of my oldest friend gave me a ten dollar present that enabled me to buy the wedding ring. From then on life was perfect.

•••••

**Donald K. McIntyre, MD**, born January 26, 1912, in Mount Vernon, New York, served in World War II as Battalion Surgeon with the 159th Infantry Regiment. He now lives in Chapel Hill.

# Early Hatteras Holidays

## Sybil Austin Skakle

Christmas is an awesome time for a child, conditioned by family and peers, as well as the unexplainable, to expect wonderful things to happen. In Hatteras, where I grew up during the thirties, in the midst of a world wide crisis known as the Great Depression, our Christmas Eve program at Hatteras Methodist Church was the most important event. For me and my siblings, activity and changes in our father's store ran a close second.

Turkey and plum pudding were not the fare we expected. We were fortunate to have a goose as the main attraction at Christmas dinner, with rutabagas, with sweet potatoes, collard greens or cabbage, and the usual pies and cakes. One we called "Poor Man Cake[1]," made without some ingredients usually expected and full of raisins, may have been a substitute for fruit cake. Pone bread[2], a heavy bread made with meal and molasses and soured before baking, was very popular in some homes. I never knew how turkey tasted until Mama decided to raise her own.

She acquired a tom and hen from somewhere and began the process of experimentation. Mama enjoyed new challenges. Later she had Rev. Bill Parkin bring her a piglet to raise and honored our pastor by naming said pig Bill. Tom turkey grew into a large, ill–tempered bird. When Mama sacrificed him for Christmas dinner, I felt no regret.

Once he caught my bare feet with his sharp talons, as I crossed the walk from wash house to our back door. I avoided him, afraid of his assaults. He attacked Daddy walking in the yard. He flew up onto his back, beating Daddy with his powerful wings.

"Get! Get you crazy bird!" Daddy cried, flailing his arms. "GET out of here!"

That turkey even went across the road to Mr. Dolph Burrus' store to take on Mr. Dolph as he got out of his truck one morning. Mr Dolph was a competitor for grocery business, but the rivalry between my father and him was friendly. Tom made his attack without any human authority. Tom was a foul fowl.

I ate turkey and too much rich chocolate candy sent to the family by Mr. Massoletti, a restaurant owner from New York City, who owned a cottage at Hatteras. I became very ill. For years I told anyone offering me turkey, "I'm allergic to turkey. It makes me sick."

Community life centered around the family, church, and school. Both Hatteras School and Hatteras Methodist Church were across the sandy road from our house. We had chapel once a week, and at Christmastime our principal read us the Christmas story from the Bible. We heard it again in Sunday School. We drew names and exchanged small gifts among our classmates at school and at church school. Our mothers saw we were provided with gifts for our teachers.

Preparation for the Christmas Eve program at our church took most of our attention and time after school as Christmas approached. If we celebrated Advent, which starts on fourth Sunday before Christmas, I do not remember. Part of our program was the enactment of the story about the Nativity and Holy Family. Which young child would be chosen for the manger created a lot of curosity for us children. My main concern was to learn songs and speeches I had to perform.

Daddy's store at Christmastime became a place of mystery and surprises as Christmas approached. Packages arrived on the freight boat *The Cathleen* from Elizabeth City, from Butler Brothers, that far–away place named Baltimore, Maryland, as well as the wholesale houses in Elizabeth City.

Shortly before Christmas, those boxes would be opened after the store had closed for the night. By next morning, exciting new things had taken place of regular merchandise on the shelves. Mona and I found it hard not to touch every item. Our young hearts were greedy. Dark cobalt blue bottles of Evening in Paris tempted us, not only to touch but to sniff. The two show cases on the dry goods side of the store were filled with sets of Evening in Paris and other kinds of cosmetic sets for both men and women. On the shelves that usually held bolts of cloth, bulk socks, and a bit of lingerie, panties specifically, now held boxed handkerchiefs, socks, ties, and a few toys—things to see and admire.

On the far side, the grocery side, a wooden bucket of mince meat sat on the counter with a large metal container of shredded coconut. Beneath that counter large boxes contained pecans, almonds, nigger toes (I never knew them as Brazil nuts as a child), and English walnuts. Stored there with the nuts were heavy, sectioned, cardboard boxes containing chocolate covered nougat, cherries, and Brazil nuts and peach blossom candy. Delightful to our eyes and noses, they tempted us as Eve was tempted in The Garden of Eden. Our desire for sweets, hers for knowledge of good and evil, caused us to disobey the authority in our lives. We ate far more candy than we were given, or Daddy knew.

Speeches were distributed at the first practice meeting at church before school recessed for Christmas. It seemed farther ahead than it probably was. We met several times after school at the white, clap–board Methodist Church next door to our school to learn and practice the songs and our speeches with the older lady volunteers, who offered their time and patience for us.

The last practice came on the afternoon of the day before the performance on Christmas Eve. By then, some men of the church had found a big cedar tree in Buxton or Trent—renamed Frisco some years later—and had stood it up in front of the dark, varnished, diagonal sheathing in the left chancel area of the church. Our excitement made practice noisy and difficult for our prompters.

Gifts we gave and received were neither plentiful nor expensive. Mama saved coupons to order gifts. Octagon Soap helped make clothes clean with boiling and scrubbing on a washboard. Octagon coupons bought good premiums.

Mothers who sewed had been stitching new clothes for weeks. Other women, who sewed for others, like Jean Austin and Eleanor Stowe, swamped with material and dreams, were driven by the holiday's deadline.

Worn shoes had to be replaced. Orders had been sent to Montgomery Ward, Sears and Roebuck, and Spiegel. People crowded the small, front entrance of the maroon–painted post office, a short distance from Rollinson Creek landing where the mail boat came when it arrived from Manteo, via other villages on Hatteras Island. Waiting for Miss Maude O'Neal, the postmaster, to sort the mail packages last caused anxiety to mount in us! Would the big, fat bags of mail contain our shoes, dresses, gifts?

When my shoes arrived from Montgomery Ward one year, I had two right shoes that did not even match. With no time to reorder and have them arrive, my older sister Jo came to my rescue by letting me wear her green suede shoes for the Christmas Eve program at church.

We expected new clothing at Christmas and Easter. That same year Mama used a soft brown dress that had belonged to sister Jo to make mine. She took the dress apart and recut each piece to sew a dress for me. I felt elegant in my lovely dress and Jo's green suede shoes. New clothes were not named as gifts, but five children appreciated they were part of our Christmas.

One Christmas Mama used her creative ability and skill with needle to make new dresses for dolls belonging to my younger sister Mona and me. My prettiest one, made from a scrap of material, was pale, pink chiffon with tiny buttons on its gathered yoke. By Christmas morning every doll had a new dress made from material from other sewing projects that Mama had saved.

Mona and I pooled our money, saved from our earnings. Mama paid us a dollar a week to help at home. We did not have allowances as such. We were expected to earn. With our money, we went down the road to Mr. Dan Oden's store to do our shopping. I remember his patience as two small girls tried to decide, and he made suggestions to fit our resources.

While we hoped to keep ours secrets, we searched for hiding places for our gifts from our family. Sometimes we found hiding places, not meaning to find them, spoiling our surprises. Strangely, it did not stop us from searching. Such contradiction!

It may have been activity that kept my family too busy to get our tree early. I think it was part of an old tradition to wait until Christmas Eve, like the celebration of Old Christmas on January 5th at Rodanthe on the northern end of the Island, when they roasted oysters and greeted Old Buck. We put our tree up later than is now the custom, but we did not take it down until after Epiphany, to us Old Christmas. The old belief was that Santa Claus decorated Christmas trees when he came on Christmas Eve.

A number of packages were piled beneath the decorated tree at church that evening when we went for the program. After we had recited our speeches, had sung our songs, someone dressed like Santa Claus gave out the gifts to those for whom they were intended. Santa gave every child a small, brown paper bag full of Christmas candy and nuts from his pack. Then home to bed, to try to stay awake to listen for the real Santa. Even if we never saw him, we knew he would leave surprises and fill our stockings, borrowed from Mama, with an orange in the toe, nuts, hard candy, and chocolates for each of us. When morning arrived, it would be Christmas at last.

Recipes:

[1] Poor Man's Cake or Hatteras Cake

*Sift together: 4 cups flour, 1 tablespoon baking powder, 2 teaspoonfuls of nutmeg, 2 teaspoonsful of cinnamon.*

*Cook 1 package raisins in enough water to cover. Save juice for batter.*

*Puree cooked raisins, add one cup shortening and 2 cups of sugar, 1 teaspoonful of salt. Mix all together and bake at 300 degrees in a greased pan of suitable size for 50–60 minutes.*

*Mix together 1/2 package of confections sugar, butter, and additional cinnamon, to taste*

## [2] Hatteras Island Pone Bread

*5c. white corn meal*
*4 c. hot water*
*1 cup sifted flour*
*1 cup cold water*
*6 tablespoons of sugar*
*2 tablespoons of shortening*
*3 tablespoons of molasses*
*1 ½ teaspoons salt*

*Put meal and molasses into bowl, add hot water and stir well. Add sugar, salt and cold water, add flour and mix well. Cover for a few hours or overnight. Melt shortening in 2 quart pan, pour in mixture and bake, covered, at 350 F for 1 ½ hours. Let stand until cool. Cut in squares like corn bread.*

●●●●●

**Sybil A. Skakle** has been writing prose and poetry since retirement in 1990 as a hospital pharmacist. She has three sons and nine grandchildren. Her articles have been published in *Our State* and *The Island Breeze*, and her poems have appeared in various publications, anthologies, and *Echoes*.

# A Car of Distinction

## Mary Ellen Priestley

When my husband, Erik, bought a 1933 Ford sedan in 1943, I attributed his satisfied grin to the fact that he had purchased for only $325 an automobile that had been cared for like a family jewel. Its former owner, a technician at a St. Louis School of Medicine where my husband taught, had polished its black four–door body lovingly every weekend for fourteen years whether it had left the home garage or not. Its Odometer read 21,689 miles and no one disputed it.

"This car will do us until we can buy a new model. At least we can go on some painting and picnic trips." Erik explained his purchase as he parked the sedan between sleek slope–shouldered new cars in front of our apartment. Painting was Sunday hobby, and lack of transportation had narrowed the subjects of his watercolors to a six–block area.

I took for granted his plan to purchase a new car a little later. After looking over our neighbors' late models, I realized that assembly lines must be pouring our horseless carriages in everything from robin's–egg blue to leopard skin. What new model could we hope to buy? But I had not reckoned with the love affair that was quickly growing between my husband and his Ford car.

"What bad taste and design in these big, fat cars!" he would say when new cars swept past us on the highway. "They crumple like tinfoil when they're hit. Notice that picture in last night's Post? New cars, but three were killed. We're safer in a pre–war car!"

One Sunday during the first weeks of life with our bargain, we were descending a gullied, hardened–mud road to the river for some painting when Alice, our painter friend with us, sniffed the air and said, "Don't I smell something burning?"

My husband, intent upon maneuvering the car among the ditches and chuck holes, didn't raise his eyes from the road. I glanced around as an odor of burning rags stung my nostrils. A curl of smoke rose from between Erik's feet.

"Stop the car!" I shouted. "We're on fire!"

The brakes were in good condition. We bounced off the windshield and shot over the front seat. Paint brushes, lunch, and tubes of paint hurtled around us. We leaped from the car, and my husband pulled up the rubber mat and yanked up the floorboards. He scooped up sand and poured it on the flames. As Alice and I recalled every fire we had ever heard of, Erik cleaned off the battery, adjusted the scorched wires, and boldly started the car again. Convinced after ten minutes that it wouldn't blow up, we crawled back in.

"That would have been a real fire if we had been in one of these low–slung new models," my professor declared later as he brushed a stormy sky on watercolor paper.

Lizzy performed numerous feats beyond the line of duty. For a passenger car, she was indestructible and of such vintage the medical researchers didn't mind driving her to the dog pound for five or six stray mongrels who would do their bit for science. It didn't matter that the dogs got sick on the way home since Lizzy could be hosed out and disinfected. The students' convertibles were hardly adaptable for this phase of research.

The Ford's squarish top had special value to my husband who has a poor sense of direction. Coming out of a building with which he is not thoroughly familiar, he might wander about for fifteen minutes getting his bearings. After he bought the Ford, he was reasonably sure of seeing the square–topped car standing out like a beacon above her streamlined, curvacious sisters. It was worth money to be able to walk confidently toward your car after one brief glance over the parking lot.

That winter we drove to Rockford, Illinois, for a Swedish Christmas holiday and found ourselves caught in an ice storm as we started back to St. Louis. Sleet turned the highway into one long icicle. Cars slid crossways. More and more of them went into the side ditches. Filling stations and cafes were crowded with holiday travelers buying chains and antifreeze. I suggested we stop and spend the night at a motel. I argued that it wasn't safe to drive.

"But I have an eight o'clock lecture tomorrow morning," my husband answered. "We'll have to do something about the tires."

He pulled off at the next side road and let enough air out of the tires to leave them soft. We made the next 200 miles to St. Louis in record ice storm time by driving down the center of the highway, moving over only when we met another car. It was beside the point to mention that Erik was clutching the steering wheel like a veteran racer. He suffered from sore muscles for a week. Or to complain when the heater failed, and I was all but congealed before we reached home.

His story of the Christmas trip, minus the drawbacks, made the round of the University for the winter season. His old Ford had purred right in home while Packards and Cadillacs were ditched and useless, strewn along the 200–mile route.

In the spring we loaned the Ford to a professor of philosophy and his wife who drove to Estes Park in Colorado and over half the Rockies without a minute's trouble and almost no oil. Good little car, they said. Not too comfortable, but in good shape.

Allusions to the car sprinkled my husband's lectures to medical students, usually in some allegory on old age or potency after seventy–five. "Gentlemen, these hormones can restore sexual vigor in an old man about as fast as high octane gas would change my old Ford into a sleek convertible. Years have done their damage," he would end with a sorrowful face as the class roared. The car came more and more to be associated with the professor.

Just as Lizzy seemed ageless and I began to foresee us photographed with her before the gates of the Ford Motor Company in the year 2000, she began to have internal trouble. Fuel pump.

Without warning, Lizzy would wheeze to a stop as the unfortunate driver pressed down desperately on the gas pedal. This behavior occurred so frequently in the left lane we found ourselves driving blocks to avoid a left turn. The fear of sitting at the head of a long line of impatient drivers while the light changed to green and then back to red gripped us as we approached traffic lights. About the sixth time that I took the wheel and steered, as Erik pushed us to the curb among honking rush–hour drivers, I made the motion that we leave the car in the no–parking zone with a "For Sale" sign attached.

"Nothing but the fuel pump," said my puffing mate. I sat in the car, hoping to ward off policemen while Erik walked to service station for our fourth fuel pump. By now, he had

314

learned to install one with a minimum of grease on trousers, shirt, and steering wheel.

An event which I thought would break the camel's back only served to strain our own sacroiliacs. A friend whom I had not seen for two years stopped over with us on her way to California. She had to make an 8:30 a.m.. train, and Erik offered to drive her to the station on our way to work. As we approached a low section of the city, the autumn morning fog grew denser until cars in the next lane were filmy outlines. As we started up a slight hill, a gasp escaped from the innards of the car. I looked at Erik's stricken face. It was eight o'clock. The gasp lengthened to a tired sputter and quit as he guided the Ford to the curb. We strained to see through the fog. Where were the taxis? Nowhere when you needed one!

"Come on," our man called. "I'll lock the car and...."

"Don't bother," I cried, dragging out one of Judith's three bags. "Maybe someone will steal it."

We inched ourselves and bags uphill to a crowded bus and squeezed on, clutching overhead straps and Judith's bags as we watched for the Union Station stop. Three minutes before train departure, we pushed Judith through the ticket gate. A porter grabbed two of her bags and they ran for her coach.

This would do it, I thought. But no, when my husband and a tennis–playing friend returned to the abandoned car after work, it started without even an added shot from the choke. We were doomed to ride in the antique forever.

Then great news! Erik learned he didn't always have to buy a new fuel pump when his machine had troubles in the intestinal tract. By drawing gas from the tank in a syringe

315

commonly used for medicinal purposes and squirting it into the carburetor, he could start the car with a minimum loss of time. The syringe stayed in the glove compartment and fell out each time I looked for a map or sunglasses.

During the winter the Ford made another niche for herself in my husband's life by serving as a mobile studio. Although he entered two or three shows a year, he guarded his amateur painter's standing jealously. He like to paint, but his love of research mixed with a Scandinavian distrust of "artiness" made him discipline himself to one painting excursion a week. That one trip, usually on a Sunday afternoon, was made come snow, ice, or in–laws.

In bad weather he propped his painting up on the dashboard, placed his paints beside him on the seat, set the jar of water on the floor, and slung his brush with abandon. Watercolor could not hurt the old car. That winter the seat covers took on the colors of a rich batik. And his store of paintings pushed the clothes out of our large closet.

Other people talked about the merits of the new automatic lock on their car doors, and we managed to say something appropriate about how ingenious the car designers must have become. We did not know we had an automatic lock until the rainy evening we offered to take a couple home from our apartment.

"Wait at the front door and I'll bring the car around," Erik said, pulling on overshoes and a raincoat. The car was parked at the rear of the building on a patch of red clay where garages were to be built

When Erik failed to appear in ten minutes, I threw a raincoat over my head and went out to see what had happened. In the half–light I saw the car, and, up on its engine, my husband, head down, posterior up.

"What are you doing?" I called.

"Opening the car door," he answered as if anyone else could have seen immediately what he was doing. I thought back over the drinks we had served. Erik's stories had got bigger as the evening went on, but....

"Have you tried the key?" I asked. "In the door?" There was no answer. I walked out gingerly to the car. There I saw that he was punching a broom handle through the open ventilator below the windshield.

"I locked the door on the driver's side," he said as he pushed the stick in short jabs at the inside door handle. "Neither side will open with a key." A path of his tracks in the orange–red clay circled the car.

The broom handle finally acted as a lever from Erik to the door handle, and the lock sprang open. I returned to our guests and Erik soon drove up.

"Good thing I put on my overshoes," he said. I looked at his feet. Great blobs of red mud fringed each foot. Brake and clutch were hidden by clay.

When we returned to the apartment after taking our friends home, I went into the living room, but Erik paused at the door to remove his muddy footgear. Then I heard him laughing, or was it moaning?

"Guess what?" he called. "I don't have my overshoes on!" He came inside minus shoes. The next morning we found the overshoes stuck in his tracks in the clay. It took about a week on off hours to clean his shoes. It was a longer time before we parked the Ford at the rear of the apartment.

In June we decided to go to New England for our vacation. But, for business reasons, we were to go by way of

Florida. I soon discovered that Erik intended to make the trip by car.

"And why not?" he asked. "It's city driving that is hard on a car. She'll be fine for a long drive."

I finally had to bribe the garage mechanic and my doctor into telling him that Lizzy and I could not make it to New England together.

Two weeks before vacation, he reluctantly bought a new car, and, not able to part with Lizzy, he sold her to an intern who commuted between the medical school and the hospital.

In spite of the elegance of the new auto, something went out of my husband. The vacation was a forced tonic to get over a lost love.

Back home, I noticed he had a shadow of whiskers on his upper lip and chin. Didn't he need a shave?

"No, I have to do something to distinguish myself as a professor," he answered. "Someone may take me for a student in this shiny new car. So I am growing a beard!"

•••••

Mary Ellen Priestley is a native of Tennessee, where she attended college. She had a double major in music and English, and she edited the college newspaper at Middle Tennessee State College. In World War II she served thirty months with the American Red Cross Club Service. She kept a journal which she is preparing for publication.

# Remembering New York's World's Fair 1939–40

## Marie P.Spinner

At our house in the summer 1939, plans for our first trip to the New York World's Fair were underway. The only topic of conversation for the last few days had been the Fair. We poured over newspapers and magazines, devouring every item related to the Fair, taking special note regarding exhibits and scheduled events. For me, going to the Fair was the most exciting event of my life!

The Fair grounds had taken almost three years to construct, employing thousands of people, who would have otherwise been out of work and in need of federal relief assistance. Businesses needed a stimulant. The Depression had not entirely departed. Thus the bright idea of the World's Fair had been formulated.

We left early on a Sunday morning for our trip to Flushing, New York—after my sisters and I helped our mother make sandwiches to be wrapped in wax paper, wash apples, which we packed into a brown, paper bag, which we put into Mother's canvas carry–all. We still had to watch our pennies because our family still felt the pinch of the depressed economy.

We were in high spirits and in our Sunday best, as we climbed into our second–hand Chrysler automobile, our first family car—bought on the installment plan. We rode toward the new Whitestone Bridge, spanning the East River. Then, as if by magic, we saw the Trylon and Perisphere in the distance. As we approached the Fair ground, they seemed to take on the proportions of some

huge pointed obelisk and gigantic ball deposited there from outer space. What a sight!

The Fair opened at 9:00 a.m. We were in line at 9:15 a.m. Admission for children was twenty–five cents and seventy–five for adults, a bit high when a subway ride cost a nickel.

The next year children could buy a special summer coupon book at their schools, but good for Wednesdays only. We bought them and took the special shuttle to the Fair. Those were wonderful Wednesdays spent at the Fair with our friends.

You who are the same age as I may remember the Fair—the seven hundred foot high Trylon and the two hundred foot wide Perisphere. They were painted white, as were many of the buildings and statues. Added bubbling fountains and waterfalls made a most dazzling scene. My first impression of the Fair was that I was entering another world—truly, a world of the future. No wonder!

Trylon was our first stop. There we rode on what was one of the world's largest escalators.

When we entered the Perisphere, we stepped onto a moving ring, where we could see the vast diorama of a *Democracity*, which sought to portray America 2039 for the theme of the Fair was Building the World of Tomorrow.

These wonders were only the beginning. Nearby stood the majestic statue of George Washington as he must have appeared at his inauguration.

Next came the Transportation Zone. At the General Motors Complex, we were treated to *Highways and Horizons*. Seated in high–sided chairs that moved over a scale model of a highway world of 1960, with express highways, huge bridges, and modern high–rise buildings, we thought it an unbelievable dream. Leaving, we were given a button with the caption: "I Have Seen the Future." I treasured that button like a medal of honor.

At the Communication Center we viewed the first television. Inside the Consolidated Edison Building we found *The City of Light*, an animated, lighted model of metropolitan New York City. Here a full day passed by in just minutes, ending with a darkening of the sky with elements of a storm. Westinghouse had a demonstration of *Electro*, a seven–foot–tall walking and talking robot.

We could not miss the Food Center. *Borden's Dairy World* had Elsie, the famous Jersey cow, while the building constructed by The Continental Baking Company resembled one of their bread wrappers, painted with blue, red and yellow dots. At the end of the Heinz tour, we were given wonderful, green pickle pins. I wore mine to school for weeks.

The Foreign Pavilions, which were very interesting and educational, gave us glimpses of the cultures of many different countries by the displays and the objects displayed. The British Pavilion had a replica of the crown jewels worn by the King and Queen of England. A copy of the original manuscript of the Magna Carta, looking so authentic that I could almost feel the ancient parchment, could be viewed behind a glass enclosure. I was more impressed than the others, because the semester before in junior high school I had studied English history. There before my eyes was one of the most important documents of all times, the ideals of which became part of the framework of our own Constitution of the United States of America.

The Canadian Pavilion was vivid with colorful displays of totem poles carved by the Indian artists of British Columbia. Two handsome Royal Mounted Police, resplendent in the scarlet uniforms, were standing at attention and were so straight and still that my little sister thought they were models. She stepped up, touched one of them on the hand. Feeling a response, she jumped back and fell against me. She whispered, "He's real!"

He never moved. One of his eyes winked. Surprised, we giggled and ran after our family.

Our own United States Building had two lofty, white towers representing the houses of our government: Senate and House of Representatives, and thirteen white columns for the original states. In the garden stood a bust of President Franklin Delano Roosevelt.

Nearly every zone of the Fair had gardens with beautiful flowers. shrubs, and trees. On that first visit we noticed that the gardens attracted the visitors' attention as much as the exhibits.

Finally, our feet needed a rest, and hunger pangs had begun. So, what better place to have our lunch than a lovely English garden on a bench under a spreading shade tree? There we ate our bag lunch, chatting and recalling our experiences so far.

After lunch, fortified, we were ready for another adventure. The first one was the three–dimensional movies where they handed special eye glasses to us to view this phenomenon.

The Parachute Jump was breath–taking to watch, but no one wanted the thrill for themselves. We were first in line for the late afternoon performance of Billy Rose's Aquacade with its spectacle of dazzling colored lights and drama taking place in an amazing pool of water. The comic clowns showing off their acrobatic skills by jumping off diving boards, and the lovely female swimmers performing aquatic dancing to music was an extravaganza never before attempted.

Mother and Father called a halt, declaring that was enough for one day. We, clutching our bags of free souvenirs and booklets, left the Fairgrounds at dusk. We climbed into the old Chrysler, weary, overwhelmed, but happy.

The New York World's Fair of 1939–40 was considered the greatest of all fairs by many people. It was a symbol of hope to a nation emerging from the Great Depression. It gave more than fifty million people passing through its gates memories that can never be forgotten.

•••••

**Marie Spinner**, of Chapel Hill, formerly of New York, a retired elementary school librarian, has studied writing at "Life Time Learners" at Norwalk Community College.

324

# Winning the War

## Mamie Christine Linthicum Dunn

Until I was seventeen years of age, I was in Miller Orphanage at the corner of Park Avenue and Memorial in Lynchburg, Virginia. My father was a blacksmith. I can remember so well how my parents were sweet, loving, kind, and good in every way to people. They were church going folks. Father was a businessman in the Christian Church, and they always went and took me.

My mother was Murray P. Thomas of Wytheville, Virginia. She was Dutch and German, her people coming from Wales. Mother was frivolous but had a good way about her. My father was a distant relation of German Jews, but was born in Rustburg, Virginia, just outside of Lynchurg in Campbell County. He used to bring me home stick peppermint and horehound candy. They (my parents) brought me up to obey and behave myself. If I did not, I got a keen switch on my legs. Little mischief there!

In those times, people bought flour, sugar, and coffee by the barrel; had to—things were hard—to keep from starving to death. Mother tried to open a store, but such few homes were about that it did not do much good.

Father was hurt when a car—the first car to come out in 1910—knocked him down. He lay in bed for four years and tried to get up and go to work, but fell. He died in 1913.

Mother tried keeping me in school and continued to work in her store, but could not do it. A friend of hers suggested she put me in an orphanage. She did not want to, but realized she had no choice.

I entered the Miller Orphanage and learned to work there. I sewed, cleaned, and cut grass and mended my own clothes. We ate beans, oatmeal, butter and bread, and drank lots of milk and buttermilk. We stayed healthy. At ten years of age I became Miss Willie Bowman's pet. Mother came to see me every Saturday. I bought her a little basket to put her letters in.

In 1920, I came back home. I was seventeen years old. I worked with mother at home, and then went to work in the hosiery mill. I could not stand the smell of the cotton, so I got a job in Caraddock at the Terry Shoe Factory. I met a few young fellows there and went out with them once or twice. Then I met the man I married, Walter Thomas Dunn.

Mother moved out about then to live with friends. She still looked her best, as always. Mother's friends were all so good to her. She went to work at the coolage at the end of Vernon Avenue and Illinois Street.

I married Walter when I was twenty–one years of age, on the 24th of December, 1926. Our daughter Ruth was born in 1927.

Walter, Ruth, and I lived a simple, happy life. I spent my life in the Christian Church in my hometown. Ruth was a sweet child, who obeyed in every way. I never had any trouble with her. Walter worked in Crutchfield's Laundry and Drycleaners on 12th Street in the business district. He was at home a lot with us and would watch Ruth while I did my housework.

We later moved to Monroe Street in a house to rent for twelve dollars a month. Walter then got a job with a dry cleaners in Rivermont making fifty dollars a week. We did very well in living expenses.

While Ruth was in school, she walked down the street and skated with her school friends. We let her go home with one where she learned to play the piano. I gave her Hawaiian guitar lessons. She played at the Mosk Theater in Richmond that summer.

She was doing well with friends and at school, and so I went to the Naval Air Base in Norfolk, Virginia, to work in blueprints at fifty–nine dollars a week. I thought if I was going to die in the war, I might as well do something for my country! Walter and I talked it over, and he said it would be okay; he would take care of Ruth for me and come down to see me now and then.

I boarded in one room while I was at work. Ruth came down once by herself. She had to stay in the room until I got off at four o'clock. She wanted to go to Newport News to see a friend, so I let her go. She went and came back all right on the ferry.

Walter came the next week, and we all took the ferry over as far as Newport News and turned around and came back. I had to go back to work. We kissed, and I cried and so did Ruth.

About four o'clock the caissons started. The sailors came and stood in front of the office. My job was to hand out ice cold rivets the width and diameter as given on the blueprints. One day, a sailor moved to one side, and I could see the headlines: VICTORY! I was one happy person; we had won the war! An officer came around and asked if I wanted to leave for home. I wrote home; it was all in the papers. I was glad I had gone, but my husband was so glad to have me back, and Ruth kicked up her heels and wanted to do things. I said, "Go to it, Honey! I'm home now and we're alive."

**Mamie Dunn** was born and raised in West Virginia. She joined The Writers' Group when she was ninety–three years old. She now lives near her family in Hillsborough, North Carolina.

# Memorial

## Willie Mae Jones

The sun casts shadows across the rough walls of granite, illuminating the quotation of Franklin Delano Roosevelt, which is carved into the granite stone, which tells about his four decades of service.

Water cascades into pools which gives cool, quiet, meditative tranquility throughout, reflecting a legacy of our history. Each room conveys, in its own way, the spirit of this man.

The memorial stands in West Potomac Park, between the Tidal Basin and the Potomac River. A sculpture of the Presidential Seal is mounted inside the entryway.

The first room introduces his early presidency, when he launched the New Deal in response to the worst economic crisis of the century. A relief sculpture depicts his first inauguration.

In the second room, sculptural groups—an urban breadline, a rural couple, and a man listening to a fireside chat—recall both the despair and the hope of the times. New Deal social and economic programs are depicted in bronze panels. A grassy knoll between the second and third rooms marks the historical point at which the president and the nation confronted World War II. In the third room Roosevelt appears as a seated figure; his beloved dog, Fala, sits nearby.

The fourth room honors the life and legacy of F.D.R. A sculptural relief of Roosevelt's funeral cortege hangs in the alcove. The statue of Eleanor Roosevelt commemorates her role as First Lady, as well as her later work as United Nations delegate and champion of human rights.

In the plaza is a timeline of important dates and events from the extraordinary life of Franklin Delano Roosevelt. My son and I walked throught the rooms. I, with a sense of living these historical times, remembered supper served early on the nights our president spoke to the nation. I felt he personally spoke to our family.

With the table cleared and dishes washed, Father advised each of us to sit in a chair around the radio so that we heard every word, which was important and could be discussed from notes written by Father and Mother. The six of us listened quietly.

I told my son how important the farm, the general store, hard work, and going to school and church were during the Great Depression and after my father's store burned to the ground. The insurance coverage was inadequate to cover the bills. My father raised vegetables, hogs, chickens, and finally secured a job working on a Works Progress Administration road project. Each morning I had to get up early to help Mama cook breakfast for eight in our family and the three boarders.

It was my job to pack my father's lunch in the shiny scrubbed syrup bucket. He wanted biscuits with beef, baked sweet potatoes, and pound cake.

We qualified for surplus commodities and received the delicious cheeses, real butter, flour, sugar, and other staples to feed a family in times of need. My mother made dresses and shirts from flour sacks.

My oldest brother planted trees in his job in the Civilian Conservation Corps, which, in later years, provided for the economic life of the community. He received $30.00 a month and a high school diploma.

During the war years, as well as later, four of my brothers served in branches of the service. Their symbol, four stars on a silk flag, hung in the front window.

My son and I remember his father's service to our country—his four bronze stars and other citations. We walked along as I read each inscription and told him about the effects of these events in the lives of our family members. For instance, the G. I. Bill, which gave four of my brothers the opportunity to attend the state universities, get jobs, social security, and later to retire with dignity and a pension. Some were able to secure loans to purchase homes at a reasonable rate of interest and to retain military life insurance. In later years, during periods of illness, each was served by the V.A. hospitals at no charge. Our country owes a debt of gratitude to the people who served in such times of need.

My son read the inscription in each room carefully and could now envision the Great Depression years that his father and I discussed throughout his and his brother's childhood.

After many hours of walking, reading inscriptions, discussing his father's and my early childhoods, we went home.

"Today, as an adult," I said to my son, "I truly feel that the freedom that each of us has can make dreams come true. I have that freedom."

The next morning early, with the dew still moist beneath our feet, our tour group walked through the F. D. R. Memorial. With my memories and views experiencing the Great Depression and World War II, I asked younger viewers and older persons their impressions and feelings which were evoked by these four rooms of history dating from 1933 to 1945.

One gray–haired man, walking with his cane, said, "It grows on you as you walk deeper into each room, as you read and remember where you were at these times of one's individual life. Imagine, four administrations—one president!"

Another visitor said, "One finds hope and peace. During those times, one could count on one another." Others added, "Moral and spiritual values that worked." "Guardian of our civil rights." "Democracy at work." "Today, it seems his actions evoked different reactions from what he intended."

A woman in her drab–colored park uniform and perky cap said, "My walks let me see, feel, and read thought–provoking words which affected the lives of people in every nation, and issues which we discuss and adapt today to a changing time."

Reflecting on the various comments of the folks who came to linger, my thoughts included the sense of worth and purpose of each individual.

The water cascades depicted Roosevelt's naval career and the healing warmth to his body.

The historic setting for the memorial gave me a feeling of the powerful blending of landscape gently softening the rough edges of the granite—that our country survived to give us a nation that has a history of individual justice, under the law. That as a family, with the restoration of faith and belief in the individual, our lives and our children's lives will be better.

**Willie Mae Jones**, a native of Louisiana, was a teacher and an administrator for forty years in the Louisiana education system. She retired to Durham, North Carolina, in 1992, and has studied writing at the Duke Institute for Learning. She has published in *"Dreaming," "Metaphor," and "Echoes."*.

# Franklin Delano Roosevelt Memorial, October, 1997

## Sybil Austin Skakle

Planes roar close overhead.
Water falls into pools at my feet.
Massive blocks of rose–gray granite
provide slates for his quotations

"We must scrupulously guard the civil rights and
civil liberties of all citizens, whatever their background."

"We must remember that any oppression, any injustice,
any hatred is a wedge designed to attack our
civilization."

As the morning grows older, as tourists
wander by to read his quotes,
reflect on them and to take pictures
odor of exhausted plane fuel hangs
heavy over Washington, DC

"May all be resolved to do all possible
because I hate war."

And so do we.

•••••

Sybil A. Skakle has been writing prose and poetry
since her retirement in 1990 as a hospital pharmacist. She
has three sons and nine grandchildren. Her articles have
been published in *Our State*, *The Island Breeze*, and
her poems have appeared in various publications,
anthologies, and *Echoes*.

# Bibliography

## Background

*The Great Depression and World War II (1930–1945)*, Volume III, Macmillan Publishing Company, New York

## About Hoboes

James R. Chiles, *Hallelujah, I'm a Bum*, Smithsonian, August, 1998.

Charles Elmer Fox, *Tales of an American Hobo*, University of Iowa Press, 1989.

Ted Conover, *Rolling Nowhere*, Viking Press, 1981.

## Life As Usual, Except...

References: Information not in my memory was found in an article "New Deal," Microsoft (R) Encarta 97 Encyclopedia (c)1993–1996 Microsoft Corporation, and "U.S. Depressions and Prosperity Since 1790," pgs. 126–127, *The World Book Encyclopedia*, (C) 1960; and I am indebted to another Hatteras native, Mildred Stowe Willis, for confirmation, names, and additional information.

# A History of the Writers' Discussion Group

## 1991

Rosella (Roz) Wolbarcht gathered many of her former writing students and announced to them that she no longer would be teaching writing. She asked them to continue their writing by forming a support group. Since that time, the Writers' Discussion Group has been led by Marjorie Svoboda.

## 1994–1995

The Writers' Discussion Group along with Margaret Valiquette co–sponsored a weekly "Writers as Readers" series at the Chapel Hill Senior Center.

## 1997

The Writers' Discussion Group published *Echoes*, a collection of prose and poetry written by fourteen of its members.

## 2000

The Writers' Discussion Group is publishing *A Generation Speaks, Voices of the Great Depression*, a collection of personal experiences of members and friends who had stories to tell.